The Company and the Union

The Company and the Union

The "Civilized Relationship"
of the General Motors Corporation
and the United Automobile Workers

by William Serrin

VINTAGE BOOKS
A Division of Random House   New York

FIRST VINTAGE BOOKS EDITION, July 1974

Copyright © 1970, 1971, 1972, 1974 by William Serrin

All rights reserved under International and Pan-
American Copyright Conventions. Published in the
United States by Random House, Inc., New York, and
simultaneously in Canada by Random House of Canada
Limited, Toronto. Originally published by Alfred A.
Knopf, Inc., in 1973.

Library of Congress Cataloging in Publication Data:

Serrin, William, date.
  The company and the union.

  Reprint of the 1973 ed. published by Knopf, New York.
  Bibliography: p.
  1. General Motors Corporation. 2. International
Union, United Automobile, Aerospace, and Agricultural
Implement Workers of America. I. Title.
[HD6976.A82U56 1974]   331.89′042′920973
ISBN 0–394–71974–3   73–17178

Manufactured in the United States of America

This book is dedicated to those people—they know who they are—who hoped that I would fail.

Contents

Acknowledgments

I am particularly indebted to Jerry M. Flint of *The New York Times* and Norman Pearlstine of the *Wall Street Journal* for their assistance and points of view; Patrick Owens of *Newsday,* who provided aid at an important juncture; Judith A. Serrin, my wife, for her encouragement and editorial work; and Ashbel Green and Daniel Okrent, of Alfred A. Knopf, for asking me to write this book and for their editorial assistance. My thanks also go to the Detroit Free Press library and the Detroit Public Library . . . and to a number of people who must go unnamed.

The Company and the Union

Chapter 1

"A strike makes ratification easier"

Everyone said no, he did not want a strike. Leonard Woodcock, president of the United Automobile Workers, said that the union approached the negotiations with a "sincere hope and desire that we can work out an agreement with General Motors without a work stoppage." A settlement without a strike, Woodcock said, "would be the greatest contribution we could make to our sorely troubled country."

Earl R. Bramblett, General Motors vice president for personnel and the corporation's top negotiator, said he believed a strike could be avoided. "There is never a good time for a strike," Bramblett said. "Everybody loses and nobody wins. It is time for both parties to accept the fact that we have a greater community of interest than of conflict." James M. Roche, the General Motors chairman, said, "I hope the negotiations can proceed without a strike."

Malcolm L. Denise, vice president for labor relations at Ford Motor Company, said, "Regardless of how strewn with obstacles the path to a peaceful settlement appears at this point . . . I am a congenital optimist."

Lynn Townsend, Chrysler Corporation chairman: "It's my hope that the industry as a whole can negotiate contracts without a strike." John D. Leary, Chrysler vice president for

The Company and the Union 4

administration and the corporation's top negotiator: "I think we can settle these negotiations without a strike."

James Hodgson, secretary of labor, said that the companies and the union faced a "real bargaining problem" but that the "magnitude of the problems is never reason for having a strike." A strike, Hodgson said, was not inevitable.

But there is much posturing, much cant, in labor negotiations, and this talk was part of it. Certainly the leadership of the union and the companies wanted to reach a settlement without a strike—if that would have been possible. But it was not. A strike has value for both sides. The union, its members badly hit by inflation, had the largest and most expensive list of demands in its history. A strike, by putting the workers on the streets, rolls the steam out of them—it reduces their demands and thus brings agreement and ratification; it also solidifies the authority of the union hierarchy. The companies—particularly the stupendously large General Motors, against whom there was great union pressure to strike—were particularly intransigent. General Motors, the victim like most businesses of rising costs, wanted to teach the union a lesson: take a strike, if it came to that, to slow cost increases and to gain concessions that would improve its flagging productivity. "A strike," explains a man who has intimately observed automobile negotiations for two decades, "does not have to be a stress to be avoided. It can be a tool for agreement." A strike, he says, often is not a "centrifugal thing but a centripetal thing."

Emil Mazey, secretary-treasurer of the United Automobile Workers and one of the union's founders, says, "I think that strikes make ratification easier. Even though the worker may not think so, when he votes on a contract he is reacting to economic pressures. I really believe that if the wife is raising hell and the bills are piling up, he may be more apt to settle than otherwise." In 1970, Mazey says, "A strike was inevitable."

. . .

As the largest and most American of industries, the automobile industry is the nation's bellwether, directly employing more than 800,000 workers; one in six jobs in America, the industry says, is linked to automobiles. More than 800,000 businesses, one out of every six firms in the country, depend upon the automobile industry. There are the parts companies (firms like Budd, Dana, Kelsey-Hayes, Bendix), glass companies (Libbey-Owens-Ford, Pittsburgh plate glass), tire companies (B.F. Goodrich, Uniroyal, Firestone, Goodyear), steel companies (U.S. Steel, Bethlehem, McLouth), aluminum companies (Kaiser, Reynolds, Alcoa), copper companies (Anaconda, Kennecott, Phelps Dodge). And there are thousands upon thousands of small suppliers, gasoline stations, and service firms, the privately owned and operated businesses that line the main streets of nearly every city in the country.

Each year the automobile industry consumes 20 per cent of the steel used in America; 11 per cent of the aluminum, 35 per cent of the zinc, 50 per cent of the lead, 60 per cent of the rubber. One out of every six retail dollars goes toward the purchase or upkeep of the automobile. "The automobile industry," Peter F. Drucker, the business analyst, has written, "stands for modern industry all over the globe. It is to the twentieth century what the Lancashire cotton mills were to the early nineteenth century: the industry of industries."

In summer, 1970, the coming automobile negotiations were to be particularly critical—the most important labor talks in a decade, the most crucial talks in the automobile industry for a quarter of a century. In the months to follow the auto talks, contracts covering more than five million workers would be negotiated—steel, copper, aluminum, can, railroads, meatpackers, the postal service, aerospace—and the auto contract would do much to establish the pattern for these talks, and thus shape the economy as the nation entered the 1970s.

In that summer of 1970, White House economists said that the nation slowly, frailly, but appreciably, had begun a recovery from the recession spawned by the Vietnam war. If this recovery was to continue, the government said, a strike must be averted. Months before, President Nixon urged the nation's unions and companies to exercise restraint as contracts were put together; and at the White House, Nixon told leading automobile executives he hoped they were not planning for a strike. A strike, the president said, would seriously damage the nation's hopes for a stabilized economy. Yet this was a strange year of many whirling currents, and people in the White House also believed that if the auto union's demands were too large, if the union seemed too greedy, it would be better if the industry took a strike to place a lid on wages.

The first issue, for the union, the companies, the workers, was wages.

The workers wanted more money; they needed more, they deserved more. The union had won a 6 per cent annual wage increase in the 1967 negotiations, but this increase had been eaten away by inflation. Workers' real income the preceding three years, Woodcock said, had fallen 7.4 per cent. The typical auto worker, the assembler, was making about 8,000 dollars a year—less than the Labor Department said was needed by a family of four to maintain a moderate standard of living. The Nixon Administration's anti-inflationary moves —increased unemployment, high interest rates—had harmed not the rich or the well-to-do, but the working class and the poor, the very people whom the inflation had hit the hardest. And now these people, epitomized by the auto worker, were being asked to lower their demands to stop inflation. At the same time, astronomical settlements, some of them greedy, had been won by other unions: a Teamster package of 1.85 dollars an hour in wage increases, or a 43 per cent increase in wage and benefits over thirty-nine months; a 41 per cent printers' settlement at The New York Times; a building trades settlement that, in the Detroit area, reached at least 23 per cent over two years. Such settlements, Woodcock said, "were not academic to us."

A second major issue: the demand for unlimited cost-of-living increases. In 1967—in the last contract negotiation before his May 1970 death—Walter Reuther had blundered and traded away an unlimited cost-of-living agreement at Ford so that the ever-restless skilled tradesmen would get 30 cents more per hour than the 20 cent increase for production workers. Union executives had not believed that inflation would be a great problem in the next three years; thus, when inflation skyrocketed, the 8-cent-a-year ceiling on cost-of-living increases that Reuther had accepted cost each union member between 700 and 1,000 dollars. Removing the ceiling, or coming close to this, Woodcock and the companies knew, was a condition of settlement.

The third major issue, early retirement, had risen in the shops as workers rebelled against the monotony, drudgery, and meaninglessness of auto factory life. The terms of the demand provided that after thirty years' service, workers would be able to retire at a pension of 500 dollars a month. No issue had more emotion attached to it. Union members wore buttons that said, simply, "30-and-out"; they shouted "30-and-out" at union meetings; men and women working in the plants pleaded with their union leaders to win 30-and-out and let them escape the shops. At Flint, Michigan, the birthplace of the union, a union man said, "If that Woodcock don't get 30-and-out, he is a short-term president."

There were other union demands: an end to compulsory overtime, a company-paid dental plan, programs to combat in-plant pollution and pollution in the dreary factory neighborhoods, inverse seniority so that when men were laid off, the older men, if they wished, would be laid off instead of young men, giving the younger men—increasingly a larger part of the work force, including many blacks who needed the money—a chance to earn extra money, and at the same time freeing the older men to their yards or deer blinds or the lakes, allowing them to see whether they would enjoy retirement.

The automobile companies, meantime, faced problems unprecedented in the industry's history.

Despite great lobbying on the industry's part, federal regulations were forcing them to place millions of dollars into intensive safety and antipollution campaigns, much of the money diverted from styling changes, long the cornerstone of the industry. There were other cost problems as well. General Motors was spending 225 million dollars a year on medical insurance for its workers, up from 180 million dollars the year before, and there were similar increases at Chrysler and Ford. Lee A. Iacocca, the swashbuckling Ford executive, complained that the cost of an appendectomy had increased 160 dollars in recent years, and that this, multiplied by scores of appendectomies throughout the Ford work force, amounted to many thousands of dollars and, goddammit, this represented costs that had to go into the price of an automobile. Labor costs throughout the industry, the executives said, had been climbing at 6.5 per cent a year the last six years, while productivity increases had been less than half that, this in an industry where productivity increases usually far surpassed the national average of 3 per cent a year.

And while costs were up, sales were down. Foreign manufacturers had moved into the American market with their excellent, low-priced small cars; by early fall they had seized an alarming 13 per cent of the market, a figure that reached 15 per cent by the end of the year, more than one out of every seven cars sold in America. Denise, the Ford labor relations vice president, said that two hundred workers were needed to manufacture every thousand cars; in a ten million, or normal, car year, he said, each percentage point of sales lost to foreign manufacturers represented one hundred thousand lost cars and twenty thousand lost jobs. Denise was engaging in press agentry; the jobs he spoke of included everything from the farmers whose cotton went into seats, to carhops and gas station attendants, to assembly-line workers. But the point was clear: foreign competition was severe.

The foreign inroads into American markets were all the more impressive since the Japanese and some European manufacturers still had not developed extensive sales and service networks, meaning that the bulk of the sales were on the two coasts, especially the West Coast, often the trend-setting area for America. This was to prompt Henry Ford II, the blunt Ford chairman who becomes especially bitter when discussing the Japanese since they have restricted American manufacturers from their markets while wreaking havoc in American markets, to warn, "Wait till the Japs hit Middle America."

To combat the foreign manufacturers, General Motors and Ford had begun manufacturing small cars of their own, the GM Vega and the Ford Pinto. Chrysler was importing two small cars, Cricket and Colt, and American Motors Corporation was producing the Gremlin. To cut costs, Ford was importing a Pinto engine from its Dagenham plant in England and its steering gear from the Ford subsidiary in Germany. And many other Pinto parts came from abroad as well. General Motors, characteristically, would not deign to depend upon foreign countries if this could be avoided; instead, it was placing its trust in American ingenuity and resourcefulness. The corporation was spending perhaps 250 million dollars to design the Vega and to construct the most automated automobile plant in America among rolling woodlots and cornfields at Lordstown, Ohio, midway between Cleveland and Pittsburgh. Automatic welding machines, including robots called Unimates, remarkable devices resembling dodo birds, were performing 95 per cent of the body welds, and it was scheduled that cars soon would be driven off the assembly line at the rate of one hundred per hour, compared to the normal run of fifty to sixty. Still, the American manufacturers were facing skillful and efficient competitors; the Germans and the

Japanese had much capital behind them and it would be a difficult struggle, particularly with the Japanese, with their amazing productivity and worker loyalty. The foreigners would not be routed as easily as the Americans had routed them ten years before, when the first generation of American compacts had been introduced.

With so many problems facing the auto companies, it seemed to some people that the industry was falling apart. Peter Drucker observed, "The whole industry is way over the hill. It's a declining industry . . . You in Detroit are the last monument to yesterday . . . You are as obsolete as the English midlands." The industry critic and business reformer, Ralph Nader, who had done more to bring about a loss of affection for the automobile than perhaps any other man, said that General Motors was obsolete, "where the Yankees were in 1963"—on the brink of collapse after years of supremacy.

The tone of the coming talks was set in a surprisingly outspoken speech by James Roche before the St. Louis Chamber of Commerce in February 1970, a speech that stunned the auto industry with its shrillness, so uncharacteristic of General Motors, a speech meant to show that inflation was the key issue for manufacturers as well as the workers, and that the union was chiefly to blame.

General Motors, Roche said, faced an acute crisis of cost. Interest rates, he said, were the highest since the Civil War. Payrolls had advanced 6 per cent; the price of steel had risen 6 per cent; lead, 24 per cent; aluminum, 4 per cent; nickel, 10 per cent—and all were continuing to rise. Industrial production, he said, had been declining for six months.

While production and labor costs were rising, Roche continued, General Motors had "been able to recover only a fraction of recent costs through greater efficiency, only another fraction through price increases."

In 1969, he said, General Motors had earned about 7 per

cent on sales—1.7 billion dollars on sales of 24.3 billion
dollars. But five years before, he noted, in 1964, General
Motors was "able to earn about 25 million dollars *more* on a
sales volume that was some 7 billion dollars *less* than in 1969."
From 1959 to 1965, output per man-hour in manufacturing
industries increased about 25 per cent each year. But from
1965 to 1969, compensation per man-hour increased about
25 per cent while output per man-hour—the vaunted productivity—rose only 9 per cent. As a result, unit labor costs
increased by 14 per cent while industrial prices rose 10 per
cent. "There is a serious question," Roche said, whether
American manufacturers could achieve the productivity to
produce the new subcompact cars as a "profitable business
venture, or whether inflated labor costs will price America
out of our own market."

Roche noted that the UAW–GM contract spoke of a
"cooperative attitude on the part of all parties" toward increasing productivity. But he declared, *Here is where management and the public have lately been shortchanged. Here is
where we have a right to more than we have been receiving.*

In 1969, Roche said, General Motors had lost 13.3 million
man-hours in work stoppages, many of them unauthorized
by the union. He said:

> The efficient production of motor vehicles—the assembly-
> line process—is nothing if not a team effort. Absenteeism
> lessens the effectiveness of all employees on the line. It
> undermines the foundation on which efficient production
> depends. It cuts into the quality standards of the product.
> It carries a price for all workers—the present and the
> absent alike—and ultimately the consumer. Many have
> suggested that higher absenteeism is a by-product of the
> affluence of the sixties. If so, I suggest that it is time the
> fundamentals of our affluence be recognized for what they
> are. Our ability to improve our standard of living depends
> directly on our willingness to work to create the goods and
> services we enjoy. . . .

In the negotiations of 1970, unions and management

must strive together to achieve regular attendance, eliminate unnecessary work stoppages and cooperate in improving quality.

We must restore the balance that has been lost between
wages and productivity. We must receive the fair day's
work for which we pay the fair day's wages . . . Nothing
less than the American future—the kind of country we will
pass on to our children—is at stake. Let us all hope that the
men of labor and the men of management will have the
vision to see the present grave imbalances and the courage
to correct them.

Not in years had an automobile executive made such a
speech. General Motors publicists stressed to journalists how
important the corporation considered the address, meaning
that they hoped it would receive prominent play in the
papers, which it did. The company, it seemed, was sending
a warning to the union: this year we will be tough, tougher
than we have ever been before.

Two months after Roche's speech, Walter Reuther replied
for the UAW at the union convention in Atlantic City. Ad-
dressing some three thousand delegates, he said, "In the last
ten years, including 1969, where Mr. Roche said they were
suffering a serious profit squeeze, the General Motors Corporation earned 14.8 billion dollars. Or, to put it another way,
every three and a half years, General Motors had an income
—a profit—equal to its total investment." Reuther declared,
"When Mr. Roche puts a story in the *Wall Street Journal* and
bemoans what he calls the profit question, we have to tell
him that the problem in America and the problem in Canada
is not the profit squeeze. The real problem is the squeeze on
the workers who haven't enough money to do the things they
need to do for their kids. That is where the squeeze is.

"Now Mr. Nixon tells us we ought to exercise restraint when
we go to the bargaining table to get our equity. They would
have the American people and the Canadian people believe
that it is the unreasonable demands of wage earners that have

fed the forces of inflation. But I want to say the record is clear: wage earners are not responsible for inflation, and as far as we are concerned UAW members are not going to be used as scapegoats in the fight against the inflation."

But if the companies were having trouble with the workers, so was the UAW.

More than 40 per cent of the union membership was under thirty. These young workers, conceded Douglas Fraser, a union vice president and director of its Chrysler Department, had "different values than people of my generation." Even Reuther, a man who had grown out of touch with young workers, admitted the change. ("Walter didn't like liquor," a journalist said, "so you can imagine what he thought of pot.") Reuther said, "There is a new breed of worker in the plant who is less willing to accept the discipline of the work place. He is unwilling to accept corporate decisions that preempt his own decisions. There is a different kind of worker than we had twenty-five or thirty years ago." A resentful local union president, an older man, said, "These people want everything handed to them on a silver platter."

The young men and women workers saw no reason to work to the bone, as their fathers had done. Their fathers hated the drudgery, the repetition of the assembly line, but they were older men and older men are not rebellious; they had seen the Depression and they remembered it; they also knew what it had been like in the plants in the days before the union; and they had, in their years in the plant, come to accept plant life as the way plant life was meant to be. The young workers had not; often, they quit or stayed home, or harassed the foremen. Fuck this, the young workers said.

That spring of 1970, at the Chrysler Sterling stamping plant in Sterling Heights, Michigan, a white working class suburb of Detroit, young workers had rebelled, refusing to work overtime after fifteen straight days on the job. What these workers were saying, according to Fraser, was, "I can meet all my worldly needs working five days a week. I've got no obligations, no family. Does the company have the right to deny me my social life?" Fraser said, "The answer, it seems to me, has to be no—the corporation doesn't have that right."

Absenteeism in the plants on weekdays had risen from 2.5 per cent during the fifties and most of the sixties to more than 5 per cent in 1970. The corporations were angered about this, yet the attendance rate at meetings of the twenty-four member General Motors board of directors was 95 per cent, meaning that the corporation directors also had a 5 per cent absenteeism rate, and directors receive six hundred to nine hundred dollars a meeting, plus enjoy a sumptuous meal. Perhaps the workers are to be praised for reporting as faithfully as they do. On Fridays and Mondays the absenteeism rate often soared to 15 per cent or more; General Motors and Ford had been forced to close plants because not enough employees had reported for work.

When this happened in Baltimore in April, with some 200 of 2,700 hourly employees skipping work, the plant manager sent letters to the workers addressed "Dear fellow employee and family," and asking for their "best effort in being at work every day on time." But such efforts showed few results. Once, says Fraser, relating a story that has been told for years in the auto industry, a questioner asked a welder why he had taken a day off, why he was willing to get by on four days of pay a week instead of five. The welder stopped, raised his welding gun, tipped back his visor, and said, "Because I can't get by in three."

To a large extent the increase in absenteeism, like many of the other problems of the work place, was due to the fact that more and more of the jobs in the plants were held by blacks, especially younger blacks. These men possessed a special hatred for factory life; to them the factory was a symbol of America, an obscene, ugly place. They resented that only factory jobs, often the worst factory jobs, were available to them, and that it seemed so difficult for them to advance.° And, in a time of black protest and aspiration, the blacks displayed their discontent: they skipped work; they refused to obey, or sullenly obeyed, the white foremen; sometimes there was sabotage; many of these young black men came from ghetto streets and brought their guns and heroin into the plants. One black worker, a militant at the Dodge plant in Hamtramck, said, "Black workers, they work on the dirtiest, nastiest, filthiest, noisiest jobs. You go find the dirtiest, nastiest, filthiest, noisiest, mother-fuckingest jobs and that's where you'll find the black man."

A perplexed Iacocca lamented, "Who am I to say what we have produced in this country . . . I don't know why some guys won't accept discipline. Maybe it's because they're young . . . I don't know why they won't recognize established order, like getting to work at eight. The son-of-a-bitch comes in at 8:40. You say, 'Didn't I tell you to come in at eight?' You say, 'Well, you bastard, I'll discipline you.' He doesn't recognize discipline or he'd have been there at eight in the first place. So rules don't work. You say, 'Ah, we'll use that old American thing, incentive. We'll pay him something if he comes in.' But he's not coming in the fifth day *now*. If we pay him more, he'll come in only three days instead of four."

Woodcock, the UAW president, said, "Maybe the Protestant ethic is breaking down." In September, two weeks before the strike deadline, Woodcock told cheering Chrysler workers that perhaps a strike would benefit this "new generation" of workers, maybe a strike would show them that "it is only through struggle" that unions achieve their demands.

° This is an old lament. In a perceptive but ignored book, *Labor and Automobiles* (New York: International Publishers), published in 1929, Robert W. Dunn declared: "The writer noticed in one Chevrolet plant that Negroes were engaged on the dirtiest, roughest and most disagreeable work . . . It is more difficult for a Negro to get promoted. Opportunities for more skilled jobs are . . . fewer for him than for the white worker."

Yet the older workers, the ones who had for so long put up with the heat, the noise, the monotony of the shops, the knowledge that as working men they were inferior to white-collar men, inferior to company executives, inferior to the young men coming out of college and joining the company at white-collar levels—these men, many of them, were becoming dissatisfied too. They were tired, they were fearful of violence, they were distressed by the blacks, fed up with factory life, with going in, doing the job, coming home. They had come to hate their jobs; they wanted out.

It was their dissatisfaction that gave rise and support to 30-and-out. Fraser, a well-liked man who had come out of the old DeSoto plants to win union office, lamented, "I feel very badly about this unhappiness, because it wasn't always that way. Guys accepted the auto shop as a fact of life and went home and, you know, in those days, the escape, the recreation, was bowling or finally buying a home, which was really something then, or raising kids. And I guess their high ambition was to get their kids in college. And they seemed reasonably happy." But now, Fraser said, now, "fellows my age—and I wouldn't want to say this in a mass meeting because it's so regrettable, guys who are fifty-one, fifty-two, fifty-three, guys I worked with, are calling me up and saying. 'Doug, you just got to get this 30-and-out. We've got to get out of here.'"

Many of these older workers seemed to have recognized that while they had worked hard all their lives, and achieved homes, cars, boats, snowmobiles, there was a hollowness in what they had achieved. Society was not working well. Taxes were rising. Wages were higher, but they did not buy what they used to. "You go into a store," a Chevrolet worker in Hamtramck said, "and you pay twenty dollars and you come out with a little dinky bag of stuff, a little dinky bag. Years ago, you paid twenty dollars—paid it in that same store—and you came out with something, a couple of big bags, maybe more." It was the workers' sons, not the sons of the rich or the intellectuals, who were being killed in Vietnam; it was the workers' lives, their homes, their children's schools, that were being threatened by crime, violence, inflation.

A concern had risen with blue-collar workers, so long ignored, soon to be ignored again. They were discussed, investigated, polled, and, in the end, characterized as insensitive, selfish, racist, crude. But the writers and pollsters mostly dealt with stereotypes, with superficialities—the number of color television sets, the snowmobiles, the two cars in the driveways. No one, not the newspapers, the magazines, the politicians, nor the union leaders, it seemed, attempted to show the white workers that so many of the practices that worked against blacks and the poor worked against them as well: the tax structure, the political structure, housing construction practices, the use of land, the priorities that put more funds into highways than into schools or hospitals; more into the war than into parks and forests; more into space exploration than into cancer, kidney, or heart research.

Many of the union's leaders and many of its members believe, probably correctly, that the UAW is the most liberal and courageous of the nation's major unions. But the union had not called a national strike against General Motors, its largest, most powerful adversary, since the winter of 1945–6, when the two locked in a bitter struggle that lasted 113 days. That historic strike, the country's first major strike after the war, impressed GM's strength and obduracy upon the union leadership, particularly upon Walter Reuther. The two sides fought the last thirty days of the strike over a one cent hourly wage increase, and toward the end, the story is told, Harry Anderson, the company negotiator, placed a penny on the bargaining table and said, "Walter, there it is, a penny. That's what this strike is all about. And you're not going to get it." And Walter never did. The union settled for the company offer. Yet, by establishing a reputation as a bold, imaginative man unafraid of even a huge company like General Motors, Reuther seized the union presidency. And the strike invigorated the union, giving it great morale for many years.

The lesson was learned, however, and in coming negotiations the UAW always turned to Ford, Chrysler, or American Motors when it named a strike target or when workers were ordered to strike. The union is a remarkably open institution, and Mazey, the secretary-treasurer, is candid in discussing why the union never went back to General Motors; it was, he says, simply a matter of being able to win larger contracts with less sacrifice at the other companies. In 1955, the union and the companies had entered into a gentlemen's agreement in which the companies that were not struck matched the agreement worked out at the target company. "It is better to make the most possible progress with the least suffering," Mazey says. "That is, if you can push around a Chrysler Corporation, this is the thing you ought to do, instead of tackling a GM, which may not give you as much and may result in a long struggle."

General Motors, of course, was often displeased with the reciprocity. The General Motors men believed the company was tougher than the other companies, and that, given GM's excellent money position and the firm's willingness to combat the union, it could force a much less costly settlement on the union than Ford or Chrysler. They believed that the other companies knuckled under and did not demonstrate the strength that should be expected from such a responsible firm as an automobile company. In 1955, when Reuther won historic supplemental unemployment benefits at Ford, forerunners of what amounts to a guaranteed annual wage, GM's Harry Anderson told him, "Walter, let me congratulate you for going to Ford. You never would have got that here." In 1964, when the union won a four hundred dollar a month early retirement program at Chrysler, the program the union now hoped to expand in the 1970 agreement, Louis G. Seaton, General Motors' chief negotiator, told Reuther he never would have got four hundred dollars at GM, at least not without "a hell of a fight."

No matter how practical this avoidance of General Motors may have been, the belief was growing in the ranks that the union lacked the courage to confront the corporation. Mazey: "The average person, the average worker, likes to take on the big guy, the giant. And GM is a giant. Chrysler, although it is the seventh largest [manufacturing] corporation in America, is looked upon as a pygmy. The average person, if we took on Chrysler, would say, 'Well, hell, you took on Chrysler and beat them. So what?'" James Hensley, vice chairman of the union's General Motors bargaining committee, said, "I think it was definitely the trend this negotiation to strike General Motors if we didn't get everything we wanted. I think everyone was ready to strike. It had been twenty-five years since General Motors had a national strike and I think people kind of felt it was their duty to take on GM rather than Ford, Chrysler, or AMC. In fact, I'm sure a lot of people would have been disappointed if we hadn't." For both leaders and workers, a strike against General Motors in 1970 was a way to establish their manhood.

General Motors workers seem to dislike GM more than Ford or Chrysler or AMC workers dislike their companies. Perhaps this is because it was at General Motors, in the famous sitdown strike of 1936–7 at Flint, Michigan, that the union won recognition. Perhaps this is because for years the union and critics of the automobile industry have said that General Motors, with its enormous size, has its tentacles deep in America, that it dictates prices, dictates to banks and suppliers, that it is the very embodiment of the avaricious and heartless American corporation. "A strike against General Motors is different from a strike against Ford or Chrysler," Fraser explained. "A strike against General Motors isn't just a strike, it's a crusade."

The key union demand, restoration of unlimited cost-of-living, further confirmed General Motors as the 1970 strike

target. The cost-of-living formula was given to the union—
not won, as the union says—by General Motors in 1948 in
an attempt to bring stability and predictability to its dealings
with the then young and raucous union. The plan was conceived in 1940 by Charles E. (Engine Charlie) Wilson, General Motors president and later secretary of defense in the
Eisenhower Administration. With the war and the difficult
1945–6 strike, General Motors for years found no opportunity
to propose cost-of-living raises. But in 1948, still disturbed
by the bitterness of the strike three years before, and believing that by putting labor relations on a stable basis there
would be no need for strikes that would cause more bitterness, Wilson proposed the cost-of-living formula and a plan
for an annual wage increase—the annual improvement factor
—based upon increases in productivity. The union, after
some hesitation, accepted the proposal.

Much of American business, like much of labor, opposed
the idea. To counter his critics, Wilson wrote in *Reader's
Digest* in 1952: "The working people did not make that inflation [of the late 1940s and early 1950s]. They only want to
catch up with it in order to be able to pay their grocery bills.
I contend that present high wages are more the result of
fundamental inflationary money pressures than of unreasonable wage pressures by the union." He then declared, in
words that General Motors men in 1970 sometimes wished
had never entered the late, beloved president's white-haired
head (sometimes, a company man said, "we would like to go
out and piss on his grave"): "Arrangements like ours, for
lifting and lowering wages in step with the cost-of-living,
are commonly called 'escalator clauses.' They are attacked by
people who insist upon talking about the 'wage-price spiral.'
We should say the 'price-wage spiral.' For it is not primarily
wages that push up prices, it is primarily prices that pull up
wages."

Now, in 1970, wishing to recover unlimited cost-of-living,
the unions decided that the best place to get it was at General

Motors. It was a matter, Mazey explains, of having "all these marvelous, those simply great quotes from Charlie Wilson, and obviously the best place to go with them was General Motors."

Even Walter Reuther, who had been avoiding General Motors, recognized the growing pressures to take on GM in 1970. At the United Automobile Workers convention, a delegate shouted from the floor that it was time, this time, after all these years, to challenge General Motors, and Reuther, quietly from the podium at the end of the huge convention hall, said, "We might just do that." The thought of closing his negotiating career (he was scheduled to retire before the next round of negotiations in 1973) with such a large, exciting battle, it can be imagined, appealed to Reuther; indeed, it was under Reuther's direction that the union built up a 120 million dollar strike fund, largest in labor history, the kind of fund a union would need to strike the largest manufacturing enterprise in history.

By the time of the union convention, Reuther was solidly behind a long list of demands, including 30-and-out, which he had long opposed. Reuther believed, as did the companies, that it was unwise for men to leave the work force at such a young age. Moreover, he believed it would be difficult to prevent these men from obtaining other jobs, which would defeat the aim of opening up jobs for younger men. But Reuther saw that a groundswell had developed behind 30-and-out, and it is a long-standing leadership technique within the UAW, as within most any political institution, not to let younger men below develop demands, win victories, and assume the status of leaders. Reuther pulled the 30-and-out demand to his chest as if it were his own. "Quite frankly," he told the convention, "if I had spent my life on the line, I would have been demanding 30-and-out long ago."

The union demands were the largest ever, and Reuther endorsed them wholeheartedly, vowing at the convention, "We are going to fight on the picket lines if necessary to get

these demands in 1970 . . . We are under no illusions that
the corporations are going to roll over and play dead." The
cost-of-living money that would have gone to the workers
if the contracts had not been changed in 1967, Reuther said,
was not to be bargained for; it was, he said, "old money," not
"new money," and all of it—26 cents per hour by the end of
April—was automatically due the workers. The workers, he
said, needed a "bill of rights" in the plants, they needed
longer vacations with vacation bonuses, a stock purchase
plan, a voice in getting the corporations to stop pollution.

Certainly much of Reuther's support for these demands
was designed to appease the workers. Much of it was the
result of Reuther's penchant for rhetoric and grand statements, for despite his many accomplishments, Reuther was
something of a windbag. Nonetheless, oddly for a man who
prized flexibility in bargaining, Reuther had painted the
union into a corner. "When you put in demands for all
groups," one company bargainer said, "you know you can't
do everything for everybody."

Then suddenly Reuther, this legendary man, was gone,
killed six weeks before the talks were to begin, when his
chartered Lear jet crashed on a rainy spring night into an
oak and jack-pine forest in northern Michigan as he headed
for the union's handsome education and recreation center
at Black Lake.

With Reuther dead, there was no one with the clout to
go to the workers—as slim as the possibilities for approval
would have been even had Reuther been alive—and say,
"This is a fine settlement; let us accept it. There is no need
for a strike." Woodcock became president, and he felt pressure—pressure from the rank-and-file, pressure to create an
image of the union as a strong institution, pressure to prove
himself, to purge the memory of Reuther and at the same
time to honor it—to strike General Motors.

In 1964 and 1967, while director of the union's General
Motors Department, Woodcock had argued that the union

should confront General Motors. He was angered when he was overruled.

Now, Woodcock knew he needed not just a large settlement but a large settlement at General Motors to enhance his political position within the UAW. He had been elected president by a thirteen to twelve vote over Fraser, and while he had the support of the most powerful members of the twenty-five member executive board, the members with the largest constituencies, he knew it was unwise to take chances. Woodcock seemed in no immediate trouble; yet, if he were branded a coward, if the settlement was not one that could be called a victory, a large victory, who could say what would happen? The union is an intensely political organization. "These guys have stereoscopic vision; it goes right around their heads," a mediator says. Gomer Goins, a Cadillac worker and member of the GM national bargaining team: "If you snooze, you lose."

Besides, it was nearly impossible for Woodcock and the union to select Chrysler or Ford. Chrysler was in financial trouble; Ford had been the target in 1955 and 1958, and in 1967, the union had staged a sixty-seven day strike at Ford. In the summer of 1970, Woodcock says, as he traveled across the country chatting with union officials and rank-and-file, breaking bread with them, taking the pulse of the membership, "Ford guys would come up to me, not say it officially in meetings, but just indicating, 'Look we've been first an awful lot . . . Don't you think we can go after the big one for a change?' " Kenneth Bannon, UAW vice president and director of its Ford Department, insisted with a straight face that "the Ford workers will walk that last mile," but a mediator says, "Those Ford workers would have crapped in their pants if Leonard had told them to go out again."

Wherever he went that summer, Woodcock says, the overwhelming sentiment was for selecting General Motors as the strike target and, if the union could not achieve the settlement it wanted, for striking the corporation. He re-

minded union men, he says, that in the past fifteen years the
union had logged more strike days at General Motors over
local and national issues than at Ford and Chrysler combined.
He reminded them, too, that the union had struck GM for
five days in 1964 over local issues. It was obvious, he told the
workers, that the union was not afraid of General Motors.
"But I didn't make a dent on those guys," Woodcock says.
"They would always reply, 'Yeah, yeah, but we never take on
number one.'" He says, "All these things, adding together,
said to me, and had said to me for quite a time, that we just
couldn't sidestep General Motors."

Clearly there had never been a situation like this—
high union demands, lower industry profits, great pressure
to take on General Motors, company determination to resist
the union—all of this muddied by Reuther's death. In May,
as plans were made to carry Reuther's body to the Henry and
Edsel Ford Auditorium for his funeral, a riverfront building
paid for by the Ford Motor Company and Ford and Lincoln-
Mercury dealers across the country, as plans were drawn to
have the auto factories across the country close for two
minutes in an unprecedented salute to the dead union leader,
the companies were already speculating what the impact of
a new man at the head of the union might be. "It's taken a
strong man to keep the situation under control," Virgil Boyd,
Chrysler vice chairman told *The New York Times*. "I hope
that whoever his successor is can exercise great internal discipline." Another company man, realizing that the new leader
might have internal difficulties, realizing that a leader who
won his demands would be strong and that it was in the
interest of the companies to have a strong, stable leadership
within the union, told the *Times*, "We may just have to pull
their chestnuts out of the fire."

Chapter 2

A civilized relationship

Inflation, the damned inflation. That was the problem, Leonard Woodcock said, just as James Roche had indicated in St. Louis in February. But whereas Roche placed the blame on rising wages, Woodcock attributed the inflation to "the war and other unnecessary, useless military spending." The key to the 1970 negotiations, he said at General Motors the day the talks began, July 15, was to protect the workers against inflation; to do that, he said, the companies must restore unlimited cost-of-living. This would be a "return to sanity. We were sold a cap on the cost of living in 1967 as being counter-inflationary. It obviously had no effect at all upon the inflationary situation . . . We want a return to basic Wilsonian principles, C. E. Wilsonian principles."

Woodcock said that the union's financial difficulties, caused by massive layoffs in its aerospace department and the huge cash outlays at the Black Lake education and recreation center (no one had foreseen Walter Reuther's insistence upon splendor or had guessed that construction costs, including labor, would soar so high), would have no effect on the negotiations. The union executive board, Woodcock said, would meet shortly to tighten the union's finances and to make staff cuts to "make absolutely sure the strike fund is fully available if we are pushed into a strike." He said that if anyone was "looking for the imminent collapse of the UAW, a la Penn Central, that is not in the cards. Like Chrysler Corporation we will take care of our financial problems."

This year, Woodcock said, the union would change its opening procedures. Irving Bluestone, appointed Woodcock's co-director at the General Motors Department when Woodcock became president, would present the union's demands as quickly as he could, perhaps finishing in two or three days. From 1961 on, Woodcock had presented only a limited number of demands each day, so that the union could publish and distribute the demands to the local unions as they were being presented to the corporation. Louis G. Seaton, the General Motors negotiator, had called this "the Perils of Pauline" approach.

Woodcock was asked when he expected an offer from the companies. "There will come a day," he said, "if they follow the script—and I'm hoping and praying for the good of the country they will get off that script and go back to the pre-1955 ways of doing things," when each company, at least in appearance, negotiated for itself, each making a separate offer. "But if they follow the script of '58, '61, '64, '67—on some day in late August or early September, by some process of osmosis, since they tell us they don't have these consultations, Chrysler Corporation in Highland Park, the Ford Motor Company in Dearborn, the General Motors Corporation here, will make an identical economic offer to this union."

Was the union, he was asked, prepared to extend its contracts past September 14?

"If we are forced to that position, and we're going to do our level best to avoid it, there will be certainly one contract that will not be extended beyond midnight, September 14."

Which contract, he was asked, would that be?

"The process for the next five or six weeks," he said, "will be to seek a volunteer."

Bramblett, the GM negotiator, declared that "continuing inflation worries everyone." But, he said, "we agree with the union that our employees are among the best protected in

the world with respect to cost-of-living." That was a wry
reference to a statement Reuther made at the union convention in April, defending the 1967 decision to permit a ceiling
on cost-of-living increases because, Reuther said, union members were already well protected against inflation.

    Next day, following the company-a-day plan Reuther
had laid down to obtain a three day run of publicity, Woodcock and the union entourage drove to the Ford World
Headquarters, a twelve story glass and aluminum building
in Dearborn, just west of Detroit.

    The headquarters, a handsome structure known as "The
Glass House," is built on farm and woodlands that Henry
Ford bought before World War I, as he was expanding the
Ford Motor Company and wanted to avoid city taxes and
higher land costs in the city. The spot for the building was
selected after World War II, at a time when Ford was outgrow-
ing its old headquarters in Dearborn. When the site was made
known to Clara Ford, Henry Ford's widow, she complained
that the tall building might spoil her view from Fair Lane,
the family estate on the banks of the Rouge River, where
old Henry had died and where she still maintained her
residence. Henry Ford II directed contractors to erect on
the proposed site a tower that was the exact height of the
planned headquarters. His grandmother stepped outside her
home, saw that her view would not be impaired, and said, all
right, Henry, build the building.

    Whereas General Motors is a corporation that is success-
ful because of its structure and organization—it overhires
and has many plodding men, but obedience to the system
and the vast resources the system has produced make it
strong—Ford is a company of personalities. It has been that
way since the days of Henry Ford, Charles Sorensen, and
Harry Bennett, and is that way today under Henry Ford II
and Lee A. Iacocca. And while General Motors is a company
of many kings (the division managers), with the kingdoms

united in a league (the corporation), Ford is a company of
one king, Henry; one prince with the king's ear, Iacocca; and
many subordinate princes, all of them possessing limited
power.

Ford's problem historically has been that even though
the Ford provides a reasonable challenge to the Chevrolet
in the low-priced market, the company's cars have been unable to crack General Motors' dominant hold on the medium
price range with Buick, Oldsmobile, and Pontiac. Ford seems
incapable of overtaking General Motors—it has done this
only three times since the Model T was abandoned—and
perhaps it never will again. But if Ford is second to General
Motors, it is small only by comparison, for it is the world's
third largest manufacturer, behind General Motors and Standard Oil of New Jersey and, even in times of recession,
it makes a great deal of money. Ford wants to retain its
position and to maintain and improve profits. In 1967, when
Ford suffered through the sixty-seven day strike, Henry
Ford II attacked what he called the monopolistic power of
the unions—language usually reserved for unions attacking
the automobile corporations. And in 1970, Malcolm Denise
passed the word to Kenneth Bannon: Ford did not want a
strike, it is someone else's turn to be struck. If the union
strikes us, be prepared for a big fight.

The union and the Ford Company negotiators met for
two hours, and when they were finished, Denise, the company's top negotiator, warned "it would be our view that it
would be inflationary" to return to unlimited cost-of-living
increases—the union's key demand. Stressing a theme Bramblett had put forth the day before, and one President Nixon
would stress later, Denise cautioned that both sides must
guard against forcing labor costs so high that American
manufacturers could not compete against the foreign manufacturers. Denise noted the wide gap between foreign and
domestic wages, and, parroting Bramblett, declared: "To
the extent that this gap becomes even wider as a result of
the upcoming negotiations, it will be even more difficult for

the domestic manufacturers to compete with foreign producers."

The foreign car invasion, so costly to the industry,
was a subject of discussion many times in the 1970 negotiations, with the companies and the government using the invasion as a reason to urge the union to exercise restraint in
its demands. Yet neither the companies nor the government
gave a complete account of the small car issue, for, as Woodcock told Denise: "The record shows that when domestic
industry competes, it can win that competition." What had
happened, Woodcock said, was that for years the domestic
industry had not wanted to compete in the small car field;
the industry's losses to the foreign manufacturers were in
large part the industry's own fault.

There was truth in this. Traditionally, American manufacturers have disliked small cars because there is little profit
in them. Style, size, luxury, power—these have been the hall-
marks in Detroit ever since Alfred P. Sloan, Jr., and William
Knudsen pioneered the annual model change in the 1920s
to create the modern automobile industry. George Walker,
the legendary Ford stylist, the quintessential stylist, a man
who owned fifty pairs of shoes and seventy suits, wore cuff-
links the size of pieces of eight, and bathed himself in Fa-
bergé, once said that Volkswagen, the car responsible for the
small car's popularity in America, was the "mystery of the
world." Volkswagen "was just a bathtub, and I've predicted
it would drop off for years," he said. "Europeans may like
it but it doesn't have any American style." Small cars, said
Ernest Breech in the 1950s, when he was Ford's executive
vice president, implied a reduction in the buyer's standard
of living. Americans, he suggested, would never be happy
with them.

Yet there is, and always has been, a need in America for
a small, economical automobile—"a good car at a low price,"
as Henry Ford said of the Model T. Indeed, Charles F. Ket-

tering, the General Motors automotive genius, inventor of the self-starter, Duco paint, and ethyl gasoline, said in 1924: "The wanton consumption of horsepower in propelling heavy motor vehicles portends disaster." The streets, he said, "are absurdly congested with these great empty vehicles" and wise manufacturers see "signs that point the way to a smaller, less expensive car."

But the American manufacturers refused to enter the small car market because of the smaller profit. A full-sized automobile, a Chevrolet, Ford, or Plymouth, with a list price of, say, 4,000 dollars, and selling at reasonable volume, will yield General Motors, perhaps, an average 250 to 300 dollars in after-tax profits. But after-tax profits on a subcompact automobile, selling for about 2,000 dollars, are perhaps half that, 125 to 150 dollars. And if volume is not high, or if the subcompacts take sales from higher priced, more profitable big cars, a firm's earnings will be badly eroded. It is even possible for the American manufacturers to lose money on subcompacts, although they insist this is not the case.

Additionally, the industry counts on high profits on options like power windows, power brakes, power seats, carpets, vinyl roofs, racing stripes, tape decks, air-conditioning. Many people who buy small cars like the Vega and Pinto are much less likely, at least when the cars are first placed on the market, to load their cars with 600 to 1,000 dollars worth of extras—much to the industry's discomfiture, since profit margins on options often run 15 per cent or more, with the margins on some—air-conditioning, for example—perhaps rising to 50 to 100 per cent.

Finally, of course, there is the problem of labor, about one-third of the cost of a company's operations. While a small car sells for 1,000 or so dollars less than a large car, substantially the same labor (9 hours of direct labor on the assembly line, 60 to 70 hours overall) goes into all cars, large or small. Obviously, it is more difficult to recover labor costs for a small car than a large car.

Foreign manufacturers are content with small cars because they are content with smaller profits—generally 2 to 4 per cent on sales. In contrast, American rates in 1969, the last pre-strike year, stood at 7 per cent for General Motors, 4.5 per cent for Ford, and 4.4 per cent for Chrysler. And this was not an especially lucrative year.

In the late 1950s and early 1960s, what was described as a small car revolution occurred as foreign companies, led by Volkswagen, swept into the American market. At one time there were seventy-seven foreign nameplates being sold in America.

What happened was that the Big Three, heady after a record 7.9 million sales in 1955, had gone berserk, giving America the tail fin, the huge tail light, unprecedented size and power: the obscene era of American chrome. At the same time, the 1958 recession struck the country, and car buyers, revolting against the large, ugly—and expensive—American cars, suddenly preferred the small, low-priced foreign model.

The Big Three, after a time of disbelief that Americans were serious about small foreign cars, were forced to retaliate, and in 1960 they brought out the compacts: Falcon, Corvair, and Valiant. The cars sold well—874,000 units that first year—and the foreign cars fell from 10 per cent of the market in 1959 to 5 per cent in 1961. Then, as soon as the foreign cars were beaten back, the Big Three began to build up the compacts, making them more powerful, making options standard equipment, increasing the size—all of this making the cars higher priced and more profitable. Sporty intermediates were introduced to skim off the top of the small car market. The style on the compacts stayed the same, but other models continued to change, and the compacts began to appear stodgy and old-fashioned. By the early 1960s, too, the recession had ended: good times were at hand again, people had more money to buy the expensive cars Detroit wanted to sell and was advertising so heavily. Only the Volks-

wagen survived to succeed again in the late 1960s and early
1970s and to bring the American manufacturers their second
—and more damaging—small car war: the war between the
Americans and the Germans and Japanese.

For years the union advocated the building of an American
small car. Before World War II, Walter Reuther and Victor
Reuther urged construction of a Victory car, a small car that
all companies would pool their resources to produce and that
each would sell at the same price, thus giving no producer
an advantage and providing the American consumer with
economical automobile transportation. The companies rejected the proposal. During the Kennedy and Johnson Ad-
ministrations, Reuther, seemingly more aware of the importance of the foreign car invasion than the manufacturers,
urged that Congress pass legislation to free the manufacturers from antitrust restraint so they could pool resources and
produce a small car. Neither the government nor the industry
was interested in the proposal. Once, in the 1960s, Leonard
Woodcock told Louis G. Seaton during a bargaining session
that General Motors should build a small car. Not to do so,
Woodcock said, was indefensible. Goddammit, Seaton said,
you are trying to tell General Motors how to run its business.
Keep quiet, he said. What we make is none of your business.

Now, at the Ford talks, Woodcock declared that had
the American manufacturers not preferred large profits and
ignored the small car market, the problem of the imports
would not exist. The companies, he said, were asking the
union to "stand still to protect the jobs of our members—
jobs in jeopardy because of an error that the manufacturers
themselves have made." The companies, he said, "can pay
the wage rates we have and will get this year and still compete" with the foreign manufacturers.

. . .

On the third day of the talks, Woodcock went to the Chrysler Corporation, driving up the Walter P. Chrysler Expressway, named to honor the company's founder. (There is no Walter P. Reuther Expressway in Detroit or, say, an Auto Workers Expressway, but in addition to the Chrysler there are the Edsel Ford and the Fisher Expressways, the latter named for the coach-building brothers instrumental in the success of GM.)

Compared to General Motors, or to Ford after its post-World War II recovery, Chrysler has periodically been in financial trouble. It was founded in 1925 from the remnants of the weakened Maxwell Motor Car Company, which Walter Chrysler had been asked by bankers to rescue. Chrysler had been a brilliant engineer at General Motors, but quit in anger at the wildcatting ways of William C. Durant, the General Motors chairman. Later, Chrysler added the Dodge Brothers Manufacturing Company, a company that had grown large from the 25 million dollars the Dodge brothers, Horace and John, made from their 20,000 dollar investment in Ford Motor Company. Henry Ford had bought out the Dodges and other stockholders in 1919 because he considered them parasitic and no longer wanted to pay dividends.

For a time in the 1930s and 1940s, as Ford floundered under the mad hatter directorship of the first Henry Ford, Chrysler was the second largest manufacturer in the industry. It fell back to third when Henry Ford II and Ernest Breech rebuilt Ford after World War II. Chrysler continued to prosper because of brilliant engineering and styling, but its plants were old and it did not build up a profitable overseas empire as Ford and General Motors did. Hard times came in the 1950s, when Chrysler pushed conservative cars, bigger on the inside, smaller on the outside, while General Motors and Ford brought out longer, lower, and wider cars. Chrysler quickly reversed itself, introducing sleek, low cars with huge fins, but the models were pushed through so quickly they had many mechanical and electrical problems. This, coupled

with the 1958 recession and charges of corruption against
the top Chrysler executives, brought a new management in
the early 1960s. Lynn Townsend, an accountant, set the new
strategy: Chrysler, because it was third, could not afford to
be an innovator; it must follow the trends set by General
Motors and Ford. By the late 1960s, the lack of innovation at
Chrysler was apparent to buyers. Chrysler did not have the
hot cars that GM and Ford had; its expensive new plants
were operating at less than capacity. It had sunk some 200
million dollars into construction of a plant in a Pennsylvania
field, but the company's sales volume is so low the plant sits
there half finished. It had placed much money into its foreign
operations, Rootes and Simca, but these firms, European left-
overs acquired late, were largely unprofitable. John J. Riccardo, Chrysler president, a man brought in to cut costs
and reduce personnel, a man who applied himself so vigorously to his task that he is known as "the flamethrower," says:
"Chrysler will always be a boom-or-bust company."

Despite Chrysler's financial problems, Woodcock told the
corporation negotiators, John Leary and William O'Brien,
that the company would not be treated differently from
General Motors or Ford. Woodcock said he "assured Chrysler that if the industry continues in its lock-stop position
that it has over the last several rounds of bargaining, and we
are forced to pick a target, they will have the privilege of
being on the list." The day before, Chrysler had announced
a second quarter profit of 8.1 million dollars, compared to a
loss of 29.4 million in the first quarter of the year. "We are
obviously very happy that the Chrysler Corporation is back
into black figures," Woodcock said. "We have never had any
doubt that Chrysler Corporation is a very sound company."
He added, "They have been, unfortunately, one of the victims of Mr. Nixon's engineered recession."

That day at Chrysler, Woodcock also made a plea for a
cause the union has championed, national health insurance.
If national health insurance were enacted, Woodcock said—

Woodcock had assumed the chairmanship of the one-hun-
dred member Committee for National Health Insurance
when Reuther, who had been chairman, died—it would
reduce the companies' health insurance premiums by at least
a third. Additionally, he said, it would mean that proper
medical care would go to "thirty million Americans who do
not get any kind of medical care—and that is a national dis-
grace." The insurance, he said, would be financed by a 2.8
per cent tax on payrolls and a 1.8 per cent tax on employees'
salaries up to 15,000 dollars. The two taxes, Woodcock said,
would provide 60 per cent of the funds for the program, the
rest coming from the general revenues of the federal government. The union asked the company to agree to "absorb
the employee tax when it comes into effect" and "more importantly, to get their support to bring it into effect."

Woodcock laughed when he was asked whether the corporation negotiators had expressed interest in the plan. "They
just listened," he said, and took pains "to point out to us that
silence did not give consent."

While Woodcock was at Ford and Chrysler, Bluestone,
as Woodcock had promised, rapidly began bringing union
position papers before the General Motors Corporation, ac-
complishing in two days what had taken eight days in 1967.

First came the many nonwage demands the union had
been formulating, often with much fanfare and headlines,
for several months: voluntary overtime, the paid dental plan,
an unbroken holiday between Christmas and New Year's,
discounts on company products—which the company had
granted for years to many white-collar workers—for blue-
collar workers and retirees, a paid holiday for workers with
more than thirty days' service on the day of the birth of a
child. The union also asked a "harmony clause," which would
pledge the corporation not to intervene in union attempts
to organize white-collar workers. Reuther had begun white-
collar organizing in the late 1950s but the companies had
thwarted his efforts, except for the unionization of some ten

thousand white-collar workers at Chrysler Corporation, by granting white-collar workers the same increases that the union negotiated for its blue-collar workers.

Reflecting the popular concern about environmental pollution, much of that pollution caused by automobiles, the union challenged General Motors to reveal how much it spends each year toward eliminating pollutants from its automobiles and plants, and for comparison, how much it spends on advertising and styling changes. "The public has been left with the impression," the union said, "that the corporation places greater emphasis on the contour of the fender than on the control of poisonous pollutants." The union also declared that union men should sit as equals with corporation executives in meetings with government officials on both pollution and automobile safety.

In a most ironic demand, the union asked that time clocks be eliminated, Bluestone saying the clocks were "nasty" examples of the double standard between white-collar and blue-collar workers—ironic because at Solidarity House, the home of the union, janitorial and secretarial personnel punch time clocks. Emil Mazey explains that the union time clocks made for greater punctuality and efficiency.

The corporation men listened attentively, not interrupting, saying little. One reason was they had no great interest in many of these demands, especially such demands as the elimination of time clocks or the disclosure of the money spent on pollution control. They knew, as did the union, that there was no possibility the demands would be agreed to, that they were simply pro forma statements, once made, quickly forgotten. The union does this at all the contract talks, listing demands it wants and will bargain for, demands it would like to have but is not ready to fight for, demands it would like to have but knows it will never get, and demands it does not care about but which look good to the members and to the public.

The company men were really interested in money—de-

mands that dealt essentially in money and would give an
indication of how much a settlement with the union would
cost the corporation. On Monday, July 20, as the second
week of talks began, Bluestone placed the major economic
demands before the corporation: what he called a "substantial" wage increase, restoration of unlimited cost-of-
living, and 30-and-out. In addition, the union asked for
changes in the supplemental unemployment program—its
form of guaranteed wage—so that in the event of major layoffs the fund could not go bankrupt and benefits be stopped.
The union asked that the company increase the amount of
money it pays into the fund (the amount stood at 5 to 7
cents an hour, depending on the size of the fund, a contribution that amounted to somewhat less than 2.5 per cent of
GM's payroll; the union asked that this be increased to 2.5
per cent), and that workers receive 80 per cent of their
weekly, straight-time pay during layoffs instead of the 95
per cent of take-home pay, with reductions for lunch and
driving costs, which they had been receiving since 1967. The
proposal would mean 10 to 15 dollars more per week for each
worker on layoff.

The union demanded that the company pay one-quarter
cent an hour per employee to establish a union educational
program, with half the sum—General Motors estimated the
fund would amount to 2.5 million dollars a year—earmarked
for the union's splendid Walter and May Reuther Education
Center at Black Lake. In a traditional rephrasing of its 1945–6
demand, the union asked that General Motors "open its
books" to allow the union and public to see whether it could
afford to meet the union's demands. Bramblett replied that
each year the company issues "one of the nation's most com-
prehensive" stockholders' reports—a report the union has
automatically received since April 1948, when it purchased
one share of General Motors stock in order to receive share-
holder information and to speak, if the union wished, at the
corporation's annual meetings. (The share was purchased

at the market price of 56 dollars. Since then, General Motors stock has split seven ways, and on July 15, the day the 1970 talks opened, GM stock stood at 65¾, making the UAW's seven shares worth 460.25 dollars.) With Bramblett's reply, the demand, which the union feels compelled to make each negotiation, was forgotten.

Bramblett said he was stunned by the union's demands. They were, he said, "more far-reaching and extensive than anything we had read or heard about." The union's argument that the typical General Motors worker did not earn enough to maintain an adequate standard of living was foolish, he said. He always had trouble "understanding these theoretical budgets which come out higher than most people make."

Bluestone, a humorless man, hair slicked down in the Robert McNamara style, said the companies always said the union's demands were more far-reaching and extensive than anything they had read or heard about.

Next day, General Motors issued what was perhaps the most harshly worded corporation statement since the angry days of 1945–6, the tone much like that Roche established in his February speech in St. Louis, the speech that accused workers of goldbricking and charged the union with shirking its contract responsibilities.

The corporation had long been critical of employee attitudes, of absenteeism, tardiness, and shoddy workmanship, but its criticism in public had always been muted. Now it seemed that the corporation had become angry and bitter, that its patience had ended—that it was going to demand that the union step in and join the company in ensuring its demands be met, that employees start coming to work on time, that they stop skipping work, that they show enthusiasm on the job, that for once, goddammit, the company get some productivity.

The forty-five-page General Motors document declared that in past negotiations the corporation had granted the union many concessions—representation, dues checkoff, the union shop—designed to assist the union in organizing and

maintaining control of workers. But the union, the corporation charged, was not living up to its part of the bargain.
The corporation declared: "Irresponsible behavior by some
UAW committeemen is contrary to the intent and purpose
of the agreement . . . and must be corrected." Management
has the right to establish reasonable production standards,
the company said, and employees have an "obligation to make
an honest effort to perform their duties in a proper manner."
Instead, the company said, "tardiness, wasting time or loiter-
ing, careless workmanship, failure to follow instructions and
abuse of employee facilities" seemed to be increasing.

The company said that production had "been disrupted
repeatedly by 'crisis' situations and strikes." Increased absenteeism "had adversely affected both product quality and
manufacturing efficiency and . . . the peace of mind and
sense of security of the vastly larger number of employees"
who report to work regularly. "A number of local unions have
resisted management efforts to maintain order and compliance
with reasonable standards of employee conduct . . ." The
number of grievances, many of them meritless, the company
said, had increased "alarmingly"—from 106,000 in 1960 to
256,000 in 1969. "The threat of a strike which can grow out
of a production standards dispute has become an instrument
in the hands of certain local unions used to harass management and to seek concessions on issues that are entirely un-
related to the merits of the production standard dispute."

Discussing the increasing costs of health and medical insurance, the company said that between October 1969 and
September 1970, it would pay 43 million dollars for hospital-
ization–surgical–medical premiums and 17 million dollars
more for drug prescriptions than during the same period the
year before. For the thirteen months beginning October
1971, the company foresaw an increase of 66 million dollars
in these costs. A vexing problem, the company said, was that
employees who quit or were fired were covered by the company-paid health and medical insurance program for a month
after they left, and that this alone would cost the corporation

2 million dollars in 1970—2 million spent on people no longer employed by General Motors. Such coverage must be ended, the corporation said.

Unethical attorneys, the corporation said, were encouraging retirees to file workmen's compensation claims based on complaints associated, in many cases, not with work-induced accidents, but "with the aging process or the ordinary diseases of life, such as arthritis and heart disease." The corporation said that claims had been filed as long as fifteen years after an employee retired.

Many workers, GM said, were claiming sickness and accident benefits for "subjective types of illnesses" such as strains, nervous conditions, mental depression, nervous exhaustion, and fatigue. Once employees were on sick leave, the company said, they often prolonged their absence, "some apparently because they simply do not wish to return" to work. Often, the corporation said, disability benefits—90 dollars a week for the typical employee, an assembler, with other workers getting up to 140 dollars weekly—were higher than wages in the communities where the workers live, thus, the corporation said, eliminating the incentive to return to work.

The corporation made two proposals to rectify these conditions: that rates not be raised as wages increase, thus keeping payments low, and that benefits vary according to seniority. Employees should become eligible for sickness and accident insurance only after a "reasonable period of service," the corporation said, "perhaps when seniority was established after ninety days on the job." The corporation proposed that employees no longer be allowed to receive both company pension benefits and workmen's compensation.

Bramblett said that the corporation's growth and profits were not automatic. He said that the union and company must cooperate to end contract abuses. Asked whether General Motors might want workers to pay health insurance premiums past a certain point, he said, "Obviously, this is a remedy that will be considered."

Now Bluestone expressed shock. The union, he said, would study the complaints, something, he said, the union was always willing to do. But it appeared to him that the company was attempting to "legislate across the board so as to deprive the many who are deserving in order to correct the abuses of a few." He said it was inconsistent for General Motors to complain about rising medical insurance costs when the corporation never worked to halt Blue Cross–Blue Shield increases when the insurance company sought them. "Everytime the Blues wanted more, the UAW has opposed it," Bluestone said. "But we never have seen the industry taking sides with us."

By the end of the week, the union had presented its demands at Ford and Chrysler, the same demands, in the main, it had made at General Motors.

Kenneth Bannon, director of the union's Ford Department, said that the key to a settlement was returning to unlimited cost-of-living. "We want to avoid a strike," Bannon said. "But there is no way of avoiding one if Ford is unwilling to move off its position on the cost-of-living." Sidney F. McKenna, director of labor relations at Ford, said that Ford had taken a sixty-seven day strike in 1967 to place a ceiling on cost-of-living increases and "we don't entertain lightly any notion of making changes in it."

Douglas Fraser, director of the Chrysler Department, was even harsher in his criticism of Chrysler's failure to contest health insurance increases than Bluestone was of General Motors. Chrysler, Fraser said, was "afraid to stand up to the medical profession." Many doctors, he said, performed unnecessary medical diagnoses for which they charged large fees. Doctors, Fraser said, "have been picking [the company's] pocket for years."

On July 27, the General Motors Corporation announced its second quarter financial figures: profits of 473 million dollars, 1.64 dollars a share, up from 448 million, 1.56 dollars a share the year before. James Roche said that it appeared the low point in automobile sales had passed and that the outlook for third quarter sales was good—provided there was no labor stoppage. Bluestone called the profits "stupendous" and said they reinforced "our claim that GM can well afford to offer substantial wage increases to its workers and meet the many other" union demands. He said: "GM has rarely been far wrong in its projections. We will rely upon their optimistic outlook"—meaning the union would use the high profit figures as justification for its demands.

If General Motors had no financial problems, the United Automobile Workers did. On July 30, the twenty-four member executive board voted to lay off some 125 of its 980 member international staff and to cut back some 10 per cent on its clerical and janitorial staff. The board also ordered reductions in travel costs and office expenditures. The union's resources, Woodcock said, stood at a record 139 million dollars, but the union, he said, had been operating at a deficit for several months.°

The talks now slipped into the somnolent subcommittee

° The 1970 financial problems were not the first the UAW has encountered. Perhaps it is a better union than a business. In 1965, the UAW had 3 million dollars in the San Francisco National Bank and 50,000 dollars in the Brighton National Bank of Brighton, Colorado, when the banks folded, taking the UAW money with them. The controller of the currency criticized the UAW for allowing "money brokers" to persuade it to place money in a California bank—only thirty months old when it collapsed— when there were reliable, established banks in Detroit. The UAW had made the decision to use the San Francisco bank so it could earn the then rather high interest rate of 4.75 per cent. For Emil Mazey, the UAW secretary-treasurer, who is proud of his reputation as financial man and watchdog of the union treasury, this was a particularly distressing matter. It was Mazey who, in 1955, first began building a union strike fund. In 1958, he is fond of recalling, when the McClellan Committee was investigating labor racketeering, it studied the UAW's records and found that the union was so stringent in its accounting procedures that Mazey had once rejected a 1.50 dollar valet bill which Walter Reuther had included on his expense account as part of the hotel bill for an out-of-town union trip. Mazey was embarrassed—and angered—by criticism over the bank failures. "You'd think I was the only guy who made this mistake," he lamented. "That's the trouble with trying to be an executive. I used to go over all these details myself, then everybody insisted I was trying to do too much. You let someone else handle something—and you end up with a $3 million headache."

stage, broken only when Ford, on July 28, like General Motors a week before, declared its concern with the problems
of the work place, particularly the rise in absenteeism.
McKenna said that while "national and plant monthly and
yearly absence levels are disturbing in themselves, they do
not tell the full story." Such figures are averages and "hide
the impact of peaks of absenteeism, suffered for instance on
Mondays and on Fridays after paydays . . . and they mask
the crippling effects often felt on a key production operation . . ." The company proposed—the proposal does not
seem too demanding—that the contract be changed to allow
the firing of a worker after three consecutive days of unauthorized absence instead of ten days as had been the practice for years. Regarding medical insurance, McKenna said
that accident and sickness benefit costs had increased 64
per cent since 1967 and that hospital and medical costs had
increased 67 per cent. To cut these increases, McKenna proposed that workers be examined by a company doctor before
being granted extensions of medical leaves and that workers
be penalized by reductions in vacation time if they stayed
off the job for extended periods.

Nelson Samp, the union's assistant Ford director, using
Bluestone's argument, said that while the union was prepared
to combat absenteeism by punishing the "real culprits," the
company was making blanket proposals that were unacceptable.

So far Woodcock had given only the broad outlines of
the wage increase the union leadership believed it needed
from the companies to avoid a strike. This came in early July,
before negotiations began, in a conversation with reporters
at Solidarity House.

What would it take, he was asked, to avoid a strike?
Would, say, an 8 per cent increase in wage and fringe benefits
satisfy the membership?

"The answer is no," Woodcock said.

Would an 8 per cent increase on top of the 26 cents an

hour in lost cost-of-living money—together about $1.75 an hour over three years—be sufficient?

"You're getting warmer," Woodcock said.

The UAW president also insisted that there was no reason why the union's demands, no matter how high, should force the companies to increase car prices, for if the companies were satisfied with a "reasonable rate of return," he said, increases would be unnecessary. For years, Woodcock said, the companies had been "overcharging the American consumer," and, he added, "If the auto companies would announce a reasonable reduction in car prices, we would be prepared to negotiate within the framework of the financial situation in which they found themselves as a result of the price cut—even if it results in some reductions in the economic gains UAW members might otherwise have made."

The offer, perfunctorily made as it had been in every negotiation since Reuther first advanced it during the 1945–6 strike, was ignored, as it always had been.

In late July and early August, during a lull in the negotiations, Woodcock set off for a series of talks with local union officials which were aimed at making himself surer of his constituency, of what the men wanted, what was important, what was not.

Then, on August 26, the companies, in the virtually simultaneous announcements they are so fond of making, said they would make initial offers to the union on September 1. This announcement set off much speculation and, for the first time in six weeks, brought excitement to the talks, since the offers would provide the first real signal of whether a settlement without a strike—the settlement everyone said the industry and the nation so sorely needed—could be achieved.

It was clear, in a time of high wage settlements and inflation, that the companies would have to grant extensive wage increases, particularly a large first-year increase. Beyond

that, the question was how far would the companies go
toward meeting the union's two other main demands: removal of the ceiling on cost-of-living and acceptance of 30-
and-out. "I hope it's a meaningful offer," Kenneth Bannon
said, "something that will lead to a settlement without a
strike."

During every negotiation the union criticizes the companies for their nearly identical offers issued simultaneously.
The companies do not admit they work together on their
offers, perhaps fearing antitrust charges. It is obvious they
do. The automotive community, for all its pretense of secrecy
and competition, is a clubby community. Men in one company know men in other companies; men move from, say,
General Motors to Ford or Chrysler (although rarely from
Ford or Chrysler to General Motors, General Motors preferring to train its own men); they see each other at charity
functions, at cocktail parties, country clubs, on the golf
courses—and in their offices. Once, a journalist in a hurry
to go upstairs at the Ford headquarters stepped, by chance,
onto the executive elevator, which begins in the executive
parking area in the basement garage and is reserved for top
management only. There, looking straight ahead, arms at
their sides, were Louis G. Seaton, the General Motors negotiator, and members of his staff, on their way to a meeting
with Ford executives. The journalist said nothing, the executives nothing—as if the journalist had stepped onto an
elevator to find a close friend with a mistress. Malcolm Denise,
Ford's top negotiator, a frank man, concedes, "It is not merely
coincidence" that the offers are usually almost identical. "After
all," he says, "the union's demands are similar. In the end, it
[the settlements] will conform to a single pattern."

Emil Mazey confesses that in some thirty-five years with
the union, he has never seen one corporation's executives
skulking in their Homburgs toward their black limousines
at the headquarters of another. But Mazey explains, "They
all belong to the same clubs, the Detroit Athletic Club, for

example, and they have many opportunities of getting together." What the hell, says Mazey, he can understand this;
in his position, he has become friendly with "most of the
corporation officials through such organizations as the United
Foundation . . . so I know all those people. You simply get
to know them. You're involved in community problems or
something, and you're having a cocktail before lunch with
the guys and first thing you know, you're talking about a
problem you have in the plants."

The company offers came at 10 a.m., September 1, two
weeks before the strike deadline, the traditional time for the
first offers.

Bramblett, who made the offer for General Motors, said
it would cost the corporation 1.4 billion dollars in wages
alone for a three year contract, adding that it was the largest
economic proposal in General Motors' history. (Each offer
made by the companies is, by definition, the largest in each
corporation's history, since it must be larger than the existing
contract.) He said it was a "sound and realistic proposal
under present economic conditions."

The companies' offers, each the same, consisted of a first-
year wage increase of 7.5 per cent: 26 to 48 cents more per
hour, including the 26 cents of disputed cost-of-living money.
They did not mention the ceiling on the cost-of-living, meaning that the eight-cent-a-year ceiling was to be retained.
They said nothing about 30-and-out, proposing instead that
pensions for employees who reach age sixty and have thirty
years' service be raised from 400 dollars to 500 dollars a
month. They demanded that workers share future increases in
medical insurance costs, and, to reduce costs and to provide
an inducement for new employees to stay on the job, they
proposed that new hiring rates not be increased, meaning
that new workers would not receive new contract rates
until they had been on the job ninety days.

The union said it was stunned by the low offers. At a news conference Bluestone said that the proposal amounted only to three-fourths of 1 per cent in new money—money beyond the disputed 26 cents. "The gap is enormous in every area," he said. "I cannot recall a time in the twenty-two years I have been here when we were as far apart this close to the expiration date."

Bluestone said: "GM may feel it has come up with a great offer, but it is essentially a hiccough."

Douglas Fraser said Chrysler's offer was "ridiculous." Kenneth Bannon said the Ford proposal was "lousy," "an insult," and "smells of greed." At General Motors, at Chrysler, at Ford, the union men packed their briefcases, walked to their cars, and drove down the freeways and through the Detroit streets to Solidarity House,* the five-story glass and aluminum union headquarters. As the union executive board met to discuss the offers, the members so angry, suddenly everything went dark. Nothing worked—lights, elevators, electric typewriters, copying machines, telephones, air-conditioners. A transformer on the roof of the building had broken down; Solidarity House—literally—had blown a fuse.

* Designed by Reuther and Oskar Stonorov, the architect who designed the Black Lake center and was killed with Reuther, Solidarity House is built on land once part of the Edsel Ford estate. The building affords the top union executives a fine view of the Detroit River and Belle Isle, the city's main park, laid out by Frederick Law Olmsted, designer of Central Park. On clear days, the men and women at Solidarity House can see north to Lake St. Clair, the pleasant lake where people from the five Grosse Pointes, many of them automobile executives, sail their yachts and drive their powerboats. Mallard ducks flap lazily through the sky and swim languidly in the black waters, and early in summer, the best view of the hydroplane races on the Detroit River is from Solidarity House, which sits in the middle of the course. Some years ago a gymnasium was made available to the union men who worked at Solidarity House, and when it was suggested that perhaps the gymnasium—by now critics referred to it as an athletic club—was extravagant for union men, Louis Seaton, the GM negotiator, said that he was pleased that the leadership had built a place to exercise and relax; if there was one thing he liked to do, Seaton said, it was to negotiate with healthy men.

The opening offers were small—far too small. The union men *and* the company men knew this. Bramblett: "We had to make that offer in total darkness because he [Woodcock] wouldn't tell us anything. So we were sure we weren't going to put anything in it that wasn't essential and necessary. It wasn't a small offer, but we made it clear at the time that this was not the last word."

The angry union men, after meeting for several hours at Solidarity House, authorized a novel strategy, which next day, September 2, was outlined to the union's General Motors, Ford, and Chrysler councils, the union representative bodies. Woodcock, trooping the line, going first to the General Motors meeting, then to the Ford and Chrysler meetings, told the one thousand delegates that there would be two strike targets, General Motors and Chrysler. If an agreement was not reached by the strike deadline, September 14, Woodcock said, the union would strike General Motors or Chrysler—or both.

The General Motors offer, he told the cheering GM delegates, was "crap." He held the proposal high for the men to see, as if it were a dead cat. He read a sentence at the end of the proposal: "The company reserves the right to withdraw this contract at 11:59 p.m., September 14." Withdraw it, hell. They can shove it, he said.

He told the Chrysler delegates: "GM is the architect of this non-offer and Chrysler is the stooge for GM." He said: "We have heard the speculation that Chrysler cannot afford a strike. If that is true, they should quit running with the pack and sticking their necks out for General Motors."

The UAW plan was simple: the union hoped to force financially weakened Chrysler to give in quickly to a package that General Motors would not accept—to peel them, one union man suggested, as one might peel a banana—then take the Chrysler settlement to General Motors and to Ford for the automatic acceptance mandated by bargaining ground rules.

Ford, Woodcock said, was exempted from a possible

strike because the union wanted the continued production of the Pinto, Ford's new subcompact, so that one major American small car would be on the market to compete with the foreign autos. The truth was, the union could not strike Ford: not only did the company not want another strike, but the Ford workers did not want one either.

Woodcock explained to the delegates that the union might exhaust its 120 million dollar strike fund. But he declared that the union, if forced, would continue a strike without a strike fund.

Later, speaking with reporters, he said that a union was not a corporation, and, unlike a corporation, when a union was out of money it was not out of business. "A union without money," he said, "is a crusade."

Woodcock does not look like a labor leader, or at least the stereotype of a labor leader, not being inclined toward huge, malodorous cigars, baggy clothes, or white socks. It is said in Detroit that it is easy, seeing Woodcock emerge from a negotiation session, to mistake him for a member of management, given his dignified appearance: sideburns at midear length, hornrimmed glasses, tasteful but not expensive suits, color-contrasted shirts, wide but not foppish ties. He is a highly intelligent man, sometimes aloof, sometimes genial. He is much unlike Reuther. Reuther was a performer, a man who loved rhetoric, who was, especially in the last decade of his life, inaccessible to men in the union and outsiders alike. Woodcock, on the other hand, dislikes rhetoric and has no special fondness for the spotlight. He is aloof to outsiders, but allies find him easy to approach; even Victor Reuther, Walter's brother, who now has questions about Woodcock's social commitments, says, "He is a very warm individual . . . you can talk to him more easily than Walter —no question about it." Because Reuther disliked alcohol, he would never sit down and have a drink with union officers or auto workers. Woodcock, however, enjoys conversation

with union officials he likes, taking a scotch or two with
them, and this, an associate says, is very valuable because it
allows union men to know each other better and work out
problems informally.

Nonetheless, a member of the union family who has
known Woodcock for years, a believer in the Reuther legend,
no lover of Woodcock, says, "Leonard has such cruelty in
him. I shouldn't say that. In fact, I'm sorry I said it. But I
think that there is that quality, the unpredictability, the
irrationality, the cruelty." He is tough, intense, forthright; he
also possesses what an associate calls "a magnificent temper."
A Michigan political figure says of Woodcock, "The son-
of-a-gun has more goddamn guts than most people I've
known in the labor movement." And Gomer Goins, a member of the union's General Motors negotiating team, says,
"He don't dilly around. He comes right to the point . . . If
he tells the General Motors bosses that he is going to do
something, if he tells them he is going to jump off the bridge,
they can be waiting for him with the stretcher, because old
Leonard, he is going to jump."

General Motors men, with whom he has worked for
years, trust Woodcock and believe he, more than Reuther
was, is a man of his word. As the summer and fall months
went by, many people, union men, company men, and outsiders, came to realize that Woodcock possessed a mind
superior to Reuther's, that while Reuther operated out of
instinct and a feel for the situation, Woodcock possessed a
far greater ability to analyze problems and—not a soul
denied this—to speak thoughtfully and concisely, that he
was a far more intellectual man than Reuther.

Before Reuther's death, Woodcock had seemingly reached
the end of his career, "a fellow of tremendous abilities," a
friend says, "acting as if things were at a dead end." His
worst time, it appears, was in the early 1960s, the high point,
not coincidentally, of Reuther's career. In the mid-1950s, it
had been accepted that Woodcock was Reuther's heir-
apparent. But Reuther, like many of high station, enjoyed

power and prominence and refused to step down. Woodcock was just two years younger than Reuther and when Reuther decided to remain as president until he was sixty-five, the mandatory union retirement age (there was talk among some men close to Reuther of changing the union constitution and waiving the retirement age), this meant that Woodcock would have been too old to run for president, for he would have been able to serve only two years before he turned sixty-five himself. Reuther began grooming Douglas Fraser, who was five years younger than Woodcock and, Reuther had decided, a man who was less volatile and better suited to succeed him.

In the early 1960s, President John Kennedy had offered Woodcock the ambassadorship to Taiwan or to Pakistan, or a subcabinet post. Woodcock decided to join the administration, but Reuther had already lost one aide, Jack Conway, to the Federal Housing Administration, and when Woodcock asked Reuther whether he could leave, Reuther said no. Woodcock, a loyalist, accepted this decision. During these same years, Woodcock had undergone what he calls an "amicable separation" from his wife, Lola, ending an often unamicable marriage of more than twenty-five years. Finally, late in 1969, he suffered a tuberculosis-like attack, perhaps a recurrence of the tuberculosis he experienced in the late 1930s, which had kept him from participating in those exciting organizational struggles of the union, including the Flint sitdowns.

In Reuther's last years, Woodcock seemed to recognize that he was trapped, that he would rise no further. Then, in May, when Reuther's plane crashed, shearing treetops to fall into the woods, Reuther's plans meant nothing.

Born in Rhode Island, reared in England, Woodcock was brought to Detroit by his family in 1926 at the age of fifteen. Like many men of modest means—including Reuther—he studied for a time at Detroit City College (later to become Wayne State University), but he was forced to drop out of college because of the Depression. He obtained a job as a clerk for a cigar company, then worked as a machine assembler at Detroit Gear and Machine Company, twelve hours a day, seven days a week, for thirty-five cents an hour. When a union of the American Federation of Labor was established at the plant, Woodcock became an organizer; when the local joined the United Automobile Workers in 1936, it was the largest of the UAW locals. After his months-long fight with tuberculosis, Woodcock spent time in the warm climates of California and Mexico, returning to the union in September 1940, when he joined the UAW's regional staff in Grand Rapids, Michigan, and helped organize the General Motors Fisher Body factory, the last unorganized plant in General Motors.

Woodcock was Socialist in those days, drawn to the movement by his father's trade unionist background. The elder Woodcock had been a member of the Independent Labor Party in England, and in Detroit, one of the first members of the Mechanics Educational Society of America, a forerunner of the UAW. Woodcock was also dissatisfied with the layoffs, the arrogance of employers, and the Depression breadlines he saw. For a time he served on the Socialist Party's national executive council although, like Reuther before him, he makes no mention of this affiliation in his union biography. By the mid-1940s, however, he had soured on the Socialists. "I was very much against the Communists," he says, "and I was increasingly unhappy with Norman Thomas' position relative to the war, because I was supportive of Britain against the Nazis." (Thomas favored a policy of neutrality for America.) In the early 1940s, Woodcock resigned from the Socialist Party, giving himself completely to the union—meaning, to Reuther.

When Reuther ran for the union presidency in 1946, Woodcock was an important member of the Reuther caucus, assigned to helping line up and count votes. After Reuther won, he named Woodcock his first administrative assistant. But Woodcock knew that if he was to rise in the union he

would have to win elective office, and union bylaws required
that only people who had worked in the plants could qualify
for elected office. So in May 1947, Reuther sent Woodcock
to Grand Rapids to log his plant time, and in November
1947, when Reuther won a second term at the Atlantic City
convention, consolidating control over the union, Woodcock
was elected a regional director. He became director of,
respectively, the union's American Motors, agricultural implement, and aerospace divisions; then, late in 1955, Reuther
named him to the union's most important staff position next
to the presidency, directorship of the General Motors Department.

In the 1970 talks, having succeeded to the presidency,
Woodcock (known to many union people as "Timber Dick")
was on his own for the first time in his thirty-five years with
the union. He seemed to enjoy the responsibility, the work,
the position. "I am always asked," he said, " 'How does it feel
to try to fill Walter Reuther's shoes?" I'm just not going to
try to fill them. I'm just going to do the best I can. And when
I made that determination, I felt very relaxed and at peace
with myself and the world." He said, "The funny thing is I've
been much more relaxed since I've been president than I
was before."

Yet Woodcock was under immense pressure in September 1970, both as a negotiator and as the man entrusted with
Reuther's mantle. The men in the ranks, he knew, were
watching him, looking to see whether he measured up.
There were the inevitable comparisons with Reuther, comparisons that, when they continued, rankled him. Earl Bramblett, his GM adversary, says: "He was new in his position
and the members no doubt expected a lot of him."

The corporations, especially General Motors, already
the object of major focus in the talks, were displeased by the
harsh language the union leaders had used to reject the offers.

Bramblett issued a special statement saying that it was unfortunate that Bluestone and the union "had seen fit to
ridicule our $1.4 billion increased wage proposal . . . We
hope the union will make a more realistic appraisal." He said
that if the offer was not acceptable, the union had an "obligation to spell out what would be acceptable." A "sure way to
back into a strike that nobody wants," Bramblett said, "is
not to let us know what it takes to avoid one."

While the offers had been scant and the union rhetoric
harsh, there still seemed reason for optimism. To begin with,
the companies had disposed of the 26 cent cost-of-living
money controversy by including the amount in the first-year
wage increase. For months the union leaders, first Reuther
and now Woodcock and Bluestone, had insisted that the 26
cents was old money, and the union did not have to bargain
for it. Obviously the companies did not accept the union
argument; yet, by proposing a wage offer greater than 26
cents, the disputed amount was there for the two sides to
build on.

Secondly, by increasing the pension benefit from 400 dollars to 500 dollars for workers who retired at age sixty after
thirty years of service, the companies had taken notice of the
500 dollars a month figure asked for under 30-and-out. Here
again was a proposal the two sides could negotiate.

The companies had made no offer toward removing the
cost-of-living ceiling, but they knew—the union leaders had
told them so repeatedly, both in public and in private—that
the ceiling must be removed if a strike was to be prevented.
Surely, it seemed, the companies were holding back in this
area for tactical reasons; surely they could not believe the
union was not prepared to fight for this demand.

Finally, the company negotiators had taken steps to stress
publicly what the union men knew privately: their proposal
was not final; a second, larger offer would be coming, and
there were still two weeks left before the strike deadline. "We
are not in a frozen position," Bramblett said. William O'Brien,

the Chrysler negotiator, said that Chrysler did not consider
its initial offer a "take-it-or-leave-it offer." For their part,
union negotiators avoided saying flatly there would be a
strike. "We would still hope we could reach an agreement,"
Bluestone said.

A major problem, said John D. Leary, Chrysler vice
president for administration, was that the union "has not
been specific enough in the economic areas" and "very little
collective bargaining has taken place." Woodcock replied,
"Collective bargaining is a mutual process" and if the negotiations were being stalled because the demands were not
specific, "the company is equally as guilty as the UAW."
But he assured the company men that the union in the next
few days would be "more concrete in areas where we have
not been specific."

On Saturday, September 5, a bright, clear, early fall day,
Woodcock went first to Chrysler and then to General Motors
to list the union's specific economic demands for the first
time, and it was the companies' turn to be stunned. They listened for an hour each as Woodcock and the other union
men ticked off the demands: a wage and benefit increase of
more than 2.50 dollars an hour, including a first-year wage
increase of 96 cents an hour; restoration of the old cost-of-
living formula; and full 30-and-out.

Leary said that the two sides were "far apart." Bramblett
said that if Woodcock was serious, if Woodcock was "fixed
on the items he gave us today," the two sides had a "real
problem." Now that he had the specifics he wanted, Bramblett
said, "I wouldn't say it makes me more optimistic. I'm more
in a state of shock." Woodcock said this was a predictable
response. "The script calls for them to pass from a state of
surprise to a state of shock," he said. But he conceded that
the two sides were as far apart as "from the fourth floor to
the sub-basement."

Bramblett believed the two sides were in an extremely dangerous position, that they were close to a strike. He explains: "You can't make a decision whether you will take a strike or not as long as you don't know what the alternative is." Until Woodcock listed the demands on September 5, ten days before the strike deadline, he says, the corporation did not know what it would take to gain a settlement without a strike. He says: "This is unusual. I mean at some point in time, you have to know what it will take to settle so that you will have a chance to settle . . . The sure way to have a strike is not to be able to find out what it will take to avoid it. As long as you don't know what the alternatives are, there is no decision to make." Woodcock's detailing of the demands, he says, "was in response to our constant griping" that the union had not made its position clear. But the union demands were so high, he says, that the union "could not have possibly been serious . . . We couldn't take it seriously; we never did announce it [the demands] publicly and they never did either."

Next day, Sunday, September 6, Woodcock flew to Washington, D.C. to appear on "Meet the Press," flying in by himself and taking a cab downtown from National Airport.

He was poised and confident on the air. The union demands, he said, while refusing to state them exactly, were within the framework of the 41 per cent package that the printers received at *The New York Times* and the 43 per cent Teamsters settlement, which he placed at 2.10 dollars an hour, not including cost-of-living allowances. A settlement on the union's terms, he said, would not be inflationary if the auto manufacturers would remove the ceiling on the cost-of-living and enable the union to accept small second- and third-year increases; otherwise, he said, the union would be forced to demand second- and third-year increases that would exceed 3 per cent, the rate of the nation's annual productivity increase and thus the definition of a noninflationary increase.

"Our members don't want a strike," the union president

said, but "we are saying that if they [the companies] will not put unrestricted cost-of-living back, they are going to put us in the position of fighting for very high increases in years two and three." Asked whether the settlement would mean an increase in auto prices, Woodcock replied that this would depend on the pricing policies of General Motors. Asked whether the union had named Chrysler as a strike target because the union believed it might cave in, Woodcock said, "I wouldn't impute caving in. We are saying to Chrysler Corporation, 'If you want to run with the pack, you can't run with the pack and at the same time tell us you have special problems.' That's why they are out in front with their uncertain ally"—General Motors.

Woodcock flew back to Detroit after the program, turning down an invitation from President Nixon who, in the midst of wooing labor for the coming election in which law and order seemed to be the important issue, had invited some two hundred labor leaders to come to the White House the next day, Labor Day, there to dine on prime ribs and to sip California wine. Woodcock said that he could not attend, that his time was consumed with the negotiations in Detroit.

George Meany, president of the AFL-CIO, from which Reuther had withdrawn the UAW in 1968, partly in a power and personality clash, partly out of anger at Meany's conservative ways, was not so reluctant to fraternize with his traditional Republican opponents. In a Labor Day interview, Meany, sounding much like a businessman, said strikes were becoming much less desirable as a negotiation weapon than they were in the early days of union development; in fact, Meany said, strikes were almost obsolete:

> The more a person has of the world's goods—you know what I mean, for himself and the family—the more conservative he becomes in the sense that if he is moving along and he sees chances of moving further along, he doesn't want to upset the machinery. You can be quite radical if you

were involved in a labor dispute where people are getting thirty cents an hour because if you pull an honest strike, all you lose is thirty cents an hour. But you have people who are making $8,000 or $9,000 a year, paying off mortgages, with kids going to college, you have an entirely different situation when you think about calling them on strike. They have got obligations that are quite costly, insurance payments and all that sort of thing. So this makes the strike much less desirable as a weapon.

Naturally, we wouldn't want to give it up as a weapon, but I can say to you quite frankly that more and more people in the trade union movement—I mean at the highest levels—are thinking of other ways to advance without the use of the strike method. While strikes have their part and all that, and we certainly have advocated for years that you have got to have the right to strike, we find more and more that strikes really don't settle a thing. Where you have a well-established industry and a well-established union, you are getting more and more to the point where a strike doesn't make sense.

The UAW, asked about Meany's views, made it clear that Meany was not speaking for Woodcock when he advanced such proposals as settling contract disputes by arbitration rather than by strikes. "In this situation, it's out," a union official said. "As far as the situation goes down the road in future auto negotiations, I would think the reaction would also be negative."

The strike deadline was a week away. Sixty-two cents in first-year wage increases separated the two sides—34 cents offered by the company, 96 cents asked by the union—plus the other issues, many of which the two sides were as far apart upon as they had been July 15 when the talks began. On Tuesday, September 8, after a fruitless three hour meeting with Chrysler negotiators, Woodcock declared, "I am a man of infinite faith, but I'm beginning to become doubtful" that a strike could be avoided.

The union now initiated its Chrysler ploy, an unorthodox attempt to push through a settlement at Chrysler—and ultimately at General Motors. The approach was direct. One item was placed before Chrysler: 30-and-out. The union said it must have a 500 dollar a month pension after thirty years' service; in return, the union said, the company would not be struck.

Union and company negotiators met three times on the union proposal, beginning Thursday, September 10, at Chrysler Headquarters in Highland Park, a seamy plant town on Detroit's north side, the town where, in 1913 and 1914, Henry Ford gave the world modern mass production by creating the moving assembly line, his men dragging a Model T chassis through the factory by rope and windlass.

At the first meeting the union agreed to put its proposals in writing. These were submitted to the corporation in a two hour meeting on Friday. The union men believed they were making progress. Howard Young, a union research specialist, says, "The kinds of questions they were asking, and their reactions, gave you the impression they were seriously considering it—it was not just that this was nonsense, that it couldn't be done." Then, at 6:30 p.m., Chrysler negotiators asked for a recess until 10 a.m. Saturday, telling Woodcock that they were seriously interested in the union's proposal but that they wanted additional time for their experts to study the plan. Plant guards—union men—told the UAW that Chrysler executives, led by Chairman Lynn Townsend and President John J. Riccardo, stayed in their offices that night until after 11 p.m. and returned early, about 7:30 a.m. on Saturday. Woodcock and Fraser believed the plan was working. When the Chrysler men asked for a recess, Woodcock says, "They said, 'Look, we're not playing games. We've got a lot of work to do.'" Fraser: "I thought we had a breakthrough."

Woodcock and Fraser, who live near each other, drove to the Chrysler Corporation together the next morning. Fraser had not told Woodcock, but some days before he had decided

that even if the Chrysler ploy fell through, if Chrysler would
not agree to give the union 30-and-out, Chrysler should not
be struck; he believed it would be too dangerous to strike
both General Motors and Chrysler. It was much too possible
that Chrysler would be unable to stand a shutdown and
would collapse, Fraser thought, like the Penn Central Railroad, and that the union would be blamed. William O'Brien,
the Chrysler negotiator, told Fraser that if the corporation
was struck, it would take the strike, and that if the strike
was of any length, Chrysler would go under. O'Brien may
have been bluffing: an alternative to collapsing was, of course,
to grant the union 30-and-out. But it was a gamble Fraser
decided the union dare not take. Now, riding in the car with
Woodcock, wondering how to tell Woodcock he had changed
his mind, Fraser was surprised when Woodcock began discussing the matter himself. Without saying so directly, Woodcock indicated that he was opposed to striking both General
Motors and Chrysler; Kenneth Bannon, Irving Bluestone, and
Emil Mazey, however, still believed that the union might
reap many benefits by striking both corporations. What was
Fraser's view? Woodcock asked. Fraser, pleased by Woodcock's indication, said that he too had changed his mind and
that he agreed with Woodcock—if the 30-and-out strategy
fell through at Chrysler and the union had to strike, the
strike should be conducted against General Motors alone.

When Woodcock and Fraser arrived at Chrysler, they
parked their car in the small parking lot near the negotiation
rooms and were ushered into a meeting on the fifth floor.
There, Leary, the chief corporation negotiator, told them
that Chrysler had decided the proposal was unacceptable.
"They just slammed the door in our faces," Woodcock says.
But the reason was apparent; Fraser says that Chrysler
feared reprisals from General Motors, that GM had made
known its opposition to any concession on 30-and-out and
torpedoed any possible agreement. O'Brien had told the union
leadership some time before that General Motors could harm

Chrysler in many ways if it chose to do so, by refusing to
raise prices high enough to cover increased costs, by bringing
pressure against Chrysler suppliers to raise prices, by cutting
off supplies that it sold to Chrysler, or by putting pressure
on the banks, which Chrysler depended on heavily.

The deadline was sixty-one hours away. On Friday—the
day before Chrysler turned down 30-and-out—General
Motors made a second offer, a proposal it estimated would
cost the corporation 1.91 billion dollars in wages and fringe
benefits, a proposal it said it was making to avert "a strike
that nobody wants."

The offer clearly represented a large increase over the
first proposal. General Motors proposed a 9.8 per cent—38
cent—wage increase, including the 26 cents, up from 7.5
per cent in the first offer. For the first time, the corporation
moved toward lifting the ceiling on cost-of-living, proposing
the ceiling be increased from 16 cents under the current
contract to 28 cents. And the corporation came closer to
30-and-out, proposing that workers be allowed to retire on
pensions of 500 dollars a month once they reached fifty-eight
years of age and thirty years' service.

In making the proposal, Bramblett again emphasized that
the offer did not represent the company's final position; yet
he also made it clear that this was the proposal around which
a settlement must be fashioned. "We never said it was take
it or leave it," he says. "But we made it clear that this wasn't
a token offer . . . it wasn't the same kind of offer as the first.
That this was a serious offer—that while it wasn't take it or
leave it, there wasn't any big bundle of money lying in the
weeds to go on top of it. We were simply trying to say, 'this
is pretty close to as far as we think we ought to go.' " Nevertheless, Woodcock displayed outrage at what he said was
the company's intransigence; the company had enunciated a
position rather than a proposal. "God has spoken," he said.
"It is up to the subjects to bow down to the ground. We
won't do it."

That Saturday, after the attempt to split Chrysler from General Motors failed, Woodcock returned to General Motors and, in a negotiation session that began at 7 p.m., he reduced the union's demands, dropping the first-year wage demand from 96 cents an hour to 61.5 cents. He refused to specify what the union wanted for wage increases in the second and third years, saying those increases would depend upon the agreement the two sides reached on cost-of-living. The sides were still 23.5 cents apart, and Bramblett said, "Time is running out." It was at this point, he says, that he realized if there ever had been a way to avoid a strike, it had disappeared. "When the union publicly announced its position of about $2.11 an hour with only another day to go—and they put that out publicly to all its members, listed it as their position, to the public and to the membership—this certainly was an indication that it would take a miracle to turn the situation around." He says, "I think it was an indication of the position that Mr. Woodcock was in . . . He probably didn't have a good idea of what it would take, at that point, to get a ratification. He was struggling with that problem. And that was why he was being evasive."

The next day, Sunday, September 14, the twenty-four member union executive board met for three hours at Solidarity House. Most officers and board members were now convinced that it was too hazardous to strike Chrysler. Still, Emil Mazey, for one, wanted to strike both corporations. "It was my feeling that Chrysler wouldn't last two weeks, and that we could get a settlement there," Mazey says. "Also, I thought that GM might want to cut a deal if it saw that Chrysler might crack." His reasoning was based in large part on his experiences in 1948, when he was acting union president as Walter Reuther lay in Henry Ford Hospital, his right arm mangled by a shotgun blast in an assassination attempt. "We struck Chrysler but got a settlement at GM while Chrysler was out," Mazey says. General Motors settled, he insists, because, "It didn't know what to expect from me.

GM feared I might shut it down, too." Some officers in the
union believe Mazey is aging; they listen to him, respect him,
indeed, have great fondness for him, but they are wary of
his advice. Still, because he is a lion in the union, he is an
important man, and it was only after some debate that
the board decided that General Motors—only General Motors
—would be struck.

Woodcock: "Psychologically, if we had gone back to
our people and told the General Motors guys, 'You've got
to step aside, we are going to take on Chrysler,' they would
have had contempt for the union. They would have been
absolutely convinced that we were afraid of General Motors,
which was a growing belief anyway. And it would have been
adventuristic, because Chrysler was not in a good position."

Fraser says that even if the union had struck Chrysler and
negotiated a large settlement, the union membership probably would have looked at the settlement, no matter how
large, and asked, "What the hell did you take on this broke
outfit for?" With that sort of thinking, Fraser says, the membership might well have rejected a Chrysler settlement, believing it was too small and that a larger settlement could
have been won at General Motors.

Victor Reuther: "I think it's quite clear they [General
Motors] blocked a settlement at Chrysler and hence threw
down a challenge to the UAW, which the UAW could not
back away from. Certainly it could not in view of the fact
that there was new leadership at the UAW helm. It would
have been interpreted as a sign of weakness."

The executive board meeting over, Woodcock walked
down the hall in Solidarity House to the Scandinavian Room,
a banquet and meeting hall, a Danish-style room with teak
furniture and white curtains that overlooks the Detroit
River. He informed the union's twelve-member General
Motors negotiating team of the union's decision: it would
strike General Motors alone. Fraser went to the telephone
and called O'Brien at Chrysler; the strike will be against

General Motors, Fraser said. O'Brien was relieved. He relayed the message to Lynn Townsend, Chrysler chairman.

Woodcock assured the negotiators that the decision, contrary to newspaper suggestions, was based on logic, that it was not made to enhance his political standing or because of his belief that the union could not, negotiation after negotiation, continue to avoid General Motors. The decision, he said, was made by the board, not by him; it was, as the union always said and was so proud of saying, a decision of the head, not of the heart. No emotion entered into the decision, he said. Neal Madsen, a crewcut, roundish negotiator from Local 160, the General Motors Technical Center in Warren, Michigan, said, Maybe just a bit, Leonard, and everyone laughed.

That night, Woodcock and the UAW's General Motors bargaining team met with the General Motors negotiators and formally notified the corporation that it was the strike target. Barring a settlement by Monday midnight—an impossibility—General Motors would be struck. Woodcock told Bramblett that he wanted to make it clear that selecting General Motors as the strike target was a decision of the union governors, not his alone, it was not a personal or political decision, nor the result of a grudge against the corporation. He said that the union believed that a settlement at Chrysler Corporation had been blocked by General Motors and it was the union's desire to negotiate not with Chrysler, the second string, but with General Motors, the company directing tactics. Bramblett replied that he was not surprised General Motors was the target. After all, he said, Woodcock had wanted to strike General Motors for years; this was well known. No, Earl, Woodcock said, without convincing him, this was, as he had said, a decision of the union, of its board members, not of the president, not of Leonard Woodcock.

The faces of the General Motors negotiators were long and sad. They had expected for months, deep down, that the corporation would be struck, but now, at the moment of being told, it seemed as if they could not believe it was happening to them, to General Motors. For some of the UAW negotiators this one moment of confronting the representatives of the world's largest industrial corporation, the manufacturing giant, and seeing the sour faces, this one moment made the strike worthwhile. Gomer Goins: "There seemed to be a kind of quietness that fell over the General Motors people. But more than a verbal or vocal standpoint was the expression on their faces. And it appeared to me from the expressions of the General Motors people—and they had the top brass right there, the personnel directors from all over the country—that they had the expressions of, well, we didn't think this could happen to us. We just don't believe it—like they were told, like the old saying is, they said it couldn't be done, and they said the UAW wouldn't do it, but the UAW did it." James Hensley, a negotiator from Anderson, Indiana, a famous union town, home of the 1935 Anderson sitdown: "They were just stunned, momentarily, just a matter of seconds. But they were stunned. And it was worth a lot of money to me just to see that." Woodcock says, "I think they had expected to be the target for quite a long time. They are as cognizant of the facts of the situation as we are." But, he says, "Expecting it and it finally happening can, sometimes, be entirely different."

Monday, the top negotiating committees did not bother to meet. At the main conference room that night, a caucus, not a union-corporation meeting, was underway. Union representatives chatted quietly with corporation executives. Men milled in the rooms and the corridors. They discussed the coming months. They made arrangements for beer that night. They bullshitted. The die cast, the union and the company men talked of shutting the plants down, not of keeping them open.

At 10 p.m., Woodcock received word from the East Coast that the locals there were walking out, even though it was only 11 p.m. on the East Coast. The workers were supposed to stay on their jobs another hour. The hell with it, Woodcock said: the deadline for the East Coast is ten o'clock, not midnight. So the strike—the ordained strike, ordained for months despite the talks and the optimism—began. Across the country in the large cities, the bleak factory towns, the blue-collar suburbs, in the farmlands where the new plants are, first on the East Coast, then spreading to the Midwest, and finally to the West, the facilities, 138 in all, in Tarrytown, New York; McKeesport, Pennsylvania; Atlanta, Georgia; Lordstown, Ohio; Livonia, Michigan; Detroit; Warren, Michigan; Edina, Minnesota; St. Louis; Oklahoma City; Beaverton, Oregon; Van Nuys and South Gate, California; plant after plant shut down.

Woodcock issued a two-page statement:

It is regrettable that a strike had to be called . . . against General Motors Corporation. The company held out no other choice.

Over the past sixty days, UAW negotiators worked in good faith and exerted every effort possible to avoid a strike by reaching agreement on a new national contract . . . UAW's efforts to speed up negotiations and to be fair and equitable in its contract proposals were not met at the bargaining table by similar willingness on the part of the corporation . . . General Motors astoundingly has sought to build an impression that it did not understand the issues at stake. This has no relationship to facts . . .

In addition to an economic offer that is less than equitable, General Motors is insisting on many important contract take-aways—many demands by management that would seriously weaken benefits and protections that UAW–GM contracts have provided for our members for many years . . .

This strike changes the entire focus of these negotiations. Where until tonight the thrust of our negotiations here involved working out terms of a new national agreement, the union and the corporation must reach a total settlement—local conditions at each of the 157 bargaining units as well as a national agreement . . .

It is our fervent hope that, for the economic and social good for all concerned and affected, this can be resolved in a minimum of time. We will make every effort possible to accomplish this and hope that the corporation will share that willingness.

Bramblett issued a two-page statement:

General Motors deeply regrets that the United Automobile Workers have decided to strike against General Motors. We believe it is also a strike against reason. We have placed on the bargaining table an economic proposal that is unprecedented in our history in the size and scope of its benefits. The union has pushed this aside, standing on demands that we conservatively estimate at more than $2.65 an hour, or an increase of over forty-five per cent for a three-year period.

An event of such gravity deserves to be placed in perspective.

Three years ago, when General Motors and the UAW signed the contract that is now expiring, the union hailed it as an "historic agreement." They said it "provides General Motors workers and their families a larger measure of economic equity than any contract we have ever negotiated." The union said that three years ago—and the union was right.

On September 11th, General Motors made its second proposal . . .

The wage increases alone in this offer totaled $1.9 billion. The UAW described it as "not an offer"—and rejected it.

So now we are on strike. Nobody really wins a strike. Every strike causes hardships—this one more than most. We are disappointed that we were unable to reach agreement. We tried hard, but the demands are just too many and too high. We stand ready to continue negotiations in the hope of an early settlement.

A reporter: "Mr. Woodcock, why have you shied away from General Motors for twenty-five years?"

Woodcock: "We haven't shied away from General Motors for twenty-five years. Bargaining with General Motors has a very unique quality. We are given the opportunity to present our case, to answer their questions. But there is no bargaining in the normal sense of the word—of them saying, 'Now, if you will do *this*, *this* might be possible.' That doesn't happen. We present our case, and we make endless arguments for it, then one day a position paper comes down and that's it."

Would Ford and Chrysler extend their contracts?

"Out of class solidarity," he said, Ford and Chrysler had refused to extend the union contracts, meaning the UAW would have to collect its own dues, a troublesome, but not insurmountable task.

Bramblett said that Woodcock had misread the second General Motors offer. "They characterized it as a position," he said. "It was not a position. It was a legitimate, very favorable proposal," a proposal, he said, that "was still on the bargaining table," and General Motors expected "to begin our bargaining on that basis."

Q. Was there more money available?
A. Well, I think we will do the bargaining in the bargaining room.
Q. Mr. Bramblett, you said before these were the strangest negotiations you had ever been in. Why are they strange?
A. It is strange to be at the end of sixty days and still be so far apart.
Q. How far apart?
A. Very far.
Q. How long, Mr. Bramblett, do you believe the strike will last?
A. I don't have any clock on that. It's been discouraging the last several days, to say the least.
Q. Could the company stand up to another 113 day strike as it had in 1945–6?

A. Well, I don't think we're going to go out of business. We're still solvent.

A newsman suggested to Woodcock that perhaps it would be difficult to resume negotiations given the bitterness that seemed to have developed between the two sides. Woodcock said no, he did not believe this would pose any insurmountable difficulties. He said: "We still have a civilized relationship."

Chapter 3

The corporation

"There is much to say about the world's largest private industrial corporation," wrote Alfred P. Sloan, Jr., who directed the General Motors Corporation from near bankruptcy to its place as the world's most powerful and most profitable manufacturing enterprise. "Its history covers the present century and many parts of the earth, wherever there is a road to travel."

There is much to say indeed. In the 1930s, when the corporation was just two decades old, *Fortune* was already calling it "not just big but colossal." Today the corporation ranks largest in category after category. With nearly 800,000 workers, it is the world's largest private employer. Paying more than 1.7 billion dollars in local, state, federal, and foreign taxes each year, it is the world's largest taxpayer. Each year, it spends more than 200 million dollars on advertising; if it cut its advertising budget in half, it would still be among the top ten advertisers.

It is the world's largest consumer of steel, copper, zinc, aluminum, brass, rubber, and glass. It sells 52 per cent of America's cars, 49 per cent of its trucks, and 80 per cent of its buses. It is the world's largest manufacturer of locomotives, refrigerators, automotive parts, cigarette lighters, and earth-moving equipment. Its finance company, General Motors Acceptance Corporation, is the nation's leading seller of short-term commercial paper. It is the largest mover of freight by railroad and the largest shipper.

The corporation's 33 divisions, with 112 U.S. manufacturing plants in 67 cities, manufacture scores of other products: jeeps, military trucks, Arma Steel, automobile radios, tape players, radars, freezers, dryers, dishwashers, air-conditioners, ice cube trays, artillery shells, self-propelled howitzers, gas turbines for aircraft, parts for space rockets and moon vehicles, marine and industrial diesel engines, garbage disposals. The corporation, with nearly 9 billion dollars in assets, transacts business with or has funds in scores of banks in virtually every major city across the country. It purchases parts and materials from 40,000 suppliers and maintains a network of 13,000 franchised dealers.

Under a plan devised in the early 1920s by its brilliant finance man, Donaldson Brown, General Motors targets its prices to bring a long-range return of 20 per cent on investment; the rate of return on investment, Brown said, was the most accurate gauge of the corporation's profitability. Brown came to General Motors from du Pont; as a matter of family pride the du Ponts had always tried to match the 20 per cent rate of return earned by the original family powder plant on the Brandywine Creek in Delaware in 1807. Between 1947 and 1969, the period between its two large postwar strikes, General Motors, the UAW points out, earned an after-tax profit of 24 billion dollars, more than 1.8 billion dollars above the 20 per cent target rate. This compared to 11.9 per cent for the rest of American heavy industry—GM had nearly double the national average. During the 1920s and 1930s, just before the passage of corporate income tax laws and then at a time when the laws confiscated a much smaller share of profits than they do today, General Motors earned an after-tax profit of 18.9 per cent on investment. When income tax laws came, General Motors increased its prices to compensate for the taxes—it did not change its profit target. In the five years immediately after World War II, the corporation earned 22.8 per cent on investment. In the years after the Korean war, the corporation earned slightly higher than 20 per cent. In 1957, the American Institute of Management said that General Motors' profits were "nothing short of phenomenal." In the 1960s, when it had some 1.6 billion dollars in cash and bonds and, embarrassingly, seemed unable to find ventures in which to invest these funds, a General Motors executive, asked by a *Wall Street Journal* correspondent what the corporation planned to do with that vast sum of money, laughed and said General Motors was "saving up to buy the federal government."

The corporation's 1969 gross revenues of 24.9 billion dollars are larger than many countries' gross national product. GMs annual operating costs are greater than those of all but about a dozen nations. Under an executive bonus system—General Motors pays its executives comparatively low salaries, then awards lucrative bonuses as incentives for good, hard work —General Motors Corporation in 1969 paid 67 officers and directors more than 18 million dollars in salaries and bonuses, nearly 13 million more than the combined salaries paid to the president of the United States, the vice president, the members of the Supreme Court, and the one hundred members of the Senate. The 18 million dollars, the United Automobile Workers said in prenegotiation fact sheets, was equal to the pay of 1,872 General Motors hourly rated men and women; the officers and directors, the UAW said, averaged 268,000 dollars apiece, while the General Motors workers, with overtime, averaged 9,599 dollars.

The General Motors executive . . . *the General Motors man* . . . the man created by Alfred P. Sloan, Jr., the organization and marketing genius who built the modern corporation, is the model for the modern organization man—the man Peter Drucker calls "the key leadership figure" of American society, the kind of man who "runs our key institutions, the large businesses and the government agencies, the armed services, the great foundations and the large universities."

Drucker writes: "Sloan set out deliberately in the early Twenties to break the traditional patterns of business organization, business management and business leadership. To do this . . . he literally had to invent almost everything that is commonplace in business today: the concept of the big business and its organization; the very idea of a systematic management with defined responsibilities and organized means of communications and decision making, management controls. . . . Above all he had to invent a person: the professional executive who is both master and servant of his creation, the large organized institution."

White, middle class men, the General Motors executives came out of high schools in the small towns of the Midwest in the 1920s or early 1930s and worked their way through college, if they attended college. They joined General Motors, and often it was their first job. They remember the Depression, but most of them kept their jobs, and for them the Depression is not the ugly scar that it is for the men on the assembly lines.

They have worked, every working day of their lives, ten, twelve, fourteen hours a day, rising early in the morning, five or six o'clock, sliding into their huge cars, and driving down the freeways from their Bloomfield Hills, Southfield, Birmingham, or Grosse Pointe homes to their offices in the General Motors Building, arriving as early as seven. They stay in their offices all day, many times leaving only for lunch in the executive dining room on the fourteenth floor or in the basement cafeteria, these being places where the men may take a quiet meal; they walk across the street to the Recess Club, or take a car downtown to the Detroit Athletic Club or the Detroit Club. But they are not pretentious men, and, many times, if work is pressing, if they are working under deadlines, they stay at their desks, eating a sandwich and an apple. Then, when the day ends—for these men it ends between six or seven o'clock, perhaps later—they take the elevator downstairs, walk to their cars, and speed up the freeways to their homes.

The wife of an automobile executive once complained to *Fortune:* "My husband and I haven't been out together after nine for six months. He's always away on business a lot and when he's home he leaves the house before seven and he gets back to dinner exhausted. Then he goes to bed. For all he gets out of it, we could be living in a cave." Roche says: "I don't have any time to myself. I leave early in the morning and get back late at night. I always work most of Saturday and at least Sunday morning. We don't have time to socialize very much." Once, at a stockholders' meeting, when General Motors executives were being vilified as grossly overpaid, Mrs. Edward N. Cole, wife of the General Motors president, a voluble, unpredictable woman, complained to journalists she knew that, why, she hardly ever saw Ed; Ed worked himself to the bone, she said, worked morning, noon, and night, and perhaps it was not worth it, not worth the money, if Ed had to work so hard only to be raked over the coals.

A Detroit minister told *Fortune:* "These men are monks —monks who've traded in their prayer books for a production line. From the way they work, I sometimes think they want to overwhelm God with their cars. It may sound odd for me to say this, but I don't give as much of myself to my church as many of them do to General Motors and Ford and the rest." And a Bloomfield Hills physician said: "To tell them to slow down is just like telling a dog he shouldn't raise his leg at a fire hydrant."

Many automobile executives dread retirement as much as they dread dying; so committed have they been to the automobile industry that when they retire, they have all day and nothing to do. They do not garden, they do not fish, they do not hunt or sail, they do not enjoy golf that much; instead, they sit caged in their large homes. Once a journalist called a retired Cadillac executive for some information, and the executive, talking freely, chatted for an hour or more. At the end of the conversation the journalist thanked the man for giving so generously of his time. "That's all right," he said, slowly, sadly. "I have all day."

Many of the wives are active in charitable activities; charities, a society writer says, assuage their guilt feelings about being so rich. Oddly, few of the sons enter the automobile industry. Most of them become doctors or lawyers or dentists; some go into government. Like the sons of the blue-collar workers, they do not wish to spend their lives as their fathers have; they do not see the lure of devoting one's life to the manufacture and sale of automobiles.

But the fathers are not unlikable. They are friendly, uncomplicated, civilized men, with whom it is pleasant to drink one or two scotches or to see a baseball or football game. They are men from the heartland, unsophisticated, uncosmopolitan; they travel, but to attend board meetings, to check on suppliers, to see why sales are down, not to look at ruins or museums; their homes have no libraries, for they read magazines not books. "I had no time for books," Alfred P. Sloan, Jr., wrote in *Adventure of a White-Collar Man*.

There is, at General Motors, a bureaucracy, a table of organization, much like that of the Army or the Catholic Church. There are formalities, uniforms, militarylike courtesies, trappings of office, chains of command.

Not surprisingly, many men in such a hierarchy become fawns, bootlickers. Dr. David Lewis, for five years a highly regarded public relations specialist at General Motors and now a professor of business history at the University of Michigan, recalls one day in the 1960s, when he was sitting on the toilet in the men's room on the eleventh floor of the General Motors Building. A colleague burst in, apparently glanced down the row of stalls until he spied a pair of shoes beneath the half door. "Is that you, Dave?" he asked. Lewis said it was, and the colleague excitedly declared that Lewis was wanted on the fourteenth floor, the executive floor. Lewis, at normal speed, emerged—to find the colleague staring at him excitedly, *holding Lewis' suit jacket.* "You're wanted on the *fourteenth floor,*" the colleague cried. Lewis says: "Everybody's always talking about the worker's dignity. Well, hell, what about my dignity?"

Once, a story goes, a General Motors public relations man discovered that Harlow Curtice, the General Motors president, possessed a fondness for smoked oysters, so he followed Curtice for an hour or more through a Bloomfield Hills cocktail party, carrying a tray of the delicacies, always a step behind and two to the right, like a general's aide, so that Curtice, without looking and without thought, could select a tasty oyster when he wished. Lewis says that it always astonished him during his years at General Motors to see forty- and fifty-year-old men, when they received a request to report to an executive on the fourteenth floor, "dogtrotting down the corridor, out the door to the elevators."

Yet Lewis says critics are incorrect when they say that all General Motors is concerned with is profit. Profits, he says, are the "number one concern, because without profits they could not continue." But, Lewis says, "I think that most of the management people think they are providing a service to America, in terms of the products they make, the jobs they offer, the supplies they buy, the transportation they provide":

> I think they care about the dignity of their workers. The workers might dispute it . . . [but] I don't think there's any doubt that General Motors knows that the morale of the workers is important and that it will do what is expected of it. And they will go to a considerable extent to do what the workers expect them to do. They will work to make them, well, contented, if not happy. I don't think they're contemptuous of their workers at all. I have the feeling that when they talk of the dignity of the individual and respect for it, they're not talking through their asses.
>
> They probably figure, without being able to say it out loud, that . . . a plant job . . . is about all the worker is

capable of doing. And they will always tell you that some
of the workers like that work, that the worker won't say it,
but that's all they want to do—that they don't want to be
foreman or sit at some desk.

If the workers really wanted to get ahead, Lewis says, the
executives believe that "undoubtedly the opportunity is there
for people who have the drive" to do what the executives did,
to move up in life. "Drive," says Lewis, "is what they regard
as being most important in success."

A journalist who has studied the corporation for years
says, "They've said all along that General Motors is a system
designed by geniuses to be run by idiots. And it pretty much
operates on its own. They never really kidded around that
you had to have brains to make it at General Motors. It helps
but what you really have to do is work your ass off. Do that
and you get along."

General Motors Corporation was not organized so
much as it was assembled, put together as one assembles a
car.

The corporation was founded on September 16, 1908—two
weeks before Henry Ford put the Model T on the market, in
a year when the American automobile industry produced
65,000 automobiles—by William Crapo (Billy) Durant, an
audacious, ambitious man, a wildcatter, a conglomerateur, a
superb salesman, a man who, Alfred P. Sloan, Jr., said, possessed one weakness: "He could create but not administer."

Grandson of a Michigan Civil War era governor and
wealthy lumber baron, Durant loved the world of men and
selling and abhorred school. At seventeen he dropped out
from school to work in the company store at one of his grandfather's lumber mills, selling cigars, patent medicines,
matches, and whisky. By 1880, when he was twenty, Durant
had opened his own insurance agency, and one day, on a
business trip through Coldwater in southern Michigan near

the Indiana border, he met a man who held a patent on a light, two-wheeled vehicle called a road cart. The man was disappointed and bitter; although the road cart was an excellent vehicle, he had been unable to convince anyone to manufacture it. The horse-drawn cart was made of wood and had few parts. It was impossible to overturn, the man said, and he took Durant on a wild ride through the wooded countryside to prove his claim. Durant was intrigued by the vehicle, for he was convinced that with financial support and proper production and merchandising methods, he could manufacture and sell the cart on a mass basis. He purchased the patent for 50 dollars, and convinced a Flint carriage manufacturer to make the carts for him for 8 dollars apiece. He and a young friend, J. Dallas Dort, a clerk in a hardware store, then established the Flint Road-Cart Company and sold the carts for 12.50 dollars each. The carts were a great success: people loved them, since they were lighter than a carriage, yet on a trip, a traveler could carry much more than on a horse. Within a few years, Durant and Dort sold 100,000 of the carts, and made handsome profits.

In 1895, with the profits from their road cart venture, Durant and Dort formed the Durant-Dort Carriage Company to manufacture full-sized carriages. At the turn of the century, the company was the leading carriage manufacturer in the nation, selling 50,000 carriages a year. Durant—forty years old—was a millionaire.

By now, the automobile was becoming increasingly popular, and it seemed that much money could be made in what had become known as the "automobile game." Durant possessed no special fondness for automobiles, having had two tortuous rides in the contraptions through the Flint countryside. But a Flint businessman told him that a Detroit motorcar company was for sale. The Buick company had been founded by David D. Buick, a plumbing merchant and inventor —one of his inventions was a process to attach porcelain to iron, which gave America the modern bathtub and toilet.

Although the firm was financially troubled, the Buick seemed an excellent vehicle and a fine investment opportunity. After two months of rigorous testing of the car, Durant concluded that the businessman was correct, and in November 1904, Durant took control of Buick.

What had been the firm's main problem, raising money to manufacture and sell the car in sufficient quantities, was no problem for the energetic, hard-selling Durant. It is said that he personally sold 500,000 dollars of the stock to acquaintances in Flint in a single day. He opened plants in Flint and Jackson, and soon was producing five to eight automobiles a week—the 1904 Buick sold for 1,250 dollars, with 125 dollars extra for a canvas top and lights. Soon Durant had established a nationwide distribution and service network and was expanding his operations in Flint, persuading Alfred Champion, a French-born, devil-may-care race driver, to establish his spark plug firm in Flint, and Charles S. Mott, an axle manufacturer, to move his firm to Flint from Utica, New York.°

By 1908, Durant was the leading automobile manufacturer in the country, selling 8,487 Buicks that year, almost as many cars as sold by Ford and Cadillac combined. By this time, too, Durant had made his famous prediction that the automobile industry soon would be selling more than 500,000 cars a year, a prediction that convinced many people Durant was daft.

To capitalize on the future he believed lay ahead, Durant

° Mott, a delightful man, went on to make millions in the automobile business and to outlive all the remarkable automotive pioneers of those exciting times: Durant, Sloan, Henry Ford, Henry Leland, John and Horace Dodge, and Walter P. Chrysler. In the 1950s and 1960s, Mott could be seen, alone, tall, well-suited, white moustache gleaming, tapping with his cane along the downtown streets in Flint, a city to which he gave millions of dollars. In 1970, at the General Motors annual meeting, Mott, still a director, was greeted by Evelyn Y. Davis, the shrill critic of corporations, dressed in a black bathing suit, wearing a paper gas mask, and waving a small American flag. Mott, ninety-five, stopped, looked the woman up and down, and declared, "Ahah, here to raise a little hell, huh?" Mott also has told an instructive story about the General Motors Corporation: in more than fifty years, in scores of board of director meetings, he cannot recall one occasion on which the directors rejected a management decision.

began to put together a consortium of companies, believing
that diversity was a necessity in the uncertain automobile
market—if one model failed, others, or even one, would capture the public fancy and pull the firm through. In 1907,
Durant tried to bring together what were then the four
largest firms in the industry: Buick, Ford, Maxwell-Briscoe,
and Reo. But Henry Ford decided that he must have the 3
million dollars that Durant offered him in cash; when Ransom
Olds, who owned Reo, heard of Ford's demand, he declared
that the 3 million dollars Durant had offered him would also
have to be in cash. Durant dealt in stock, not money, and
the negotiations collapsed.

Next year, Durant approached J. P. Morgan & Company
of New York for financial backing for a proposed amalgama-
tion called International Motors. He was turned down, however, because a Morgan attorney objected to his wildcatting
ways. Several weeks later, Durant obtained the necessary
resources, a combination of cash and stock, on his own. The
Morgan attorney sent word that he believed Durant should
not use the name International Motors—that he, the attorney,
had conceived the name and Durant should come up with his
own name. Durant, sitting at his desk, took out an envelope
on which was written International Motors, thought about the
matter, and after a time, almost carelessly, scratched out
International Motors and wrote General Motors.

Largely with stocks and bonds of other companies, Durant
incorporated General Motors Company as a holding company
in New Jersey, where corporation laws were less stringent
than in Michigan or New York. In October 1908, Durant
brought Buick into General Motors, and then Olds and Oakland, both largely through the exchange of stock. In 1909, he
purchased Cadillac Motor Company for 4.5 million in cash,
at that time the largest cash sale in the automobile industry.

Soon the irrepressible expansionist was in trouble. General
Motors reported a profit of 9 million dollars in 1908 and of
10.2 million dollars in 1909; but the 1909 profits represented an

increase of only 1.2 million even though sales increased 10 million dollars. Some of the firms that Durant brought into General Motors, firms for which he paid millions of dollars in cash or stock, were worthless. The major example: Heany Lamp Company, which claimed a patent for a tungsten lamp. Durant paid 7 million dollars, mostly in stock, for the Heany Company, more than he paid for Buick and Olds combined, only to have the government throw out the patent application and thus render the company virtually worthless.

Buick, the base of the company, had the highest net worth of any company in the automobile industry. But the other firms in Durant's consortium constituted too large a drain on finances. In May 1910, construction stopped at Buick's Flint plants; there were large layoffs and payrolls could hardly be met. A Boston distributor saved Buick on one occasion by shipping cash to Flint in suitcases; had the money gone through the banks, the banks would have seized it to apply against unpaid loans.

Durant, in desperate need of funds, went West, believing the Western financiers more venturesome than the conservative Easterners, who still regarded the automobile as a frill for the rich. He asked for funds at banks in Kansas City, Chicago, and St. Louis, but was turned down. One night, as the distressed but still spirited Durant returned to Michigan, the train stopped in Elkhart, Indiana, in a driving rain. Durant looked out the window of his coach and at the far end of the street, he faintly made out a sign through the rain: BANK. Durant shook his friend, A. H. Goss. "Wake up, Goss," he said, "there's one bank we missed."

By the fall of 1910, bankruptcy seemed inevitable. But in November, two Eastern investment concerns formed a syndicate under the leadership of James J. Storrow to keep the corporation alive. The investors' terms were stiff: they agreed to a 15-million-dollar, five-year loan at 6 per cent, but they took 2.5 million dollars off the top, meaning General Motors received 12.5 million, and they also took 6 million dollars in

General Motors stock as part of their commission. They demanded that Durant relinquish his duties as chief executive, although they allowed him to retain his seat on the board of directors. Still, the loan was worth the price since it saved the corporation.

Yet the firm was in such trouble that the bankers thought of dissolving it and salvaging Buick and Cadillac as independent companies. General Motors was kept alive at the urging of Henry Leland, the elderly, bearded chief of Cadillac, who pledged his own and Cadillac's resources to the corporation. The bankers proved conservative yet efficient administrators. Standardized accounting and reporting procedures were initiated. General Motors Export Company, General Motors Truck Company, and General Motors of Canada were organized; unprofitable subsidiaries, including the Heany Company, were eliminated. Storrow seems to have been very skilled at selecting talented executives. In 1910, needing a new man to head Buick, Storrow asked Durant for a recommendation, and Durant suggested Charles W. Nash, who, the story goes, Durant had spotted years before as Nash worked cutting Durant's lawn. Nash, orphaned in boyhood, bound over to an Illinois farmer from whom he ran away at age twelve, worked on the lawn with such industry that Durant gave him a job polishing lamps at his carriage company for seventy-five cents a day. He then went on to display such intelligence and business sense that he rose to general superintendent. Promoted to the Buick directorship, he performed so well that he was named General Motors president in 1912. His replacement at Buick was a man no less talented, Walter P. Chrysler, whom Storrow had met in the railroad industry at Pittsburgh. He persuaded Nash to hire Chrysler, who was so excited by the new automobile business that he accepted a salary of six thousand a year even though he had been making twelve thousand working for the railroad.

Buick, under Nash and Chrysler, and Cadillac, under Leland, were the mainstays of the corporation, contributing important auto innovations and major revenue to the parent organization. In 1910, for example, Cadillac introduced the closed car, and Buick brought out the electric horn; in 1911, Cadillac introduced the electric self-starter, which for the first time made automobiles convenient for women to operate.* The corporation was sound for the first time in years. At the board meeting in September 1915, General Motors declared a fifty dollar cash dividend, then the highest in the history of the New York Stock Exchange.

The resolute Durant, meanwhile, was quietly at work concocting a way to reacquire control of General Motors. In November 1911, he and Louis Chevrolet, a huge, moustached race driver, organized the Chevrolet Motor Company and marketed a powerful, high-speed car that sold more than 3,000 units the first year.† Durant, believing that larger sales and profits lay with lightweight, low-priced cars, dropped the large car the next year, and brought out a small, cheap auto, still calling it the Chevrolet to capitalize on the race driver's fame. The switch to a small car so piqued Chevrolet that he quit, selling his stock to Durant for cents on the dollar. Durant was correct in his interpretation of the market: the first model, brought out in 1914, sold all the units that Durant could manu-

* Henry Leland and Charles F. (Boss) Kettering, General Motors' famed inventor, were responsible for the self-starter. George Carter, inventor of the Cartercar and a friend of Leland's, was motoring in Belle Isle, Detroit's park, one winter morning and chanced upon a woman whose car had stalled and who was having difficulty starting it with the hand crank. Carter gallantly attempted to start the automobile; the crank spun backward, striking his face and breaking his jaw. He was taken to a hospital, but gangrene set in and Carter died. Leland was immensely saddened by Carter's death, and told Kettering that what the industry needed was a self-starter to prevent future tragedies. Kettering set to work and after several months he fabricated a self-starter from an old storage battery, the same kind of battery he had used in inventing an electric cash register for National Cash Register. He took it to Detroit, where he demonstrated it for skeptical Cadillac engineers. It worked and was introduced as standard equipment on the 1912 Cadillac.

† When Louis and his brother, Arthur, first came to Flint, Durant had them race on a small dirt track behind the Buick factory. Louis won, but Durant hired Arthur as his personal chauffeur; Arthur, Durant said, took no chances.

facture; in 1915, the famous Chevrolet 490, priced fifty dollars above the Model T, sold extremely well, earning the new company more than a million dollars.

In early 1915, Durant announced that he would exchange the highly valued Chevrolet stock for General Motors stock at the rate of five to one. General Motors stock was greatly undervalued at the time since the bankers in control refused to pay dividends until the September board meeting, and hundreds of General Motors stockholders, including many of Durant's friends, rushed to exchange their stock, convinced that any company run by Durant would soon be earning large profits and paying large dividends.

The certificates came in so fast, it is said, that they were stored in bushel baskets in Durant's offices in New York. On September 16, 1915, seven years after he had formed the company, five years after he had been embarrassingly dismissed, a smiling Durant, his pockets bulging with stock certificates, walked into the meeting of the board of directors and matter-of-factly informed the surprised bankers, "Gentlemen, I control this company." As he acquired General Motors stock, Durant had made friends with John J. Raskob, financial adviser to Pierre S. du Pont, president of the du Pont Company, and Raskob convinced du Pont to invest money in General Motors. That November the Durant-controlled board elected du Pont the General Motors chairman, a position he would hold for thirteen years. Nash, far too conservative for the daring Durant, resigned the presidency in June 1916, later forming the extremely profitable Nash Motor Car Company in Kenosha, Wisconsin. Durant assumed the presidency. "The big show," Sloan wrote in *My Years with General Motors,* "was on again."

Durant took many actions that were important to the future of General Motors. On October 13, 1916, he organized General Motors Corporation of Delaware, an operating corporation, to replace the existing General Motors, a holding company. Capitalization was increased from 60 million dollars to 100 million. Durant created the separate United Motors Corporation, a combination of parts and accessory firms; he bought the Hyatt Roller Bearing Company, a successful automobile industry supplier, from Sloan for 13.5 million dollars, and made Sloan the United Motors president. He then folded a number of other firms into United Motors: New Departure Manufacturing Company, maker of ball bearings; Remy Electric Company, maker of electrical starting and ignition equipment; Dayton Engineering Laboratories, known as Delco, maker of electric equipment—this acquisition brought Charles Kettering to General Motors—and the Perlman Rim Company, maker of wheel rims. In 1918, United Motors assets were acquired by General Motors for 44 million dollars.

By now, Durant was moving into an expanded financial alliance with the du Pont interests. World War I would soon be over and the firm would lose its lucrative munitions contracts. Raskob, du Pont's adviser, convinced the du Pont chairman that increasing his investments in the automobile industry was sound, writing du Pont with remarkable prescience: "The General Motors Company today occupies a unique position in the automobile industry and . . . with proper management will show results in the future second to none in any American industry." Additionally, Raskob and du Pont were confident that by acquiring control of General Motors they would insure a major market for their chemical products such as Pyralin, Fabrikoid, paint and varnish.

In December 1918, the du Pont interest purchased 25 million dollars of General Motors and Chevrolet stock and later increased their holdings to more than 43 million, 26.4 per cent of the corporation, the funds largely coming from the great profits the firm was making selling explosives to the American and allied governments fighting in Europe. By December 1919, the du Pont company had invested some 49 million dollars in General Motors, and owned 28.7 per cent of the corporation's common stock.

With these new funds, Durant at the end of the war

moved into what business historian Alfred D. Chandler, Jr., called "one of the most ambitious expansion programs ever proposed in American industry." As in the past, some of the acquisitions made fortunes, some lost fortunes. General Motors acquired Durant's old company, Chevrolet, a large part of which was already owned by du Pont, and, for 30 million dollars, GM acquired a 60 per cent interest in the Fisher Body Company; both acquisitions were extremely profitable. One day in 1918, Durant visited a dirty Detroit attic with a financially troubled friend, Alfred Mellowes, and then wrote out a 56,366.50 dollar personal check for Mellowes' Guardian Frigerator Company which consisted of the few pieces of equipment in the attic. Its production at that time stood at about forty units a year. When the board of directors asked what an automobile company was doing making electric refrigerators, Durant explained that he saw an excellent future for refrigerators, a future perhaps second only to that for the automobile industry. Anyway, he said, refrigerators and automobiles were similar, each a box with a motor. The next year, Durant sold the company to General Motors for what it had cost him. Five years later, the company, renamed Frigidaire, was making twenty thousand refrigerators a year and for the first time turned a profit. In 1925, it produced 56,500 units and the company, the largest of its kind, was selling refrigerators throughout the world.

Durant also saw an excellent future for General Motors in the farm tractor business, and merged three agricultural firms into the Samson Sieve Grip Tractor Company to produce an experimental tractor called the "Iron Horse," an endeavor that Sloan later charitably described as "very unprofitable." It was abandoned in 1920 after General Motors had sunk 30 million dollars into the venture.

By the spring and early summer of 1920, the overextended Durant had steered General Motors into grave organizational and financial difficulties once again. The top executives possessed little control over the virtually autonomous division heads; the unpredictable Durant meddled with subordinates or completely ignored them, depending upon his whim. In *Adventures of a White-Collar Man*, Sloan describes how Durant decided upon the purchase of land for a new company headquarters, the General Motors Building; it is a charming, instructive example of Durant's method of conducting business: "I can see Mr. Durant now. He started at the corner of Cass Avenue, paced a certain distance west on West Grand Boulevard . . . Then he stopped, for no apparent reason, at some apartment houses. . . . He said that this was about the ground he wanted, and turned to me and said, as well as I can remember, 'Alfred, will you go buy these properties for us and Mr. Prentis [M. L. Prentis, corporation financial officer] will pay whatever you decide to pay for them.'"

Before the General Motors Building was completed—the building today bears several old-English style D's above the main entrance and high on the sides, for Durant intended to call it the Durant Building—it cost 20 million dollars. Even with so large a project, Sloan said, "That was Mr. Durant's way of operating, right out of his head."

Durant's business techniques helped cause the departure of two of his most brilliant executives, both automotive giants: Henry Leland and Walter P. Chrysler. Leland left Cadillac in 1917, at age seventy-two, ostensibly to manufacture aircraft engines. Mostly, however, Leland disliked Durant's unpredictability. Leland organized the Lincoln Motor Car Company —named after Abraham Lincoln, the man for whom he had cast his first vote in 1864—and during the war the company built 6,500 Liberty engines for the government. Afterward, Leland produced the excellent Lincoln automobile; the firm was taken over by Henry Ford in 1922.

Chrysler left in anger because Durant interfered with his running of the Buick Division. After much time and effort, Chrysler had retained the A. O. Smith Company, of Janesville, Wisconsin, the foremost manufacturer of automobile frames, to build frames for Buick. Durant, however, in a speech in

Flint, announced that General Motors would construct an
expensive plant at Flint to build Buick frames. This pleased
the Flint city fathers, but not Chrysler. He stormed to Detroit
to argue the matter with Durant; Durant, not out of rudeness,
perhaps, but because he was taken with other matters and
found it hard to turn down interruptions from friends, kept
Chrysler waiting in his outer office for hours. Chrysler fumed.
Finally, he stalked in, quit, and stalked out. Sloan, whose
office was then adjacent to Durant's, recalled: "I remember
the day. He banged the door on the way out, and out of that
bang came eventually the Chrysler Corporation."

By early summer of 1920, the company was in jeopardy.
Requests for regional managers to slash inventories went
unheeded, and in June 1920, trainloads of undelivered cars
stood in railroad yards in Western cities. In September, the
brief but bitter postwar recession struck the industry. Within
a month many divisions were having difficulty meeting payrolls. Some 64 million dollars that had been earmarked for
expansion was used for operating expenses; still, the company
had to borrow more than 80 million to meet its obligations.
By November, almost the entire corporation, except for Buick
and Cadillac, had halted production.

On November 11, Durant, having given no hint of the corporation's difficulties, invited du Pont and Raskob to lunch,
as though he simply was acting the part of the civilized businessman. To du Pont and Raskob's astonishment, he announced that he and the corporation were "in the hands of the
bankers"—the bankers had asked for his resignation and he
intended to comply.

For months, as du Pont and Raskob were to learn in the
next few days, Durant had been purchasing large quantities
of General Motors stock, apparently in an attempt to bolster
its price. But by midsummer, the price had dropped from fifty
to fifteen dollars a share. Durant had no personal books or
detailed records—it is said he had more than seventy broker-
age accounts—but after some figuring he estimated his debts
as more than 30 million dollars.

Du Pont was worried. He believed that if Durant's plight, or that of the corporation, became known, General Motors might fold and the financial panic on Wall Street might be so worsened that a depression would occur. After four days of furious activity, the du Ponts and the bankers from the Morgan interests put together a syndicate to assume Durant's debts. Like the Eastern bankers a decade before, they insisted on harsh terms, demanding Durant's 2.5 million shares in stock, but giving him in turn 40 per cent interest in their syndicate, which in 1921 he sold to them for 230,000 shares of General Motors stock, then valued at 2.9 million dollars. Durant once again was forced to resign the General Motors presidency; he did it calmly at a board meeting, smiling pleasantly, Sloan wrote, "as if it were a routine matter. . . ."

Theodore F. MacManus and Norman Beasley, in *Men, Money and Motors*, a flavorful account of the early days of the industry, described the atmosphere the day Durant stepped down:

> As he passed down the corridor, he paused to shake hands with old associates and with the smile still playing about his lips, he murmured:
> "Well, May first is usually the national moving day but we seem to have changed it into December first."
> A nod and he was gone.
> In the seclusion of their own offices, where no one could see, there were General Motors executives who wept that afternoon.

Durant, not unexpectedly, was soon back in the automobile industry. Within a few months, he raised some 7 million dollars and formed Durant Motors, which went on to produce the Durant, Flint, Star, and Locomobile. The Durant, particularly, was an excellent automobile. But once again, Durant was wiped out, this time by the Depression, and in 1933, Durant Motors was liquidated. In 1936, at seventy-five, Durant declared himself bankrupt, listing liabilities of 914,000 dollars and assets of 250—his clothes. He later opened a supermarket in Asbury Park, New Jersey, and promoted a chain of bowling alleys, believing with characteristic foresightedness that bowling would be the family sport of the future. But he was short of cash and in ill health, and the venture collapsed. In 1940, when General Motors celebrated the manufacture of its twenty-five-millionth automobile with elaborate ceremonies at Flint, Durant shared the platform at Sloan's request. Having Durant there, Sloan told the General Motors employees and members of their families, was "one of the happiest moments of my business life." Five years later, his fortune gone, Durant died in a small apartment overlooking Central Park in New York.

Du Pont, fifty, already retired as head of the du Pont Company, replaced Durant as General Motors president, but with great reluctance. Du Pont possessed no special fondness for New York or Detroit, preferring his magnificent estate in the Pennsylvania countryside, just outside Wilmington, Delaware. However, he gave in to the pleadings of a number of General Motors executives, among them Sloan, who believed that du Pont was the one man who could command the prestige and respect that the demoralized and nearly bankrupt organization required in its chief executive. Du Pont said he would do "whatever they thought best [but] that . . . I was only to stay there until a better posted man could be found to take the job."

It was obvious, immediately, that the better posted man was Sloan, the roller-bearing entrepreneur, who in an incredibly long career, more than thirty years as the corporation's chief executive, was to become perhaps the most important American business figure of the twentieth century—the man who would transform the corporation into such a huge, vitally important institution and give the corporation the character and philosophy it possesses to this day.

Even while du Pont was president, it was Sloan who

functioned as chief operating officer. Three years later, in May 1923, Sloan succeeded him. "The responsibility of General Motors now became mine," Sloan wrote in *Adventures of a White-Collar Man*. "I believe it is reasonable to say that no greater opportunity for accomplishment ever was given to any individual in industry than was given to me when I became president. . . . I determined right then and there that everything I had was to be given to the cause. No sacrifice of time, effort or my own convenience was to be too great. There were to be no reservations and no alibis."

For Sloan, it was the corporation that mattered, the corporation above everything. A millionaire much of his life, for years the highest paid businessman in America, Sloan had no excessively rich tastes. He and his wife seldom entertained. He disliked golf as a waste of time. It is said he seldom laughed. He owned a 236-foot yacht, with a crew of forty-three, the *Rene*, purchased for a million dollars after associates urged him to find a hobby, but he seldom sailed it and he later sold it off for 175,000 dollars. "Everything," *Fortune* said, "has gone into the job."

Sloan—and the men who run General Motors today practice a business philosophy, a philosophy of social thought, a mode of life, a mode of dress much like he practiced—was an old-fashioned man. He believed in the efficacy of work, and that by diligence and intelligence one could find one's way to the top. He wrote in *Adventures of a White-Collar Man:* "Think of the corporation as a pyramid of opportunities from the bottom toward the top with thousands of chances for advancement. Only capacity limited any worker's chance to grow, to develop his ability to make a greater contribution to the whole and to improve his own position as well. The routes to the heights in the automobile industry were open to all, even though increasingly and inexorably the big chances beckoned to those with unusual qualifications and with trained minds. The Fisher brothers had climbed. Chrysler had climbed. Knudsen had climbed. And in the General Mo-

tors organization thousands of others had climbed to some
degree of eminence within the structure."

His writings are laced with homilies of the quiet, middle
class life from which he rose:

> *Technological progress—and it is a pity more do not ap-
> preciate it—is the one sound approach to increased employ-
> ment and higher wages.*

> *Now what about today's eager and ambitious young men,
> eager to qualify for the more important responsibilities?
> That is a question I am asked thousands of times every
> year. Many are discouraged because they believe opportu-
> nity is lacking. They see millions out of work and cannot
> get jobs themselves. They do not see how further accom-
> plishment is possible. But there is no justification for this
> feeling. Things are different! Importantly different! Yet
> the world is in no sense finished in its building. Men have
> only started. The greatest opportunities lie ahead!*

> *Sooner or later we must learn that only by more work and
> still more work—always efficiently used—can we capitalize
> our unlimited opportunities, can we give employment to
> the millions of unemployed; can we put to work the billions
> of idle money and make use of our resources of raw ma-
> terials, whether in the form of more things for more people
> or for defending ourselves against aggression.*

> *Growth, or striving for it, is, I believe, essential to the good
> health of an enterprise. Deliberately to stop growing is to
> suffocate.*

Although he was six feet tall with long features that in
photographs made him look like a large man, Sloan weighed
just 130 pounds. He was, from at least the mid-1930s on,
partially deaf and because of this at times he talked quietly,
almost in a whisper, and at other times he practically shouted.
In his later years he felt comfortable talking only with close,
long-time associates; often, with groups of people, he spoke
little or said nothing. Throughout his life, his voice carried
the traces of his childhood Brooklyn accent.

Few people, once Sloan reached the top at General Motors, called him by his first name; always it was *Mr. Sloan*. Yet his associates considered him a friendly, warm man. Peter F. Drucker came to know Sloan during his two year study of the corporation that resulted in his book, *Concept of the Corporation*. Drucker says Sloan was "not a gregarious person . . . even in his youth he had been a solitary fellow." But he was, Drucker says, a man who fashioned enduring friendships and who could be immensely kind toward people. One General Motors executive told Drucker: "When I first had to appear before the executive committee, I got so flustered that I made a complete ass of myself. I would have killed myself off but for Mr. Sloan, who deliberately made the same ass of himself to save me."

But as kind as he could be to individuals, it was the corporation that mattered, the corporation to which he devoted almost every moment, almost every thought. In the early 1920s, the story is told, when Sloan set up the General Motors bonus system—which is a cornerstone of GM's success—one executive could not obtain the 25,000 dollars necessary to participate in the program. Sloan loaned him the money out of personal funds. The loan was later repaid; the man went on to a fine career and earned a large sum in the bonus plan. Thirty years later, when the man retired, he journeyed to New York to say goodbye to the man who had befriended him, who had been his chief executive for so long. Sloan saw him for five minutes.

Born May 23, 1875, in New Haven, Connecticut, the son of a comfortable tea and coffee importer, Sloan was the eldest of five children. When he was ten, the family moved to Brooklyn, where he attended public school and then Brooklyn Polytechnic Institute. Machines, not importing, fascinated Sloan, and he turned from his family's business to become an engineer. In 1892, he enrolled at Massachusetts Institute of Technology. A brilliant student, he completed the four year course in three years, and graduated in 1895 with a bachelor of science degree in electrical engineering. He was twenty, the youngest in his class.

Anxious to marry his school sweetheart, Sloan obtained a position as a draftsman for a small, nearly bankrupt Newark firm, the Hyatt Company, which was founded by John Wesley Hyatt, who invented celluloid not for photographic film, as it became used, but as it was never used, to substitute for ivory in billiard balls. The company was engaged in the manufacture of what were called Hyatt flexible roller bearings, a revolutionary product because at that time the regular bearings made of steel were rigid, wore easily, and quickly wore out what they touched.

Sloan disliked the shabby Hyatt factory, then located near the Newark dump, and after a time left to join an ex-Navy lieutenant in an ill-fated venture selling refrigeration units, a primitive form of air-conditioning, for New York apartments. He returned to Hyatt as a full partner after his father invested 5,000 dollars in the firm. Sloan earned 175 dollars a month as general manager—a few months later, at twenty-four, he became president—and his friend and partner, Peter Steenstrup, was business manager. The two applied themselves diligently, and within six months the firm earned a profit of 12,000 dollars.

Then, in 1899, the firm received an unusual inquiry from Elwood G. Haynes, an inventor in Kokomo, Indiana, who was tinkering with a gasoline-powered automobile, producing a few cars each year. Sloan and Steenstrup were not particularly excited; cars were still considered, Sloan recalled, not only "impractical toys . . . but a dangerous nuisance." But the two remembered Hyatt's maxim for success: "Find a market for antifriction bearings anywhere there was a turning wheel." So Steenstrup took the train to Kokomo, met Haynes, and took the order. "That," Sloan said, "was the beginning of our real adventures."

Not long after, Steenstrup obtained a trial order for 120

bearings from the Olds Motors Works in Lansing, Michigan, the company that was producing the famous Olds runabout, settling upon this car because its other models had been destroyed in a disastrous fire in its Detroit plant. A few months later the breakthrough came: large orders from C. S. Mott's Weston-Mott Company, which was making axles for Cadillac and Buick and other firms; from Henry Ford, who was experimenting with a number of models, later to settle upon the Model T; and from William Durant. By 1916, the Hyatt Company was grossing 10 million dollars and earning profits of more than one million a year. Before he was forty, Sloan, like Durant, was a millionaire.

In the spring of 1916, Durant moved to expand his newly reacquired General Motors, and approached Sloan with an offer to buy Hyatt. Sloan was then doing more than half his business with Ford and a substantial part with General Motors. He realized that if either firm were to begin making its own bearings, or switched to another kind of bearings—the automotive supplier business is a volatile business today in large part for the same reason—the company would quickly sink into trouble. Deciding it was wise to accept Durant's offer, he met with his board of directors, settled upon a "proper price," and returned to see Durant. He later conceded that he was influenced by the knowledge that Durant was inclined to be generous and not to haggle over the price of a firm he wanted to buy.

Sloan recalled the meeting in his memoirs:

"Well, Mr. Sloan," he said pleasantly, "have you got a price in mind now?"

"Yes, Mr. Durant, I think about fifteen million dollars."

Mr. Durant never batted an eye or ceased to smile and his teeth were very white.

"I'm still interested, Mr. Sloan."

Sloan entered negotiations with two of Durant's agents, and settled for 13.5 million. "I have always thought I could have got the fifteen million dollars," he wrote, "if my nerve had held out."

Hyatt was blended into Durant's United Motors Corporation and Sloan became the corporation's president. By necessity, he began to formulate a plan to control the many largely autonomous parts and accessories companies, and this marked the beginning of his famous plan—later to be implemented throughout the General Motors Corporation—of centralized control with decentralized operations. "All that held United Motors together in its beginning," Sloan wrote in *My Years with General Motors*, "was the concept of automotive parts and accessories . . . for the first time [I] learned something about getting decentralized management to yield some of its functions for the common good. . . . By placing each division on its own profit-making basis, I gave the general office a common measure of efficiency by which to judge the contribution of each division by the whole . . . I devised a system of standard accounting . . ."

Even before he joined General Motors, Sloan had discussed the "question of interdivisional relations" with Durant, and now, at United Motors, Sloan was appointed chairman of a committee to "formulate rules and regulations" for a more efficient operation of the General Motors corporation. He completed his task in the summer of 1919, and on December 6, 1919, presented his report to the corporation's executive committee, to which he had been appointed the year before. He wrote: "The profit resulting from any business considered abstractly, is no real measure of the merits of that particular business. An operation making $100,000 per year may be a very profitable business justifying expansion and the use of all the additional capital that it can profitably employ. On the other hand, a business making $10,000,000 a year may be a very unprofitable one . . . even justifying liquidation unless more profitable returns can be obtained. It is not, therefore, a matter of amount of profit but of the relation of that profit to the real worth of invested capital within the business. . . ." This was, Sloan wrote, as far as he knew, "the first written statement of the broad principles of financial control in General Motors."

About this same time, late in 1919 and early in 1920, Sloan, like many other General Motors executives, had become disenchanted with the chaotic organization that existed under Durant. In a period of weeks, Sloan put together a reorganization plan, based upon his experiences at United Motors and his knowledge of du Pont operations. Circulated unofficially, the plan, called simply the "Organization Study," became, Sloan wrote, "a kind of 'best seller' in the corporation."

Durant expressed interest but did not act on the plan, and Sloan was so disturbed by the continuing chaos in the corporation that he almost decided to resign. Perhaps he even made that decision for he went to London on a vacation with his wife and he purchased a Rolls Royce in preparation for a tour of the Continent. When he returned to his office, however, he sensed that Durant's and the corporation's problems were coming to a head, that they would soon be resolved one way or the other, and he decided to "ride along awhile and see what happens." In September 1920, he sent a copy of the reorganization plan to du Pont; du Pont thanked him for this and kept the plan in mind.

At the time of Durant's leaving and the coming of the new du Pont–Sloan administration, General Motors was in a precarious position due to Durant's wild expansionism and central management's inability to control divisions, all this exacerbated by the panic of 1920. "We are," du Pont told his executives, "in a receivership of our own." The corporation possessed almost no cash. The profitable Buick division made a practice of keeping large cash balances and delaying its reports to central headquarters; when the corporation needed funds, the treasurer, M. L. Prentis, would, Sloan reported, "try to guess how much Buick actually had and how much he could probably get from them." Then Prentis would go to Flint, discuss general business subjects and perhaps topics of the day as well, and finally, at the last moment, bring up the subject of cash and dicker over a transfer of funds from the division to

the corporation. Storage yards across the country were piled
with inventory that had been purchased at war and postwar
inflated prices. Now, prices had fallen, costing the corporation
hundreds of thousands of dollars. For a time in Detroit the
unfinished General Motors Building was boarded up.

In testimony during the 1952 du Pont–General Motors
antitrust case brought by the Justice Department,° Sloan recalled that only Buick and Cadillac were on a sound basis. He
said, "The other cars were very bad. Chevrolet was a mess,
Oakland and Olds were about the same category. There was
practically no coordination or planning of the products in
relation to the then-existing market. The cars were brought
into existence sometimes, it seemed to me, in a very haphazard
way; there was no proper engineering coordination between
the various parts of the car. It was something like a man want-
ing to get a new change of clothes and he goes and buys a
coat in one place and a pair of trousers in another, and a vest
in another, and all different fits, and you don't get a complete
ensemble." He said in *My Years with General Motors:* "There
was a lack of control and of any means of control in operations
and finance, and a lack of adequate information about anything. In short, there was just about as much crisis, inside or
outside, as you could wish for if you liked that sort of thing."

A new plan for the organization of the corporation was
urgently needed, and, at the end of 1920, du Pont recommended Sloan's proposal to the General Motors board of
directors. It was adopted on January 3, 1921, and is the plan,
without major revision, under which the corporation operates
today.

° In 1949, the Justice Department charged that the du Pont interests'
acquisition of GM stock constituted a violation of antitrust laws, and
sued to have them ordered to divest themselves of this stock. The case
was dismissed by a federal court in Chicago in 1953, but in 1961, on appeal,
the U.S. Supreme Court voted four to three to reverse the decision, and the
du Pont interests were forced to sell their GM holdings, some 63 million
shares, 23 per cent of GM's common stock, then worth about 2.7 billion
dollars. Congress passed a special tax law to allow the du Pont interests to
dispose of the stock without suffering crippling tax losses.

For all its long-term importance the plan was remarkably
simple—"primitive," Sloan said later, "by comparison with
present-day knowledge or management." What Sloan did was
merely impose a more formal method of control upon what
was then a loosely organized corporation structure of sixty
or more largely autonomous organizations. The organizations
were grouped into divisions according to function. Division
managers retained much autonomy, as they do today, but
centralized control was placed in the hands of what was to
become a largely expanded central office headed by general
executives and staff officers. The plan, Sloan wrote, represented a "happy medium . . . between the extremes of pure
centralization and pure decentralization." Two premises were
involved, he said: one, that "certain central organization
functions are absolutely essential to the logical development
and proper control of the corporation's activities," and, two,
that each division "headed by its chief executive shall be complete in every necessary function and able to exercise full
initiative and logical development."

Sloan wrote in *My Years with General Motors:*

> The new policy asked that the corporation neither remain
> as it was, a weak form of organization, nor become a rigid,
> command form. But the actual forms of organization that
> were to evolve in the future under a new administration—
> what exactly, for example, would remain a divisional re-
> sponsibility and what would be co-ordinated, and what
> would be policy and what would be administration—could
> not be deduced by a process of logic from the "Organiza-
> tion Study." Even mistakes played a large part in the actual
> events . . . and if our competitors—Mr. Ford among them
> —had not made some of considerable magnitude, and we
> had not reversed certain of ours, the position of General
> Motors would be different from what it is today . . . [But
> if] we lacked experience in operations, we did not lack
> energy in overcoming this deficiency.

It took the greater part of four years to put the plan fully
into operation, a difficult and exacting task. Duties had to be

defined specifically, and channels of communication had to
be opened between the divisions and the central headquarters.
Sloan performed remarkably, at times forceful, at times tact-
ful and patient. He explained his management style: "I sell
my ideas to my associates if I can. I accept their judgment if
they convince me, as they frequently do, that I am wrong. I
prefer to appeal to the intelligence of a man rather than attempt to exercise authority over him." In the years of reorganization, he visited scores of cities in the United States, sometimes calling on from five to ten dealers a day. "I meet them
in their own places of business," he said, "talk with them
across their own desks and solicit from them suggestions and
criticism as to their relations with the corporation." Sloan was
an imposing figure, and his visits were not quickly forgotten.
Always dapper, he arrived dressed in what was then the height
of fashion: a dark, double-breasted suit, a high, starched collar, a conservative tie fixed with a pearl stickpin, spats, handsome shoes, a handkerchief in his breast pocket.

When Sloan completed the reorganization in 1924, he had
developed the first scientific method for running the large
corporation, a plan that was followed by many other businesses
in America and abroad.

While the new concept of the corporation was being implemented, Sloan was at work studying the market and attempting to build up a product line that would capture the
public fancy.

Demand for automobiles had returned with the end of
the 1920–1 recession. But by 1924, the market had reached
a plateau of 3.5 million cars a year, and, except for 1929, when
Henry Ford brought out the Model A, industry sales did not
exceed 4 million cars a year until the great period of economic
growth after World War II. Chandler, the automotive industry
historian, points out, "Expansion of output by one company
could come only at the expense of another. Such competition
for a larger share of a market of relatively fixed size put a
premium on the use of product differentiation, mass advertis-

ing, consumer financing. . . ." And all the important market innovations—the complete product line, the annual model change, mass advertising—all these were conceived in the 1920s by Sloan.

In June 1921, the General Motors executive committee approved a long-range product policy calling for the establishment of a "complete line of motor cars from the lowest to the highest price." The idea was as elementary, Sloan later conceded, as "a shoe manufacturer proposing to sell shoes in more than one size." But Peter F. Drucker says this policy—Sloan's understanding of the market as a "homogenous market differentiated by income groups" and his plan to produce a "car for every purse and purpose"—was Sloan's most important contribution to General Motors, more important, Drucker contends, than the new corporate structure.

The problem in the early 1920s, Sloan said, was that although the corporation marketed seven makes of automobiles—Cadillac, Buick, Oakland, Oldsmobile, Scripps-Booth, Sheridan, and Chevrolet—only Cadillac, in the high-priced field, and Buick, in the middle-priced field, were organized under "clear divisional concepts." The other divisions competed among themselves for the same buyers. Sloan had two major goals: to build up the Oakland, later Pontiac, in the middle-price range and to build up Chevrolet, which had almost gone bankrupt, in the low-priced field to compete with the Model T.

In 1925, the corporation began its moves in the market place. That year it introduced the middle-priced, six-cylinder Pontiac, priced just above the Chevrolet, to improve its position in the middle-priced area of the market. It also introduced the famous 1925 Chevrolet, a long, closed-body model with sleek Duco finish, a one-piece windshield, and automatic windshield wipers.

Even though the Chevrolet's prime competition was the Model T, the executive committee did not want to sell it at exactly the same price, but rather wanted to build it a little better and price it a little higher. Sloan, stating marketing

philosophy that prevails today, declared: "We proposed . . .
that General Motors should place its cars at the top of each
price range and make them of such quality that they would
attract sales from below that price, selling to those customers
who might be willing to pay a little more for the additional
quality, and attract sales also from above that price, selling to
those customers who would see the price advantage in a car
of close to the quality of higher-priced competition."

Chevrolet sales in 1925 increased 64 per cent. In 1926,
Chevrolet sales reached 732,000; Model T sales, while still far
above Chevrolet, fell for the third consecutive year. It was
not only the engineering or technological improvements that
sold the Chevrolet, but also the fact that Sloan and other General Motors executives had hit upon a new marketing strategy:
the annual model change. This was General Motors' shrewd
answer to the problem of market saturation; if the new cars
looked different, Sloan reasoned, last year's car would look
old. "Many will wonder why the automobile industry brings
out a new model every year," he wrote in *Adventures of a
White-Collar Man.* "The reason is simple. We want to make
available to you, as rapidly as we can, the most advanced
knowledge and practice in the building of motorcars. We want
to make you dissatisfied with your current car so you will buy
a new [one]—you who can afford it. . . ."

Chevrolet sales were also boosted by the aggressive sales-
manship of Richard Grant, known as "Dynamic Dick" or the
"Little Giant," whom *Fortune* in 1939 called "one of the
greatest salesmen this nation of salesmen has produced."

A 1901 Harvard graduate, Grant had gone to work for
John H. Patterson of National Cash Register in Dayton, Ohio
—the man who invented direct mail advertising, the yearly
quota, the annual convention, and the sales contest. He became Patterson's general sales manager, and was hired by
Charles F. Kettering to manage the Delco light division. Grant
joined General Motors when it acquired Delco. He took over
Frigidaire when Sloan moved it from Detroit to Dayton in

1921, and he made it the world's largest seller of electric refrigerators. In 1924, he became sales manager of Chevrolet.

Using auto registration figures from R. L. Polk Company, Grant began making detailed checks on the performance of each Chevrolet dealer. He inaugurated an extensive dealer accounting system. In 1925, he increased the dealer discounts from 21 to 24 per cent, while Ford was allowing just 17 per cent. He increased the number of Chevrolet dealers from 6,700 in 1925 to 10,600 in 1929. Instead of basing sales projections on planned production, he informed William Knudsen, the Chevrolet general manager, of the number of automobiles he believed he could sell—and Knudsen based production on Grant's projections. The aggressive sales campaign, combined with the changes that improved the Chevrolet and the annual style changes, had its effect. In May 1927, Henry Ford shut down his massive Rouge plant and discontinued the Model T, made obsolete by the Chevrolet. He brought out the Model A in 1928, and it outsold the Chevrolet in 1929, 1931, and 1936. But Chevrolet, under Knudsen, could not be headed. Four-wheel brakes were added in 1928 and a six-cylinder engine in 1929 to combat the Model A. Ford was assigned to second place, to which it seems eternally condemned.

In 1931, advertising representatives from the *Saturday Evening Post* told Grant that according to a *Post* survey, three-fourths of all car buyers decided what car they would purchase before they visited a dealer. This was, said Grant, a "real jolt." After surveys by *Collier's* substantiated the *Post*, Sloan authorized the first of the corporation's massive advertising campaigns—and from then on General Motors was one of the world's largest advertisers.

The product plan of 1921 had emphasized the "very great importance of styling in selling," and Sloan instituted this philosophy as dogma at General Motors. The man who brought styling to General Motors was Harley Earl, perhaps the greatest stylist the industry has known. Son of a Los Angeles carriage manufacturer, Earl was working for the Don Lee studios in Hollywood when he was discovered in 1926 by Lawrence Fisher, one of the seven Fisher brothers and general manager of the Cadillac Division. Earl was doing many things that the Detroit executives had never seen—doing what the hot rod stylists would do thirty years later—building custom cars. He designed a 25,000 dollar Pierce-Arrow for Fatty Arbuckle, a custom Locomobile for Cecil B. DeMille, cars for Wallace Reid and Mary Pickford, a car for Tom Mix with a saddle on the hood and the brand "TM" on the doors.

Fisher brought Earl to Detroit and he designed the classic 1927 LaSalle. Sloan was so impressed that he brought Earl to the central staff and named him head of the new Art and Color Section, known today as the Styling Section. More than any other man, Earl was responsible for the style of the modern automobile. One day he rubbed the running board off an auto in a sketch, thus eliminating that superfluity from the American car. He eliminated the exposed spare tire. He devised the wraparound window, the enclosed trunk, the hardtop, the two-tone paint job and, in the 1940s, the tail fin, which he conceived during World War II. On a visit to an Air Force base in Arizona, he saw a number of P-38 fighter planes with their soaring tails, and proceeded to obtain permission from the Air Force for his designers to study them. The first tail fins appeared on the 1948 Cadillac, and in the 1950s they spread throughout much of the industry.

Fortune said of Earl: "He is the designer *pur sang*, employs no engineers and avoids engineering influence so far as he can, fearing his designs might suffer if he knew too much about the workings of the car beneath. This approach is, of course, an anathema to those industrial designers who believe that all form should be dictated by function. But such criticism would sound as out of place in Mr. Earl's *moderne* workrooms as would a reproach to Darryl Zanuck for not eschewing happy endings. They argue (or veto) him out of his extremisms, but there is a residue of pure, unfunctional style in the grille, hood, fenders, ornamentations, and lines of every GM car that is Mr. Earl's own contribution and is unquestionably a primary factor in how well it sells."

By the beginning of the 1930s, General Motors had done what had seemed inconceivable: passed Ford to win first place in the automobile industry. By the mid-1930s, it was, according to Wall Street analysts, "the best-managed big corporation in America." Even during the Depression, when sales dropped 70 per cent, General Motors never failed to earn a profit or to pay a dividend. Between 1927 and 1957, General Motors averaged an annual profit of 173.2 million dollars, the largest of any corporation in America.

The corporation was thus established, and despite the passage of forty years, despite the parade of executives like Charles Wilson, Albert Bradley, Harlow Curtice, Frederic Donner, James Roche, Richard Gerstenberg, General Motors' marketing policies and management structure are much the same as they were when Sloan instituted them in the 1920s. "We have never deviated from it," Sloan wrote in 1940, "and I hope we never will." Roche says: "Mr. Sloan handled the organization very well at General Motors. His policies have stood the test of time very well. They have been modified as conditions demanded." For example, a central labor relations office was created in the 1930s and, in the late 1960s and the early 1970s, some assembly plants were organized into a separate General Motors Assembly Division. The modifications have been instituted for increased efficiency, the corporation says, but also perhaps to make it harder for the Justice Department, should it ever have a mind to break up the corporation. In recent years, forced by the government to spend money for pollution- and safety-research, the company has reduced emphasis on the annual model change.

Not only the policies of Alfred Sloan but also, more tellingly, his philosophy of conservatism and caution has remained in force all these years. "It has to be cautious," Roche says of the corporation. "We have great responsibilities. . . . I hope we always will be cautious." Part of the caution may be traced

to arrogance. The men who run General Motors do not understand and are insulted by criticism. They are successful, their
corporation is successful, and they do not see any reason to
change unless they are forced to do so.

The General Motors executives were surprised by the rise
of the United Automobile Workers in the 1930s and 1940s,
surprised at the bitterness of the union's attack. They could
not conceive what the grievances of the workers might be,
nor could they imagine that General Motors had not done all
that might be expected of an enlightened employer. Sloan
took great pride in the corporation's record. John J. Raskob
had instituted a savings and investment plan in 1919. In the
1920s, Sloan wrote, the corporation was providing many benefits: "first-rate medical services, fine cafeterias, locker rooms,
showers, and parking lots for our employees." During the early
1930s, General Motors guaranteed workers with more than
five years' seniority 60 per cent of their regular forty hour
pay; when the worker did not work forty hours, the company
advanced the difference in pay, and when he worked more
than forty hours, he paid the company back without interest.
The company built homes for many workers and at times
paid Christmas bonuses.

Even after the 1936–7 sitdown strike, Sloan was defending
the dignity of the General Motors worker and, as the executives do today, the dignity of the General Motors job. In
a signed advertisement in *Fortune* in 1939, he wrote:

> To the popular mind, mention of the automobile worker is
> likely to call up a picture of endless rows of men bending
> over an assembly line performing the same simple task over
> and over again all day long.
>
> Just how incomplete and inaccurate this picture is can
> be shown by citing a few facts about General Motors em-
> ployees and the work they do.
>
> Men of literally hundreds of different skills, trades and
> occupations are represented—such as machine tool crane
> operators, electrical workers, painters, blacksmiths, car-

penters, bricklayers, body builders, welders and upholstery
workers.

The rate paid General Motors hourly workers in the
United States is more than a third higher than in 1929,
and more than forty per cent better than the average of all
manufacturing industries—high wages made possible by
the high productivity resulting from technological progress,
the use of the latest instruments of production. But even
more important is the annual income of these workers,
which is well above the national average . . .

In short, the true picture of the General Motors worker
is a picture of a typical American at work—following an
individual trade or occupation, living a typically good American life, enjoying a better than average job, income and
chance for advancement. . . .

Just as they were surprised by the labor movement, so
too were the men who run General Motors surprised by the
attack of the civil rights activists, the safety and pollution
control advocates, and the business reformers of the 1960s
and 1970s. As it did with the unions in the 1930s, the corporation, unprepared, blundered at first, aiding the enemies and
producing much adverse publicity. Then the corporation, so
huge, so many resources at its command—the consummate
master of the counterattack—struck back and the enemies
were, if not defeated, severely blunted.

General Motors has advanced in recent years, given the
views and practices of the past. The corporation has put 1.1
million dollars into a black housing development in Pontiac,
Michigan, and another one million dollars into a development
in Flint, Michigan, both large company towns. General Motors
Institute, the corporation's West Point, graduated its first
black in 1967; since then the corporation has sought out black
students for GMI, and by 1972 had graduated 14 blacks. Its
cars have become safer, its engines cleaner than a few years
ago.

"This idea that GM is insensitive, it just ain't true," says Peter Drucker. He says: "Sloan was deeply concerned about the unemployed, about training. The General Motors Institute was Sloan's creation—now that is not the view of a man who did not have responsibility." He says that General Motors "single-handedly developed the standards for safer highways" and that its actions in the 1920s in supplying capital to its dealers predated the philosophy for the Small Business Administration. He says, "Nobody has pointed out that when it comes to blacks, GM has probably done the pioneering work in industry. GM was the first one to tackle minority employment—and fight its own foremen on the issue. And has anybody mentioned that? No."

GM developed the first safety column on an American automobile and then brought out an improved, second-generation safety column. It produced the first side impact bar and was the first manufacturer to begin moving away from hard tops toward the safer sedans. It was the first company to modify its engines to run on nonleaded gasoline.

But General Motors remains a cautious, conservative corporation, a barrier to advancement in many areas. It is concerned only defensively about the effects of the automobile: traffic deaths, air pollution, the devastation that freeways inflict on farms, forests, and cities. The corporation wishes only to defend its competitive position, to preserve the automobile, not to make bold, imaginative moves toward developing new transportation systems. Secrecy and solidarity remain bywords at General Motors. The men who move up in the corporation are not men who fight the old guard, who propose new ideas. It is the spokesmen, the engineers, the financial men who advance, not the safety or pollution hawks. There is no appeal process for engineers or scientists who believe corporation practices are injurious to people who buy or use automobiles.

There is no question that much of General Motors' efforts in these fields is done as much to silence critics, to seize issues, as to assist the cause of black aspiration or to combat the problems of automobile fatalities and injuries or to reduce the nation's air pollution. For years the corporation refused to bring any meaningful numbers of blacks into the corporation, either on the factory floor or in executive offices, and it bitterly resisted the government on safety and pollution standards. Now, to read the corporation brochures, to hear the speeches of the executives, to read or listen to the advertisements, the corporation from its very creation, especially in today's time of social concern, has been the paradigm of the concerned, enlightened enterprise. "We were constantly image building," says Dr. David Lewis of his years in General Motors public relations, "trying to make a silk purse out of a sow's ear." One of the reasons he quit, he said, is that his work made him feel "like a piano player in a house of prostitution."

Dr. Lewis recalls that early in the 1960s there were two blacks employed at the General Motors Building among 3,500 GM employees. He says, "Ralph Bunche could literally not have got a job as a janitor in those days." He remembers attending a seminar at the University of Wisconsin on problems that would occur in the 1960s; one problem, the men at the seminar were told, would be a rise in black aspiration. Lewis says he returned to General Motors and, in a conversation with Anthony De Lorenzo, vice president for public relations, asked what would happen if *Ebony* or *Jet* sent a reporter to Detroit to probe black employment at General Motors. He recalls that De Lorenzo said, "We'll just have to get the boys over in public relations to put on blackface and give a damn good minstrel show." Behind this joke, Lewis says, was De Lorenzo's belief—the corporation's belief—that General Motors was a white man's corporation and it was going to stay a white man's corporation.

In May 1971, at the General Motors annual meeting, a young minister from Dayton, Ohio, a critic of the corporation's conduct, asked Roche why General Motors was not more responsive to the public. Who runs this corporation? he protested. "We are a public corporation," Roche said, "owned by free, white . . ."—and then, after gasps and laughter from the audience—"and . . . and . . . and black and yellow people all over the world. . . ." At a press conference afterward, Roche said he was referring to GM's worldwide operations. What he actually was referring to, said Joseph Onek, a director of the "Campaign GM" reform group, was the phrase "free, white and 21," an example, Onek said, of the "country club mentality" that prevails at the corporation.

Profits are what General Motors is concerned about, profits above all, and thus the corporation, unsure, afraid, refuses to speak out, refuses to take positions, concerned that anything it might do will backfire and reduce profits. Many top executives are determined, for example, that they will never let another corporate official leave to take a government post. The corporation approved the resignation of Charles E. Wilson as General Motors president to become secretary of defense in the Eisenhower Administration, but Wilson's combativeness and tactlessness drew considerable criticism, and this criticism was injurious to General Motors and was deeply resented. Moreover, Wilson was forced to be extremely careful not to give, or appear to give, the corporation any favored treatment or contracts. The damage to GM from publicity unfavorable to Wilson, the executives believe, was substantial —and on top of this they did not receive increased government business. The same fear of public reaction helps explain the corporation's refusal, even though many critics have asked, to take a stand against the Vietnam war, which is where many of the weapons and military vehicles the corporation makes are utilized. "We can have our opinions as an individual," Roche says, "but as a corporation we feel an obligation to do what the United States government asks us to do."

General Motors refuses to apply its manufacturing expertise to factory-built housing or to mass transit, two areas in which the corporation has the skills to provide an immense service to the nation. If one has seen the Lordstown, Ohio, plant where giant robots perform automatic welds, where the paint booth is so marvelously clean that workers do not wear masks or coveralls, one recognizes the great manufacturing genius at work in the production of automobiles.

With thousands of skilled engineers, General Motors, Ralph Nader says, is "sitting on an incredible talent . . . in effect stifling the creativity of the kind of talent that these industries monopolize."

Certainly the corporation with sixty-five years of automobile manufacture, had it committed itself to the task, could have developed an automobile that would for all practical purposes be fatality free; certainly since 1954, when automobiles were identified as a major source of air pollution, the corporation could have developed a pollution-free automobile with a comparatively small appropriation each year.

Dr. Lewis recalls the mid-1960s: "If one suggested that advances in vehicle safety design, some of them already developed and proven out, be built into cars, he was reminded, A, that safety doesn't sell cars; B, that safety features cost money and that anything that drives up the cost of the product drives down sales volume; and, C, that cars already are safe, and that poor drivers and inadequate highways are the real safety culprits, not cars."

Developing a pollution-free automobile, Ralph Nader says, "isn't one of this century's great technological challenges. It may be one of the great public health problems, but it's not a grave technological problem. GM has solved far more difficult problems in automating its machinery." If nothing else, Nader says, "Automobile executives personally must dislike pollution, judging by where they establish their homes. . . . I never saw a corporation president who lives in a cushy neighborhood relationship with his beloved smokestacks."

Critics estimate that the corporation has spent as much as 1.5 billion dollars on the annual model change; General Motors disputes this figure, putting the cost at 105 to 140 dollars an

automobile. Whatever figure is used, the corporation has spent
an immense amount of money making one year's cars different
from the previous year's. If models were not changed, critics
estimate, cars would sell for perhaps several hundred dollars
less than they do.

In the 1960s, General Motors spent some 250 million
dollars to change its corporate identity signs, the new motto
being emblazoned across the country in blue and white, "GM
—Mark of Excellence." The cost was many times the amount
—15 million to 25 million dollars—then being spent each year
to produce a pollution-free automobile.

The corporation's public advisory committee, appointed
after critics condemned the lack of a public review apparatus,
is a sham, composed of five board members—non-officers, but
men with the upbringing, concern, and philosophy of the General Motors executives themselves. The scientists General
Motors has placed on its scientific advisory committee are men
with prestige in the American scientific establishment but
unlikely to suggest, certainly unlikely to bring to pass, any new
philosophies or meaningful programs.

Dr. Lewis says, "The GM system works against the social
system. There is always that conflict. The stylist might see
something that should be changed, but the division manager,
conscious of the need to maximize profits, will say no." A few
nonconformists always slip through, Lewis says. "Each department of about 150 or 200 can take one of them with grace.
If there are more than that, however, it's no good. But ultimately, the non-conformists either leave or compromise. The
bonus system does a great deal to keep people at GM and
keep them loyal."

In the late 1960s, a small group of young, middle-echelon
General Motors executives met for a time in New York and
drew up a reform program that they hoped to present to like-
minded young men and eventually take to the top men of
the corporation in an attempt to change General Motors' position on such issues as hiring minority members, providing

financial assistance to black capitalist groups, and being more diligent about safety and auto pollution problems. The reformers failed. One of them, Ken Christy, who edited *GM World*, a corporation house organ, says, "We fell flat. . . . We would show this to hand-selected people that we knew . . . we sat around and picked a few to widen the circle a bit, and we didn't pick up anyone. They were afraid to tie their name to such a radical, frightening thing as a reform group. And that taught us really how futile it all can be and how sad that state of affairs is. . . . It [the corporation] had taken what we thought were fairly liberal, socially conscious, responsible people with some brains and scared them into submission."

Perhaps not much scaring was needed. While young people of America in the 1960s and 1970s may be more liberal and more radical than the young people of the 1940s and 1950s, General Motors continues to hire the hard-working, middle-of-the-road young men it has recruited for decades. "They must be breeding them," says Nader. Roche says, "We're getting the people that we want. There will always be people who are willing to work the ten to twelve hour day, and we're going to look for them, too, if that's what we need."

In many respects, General Motors executives considered the challenges of the 1960s and 1970s as a sign that American society—the society that had nurtured General Motors, that had allowed it to exist—was deteriorating. General Motors feels a personal responsibility to America—as it sees America —and the executives decided it was time to speak out. "As serious as are the problems of environmental pollution, there is another form of pollution which should concern us at least as much," Roche declared in May 1970, before the New York Chamber of Commerce. "This is the relatively recent pollution of American ideals and of our society's standards of behavior. They say our society is materialistic, that we attach a dollar sign to too many values, that we sacrifice cultural and spiritual values for material comforts and possessions. . . . I submit that profit and social progress go hand in hand. . . .

Our American system, the profit system—or free enterprise, or capitalism, call it what you will—has produced a far better social product than any other system I know about."

The answer to the problems of the country, Roche confided to an acquaintance one night, in a pleasant chat in the General Motors plane high above America, was hard work and dedication to the old ideals. Old ideals like showing up at the plant every day and on time, like working hard, obeying one's superiors. General Motors feels it has a responsibility—a duty, an honor—to try to do something about this. And as a complement to this sense of responsibility, the corporation has its sense of history, governed by a single, immutable law: *GM does not change.* It alters policies, alters practices; it bends with the winds of change; it gives the appearance of change. But on fundamental, meaningful issues, it *does not change.* In September 1970, as the corporation sat down at the bargaining table, it most definitely was not going to change.

Chapter 4

The union

The United Automobile Workers, 1.2 million members strong, was a child of the Depression, a child of the arrogance and intransigence of employers who treated workers not like men and women but like machines. Men would come to the factory, queue up or sit against the fences, and after hours of waiting be told there was no work. Often the men walked to work and walked home because they did not have the dime for the streetcar. Sometimes, too, the men and women who did ride the streetcars fell asleep from the weariness of the production lines; it was the job of the conductor to know where each man and woman got off: he would walk up and down the aisles and shake them before their stop.

A retired Ford worker states: "You know what they done at Ford's? And this is the goddarnest truth. They had the servicemen follow you into the restrooms and you're sitting in there, and he made you get up and lift the toilet seat to see if you were doing something. And if you wasn't you was fired." A widow of a Ford worker: "Before the UAW came in, why we never knew when our husbands would come home and say, 'I'm fired.' Here you may have been pregnant, had a doctor bill to take care of, a sick child . . . besides you maybe had parents to take care of and your bills was piled up. And sometimes the husband would get another job under an assumed name, and the lousy spies, factory spies, would come in and spy him and say, 'Your name is John. How come your name is Al?' And he was fired." A worker at the General Motors Livonia plant, a member of UAW Local 174—the old Westside local that Walter Reuther led on the Kelsey-Hayes Company sitdown strike in December 1936: "You were just a badge number years ago."

The auto companies engaged in espionage to ferret out union sympathizers and to block union organization. The La Follette Senate Investigating Committee called the General Motors intelligence network a "far-flung industrial Cheka," and estimated that between January 1934 and July 1937 the corporation spent nearly one million dollars to spy on workers suspected of having union sympathies. That estimate was based on only partial knowledge: when the committee sub-poenaed Harry Anderson, General Motors labor relations director, Anderson destroyed the files of William Knudsen and Charles E. Wilson.° The notorious Ford Service Depart-ment, however, was far more extensive and a far greater barrier to organization. Made up of ex-cops, ex-athletes, thugs, and racketeers, the Service Department in the mid-1930s numbered more than three thousand men, perhaps the largest private police force ever assembled.

Harry Bennett, the ex-sailor and ex-pugilist who headed the department, conceded there were a "lot of tough bastards" in it, but insisted, "every goddam one of them is a gentleman." That was hardly the case. In *The Legend of Henry Ford,*

° General Motors did not, it appears, discontinue this practice. Dr. David Lewis says that in the early 1960s Anthony De Lorenzo, GM vice president for public relations, became fearful that the Kefauver committee would subpoena General Motors files. De Lorenzo summoned Lewis and instructed him to destroy the files of the General Motors public relations committee. Lewis gathered both sets of the files, one from New York, the other from Detroit. A historian, he could not compel himself to destroy the files, so he retained them in his office. A year later there were again rumors that the files would be subpoenaed, and De Lorenzo said to Lewis how far-seeing they had been in destroying the files. Lewis pondered whether to lie or to confess. He confessed, and De Lorenzo was enraged. Goddammit, he ordered, destroy those files. Lewis satisfied De Lorenzo's request.

Keith Sward said that "no *condottieri* employed by a warring
Italian prince of the fifteenth century were more formidable"
than the Ford servicemen. Bennett himself admitted that
many racketeers were associated with the department, among
them Joe Tocco, Joseph Palma, and Chester (Chet) LaMare.
LaMare made an estimated 100,000 dollars running the fruit
concession that Henry Ford set up so the Rouge workers
could enjoy the good health Ford believed was associated
with a daily apple or pear. Big-time gangsters ran the fruit
concession, Bennett said in *We Never Called Him Henry*, because the small-time gangsters who had run it could not stop
getting involved in bloodshed. With LaMare in charge, Bennett said, there was no violence, although Bennett conceded,
"Chet didn't know the difference between an orange and a
banana."

On the night shift, Bennett's servicemen often shocked
Ford workers by leaping in front of them in the dark, flashing
a light in their eyes and demanding, "Where did you get that
badge?" and, "Who is your boss?" They also practiced a technique called "shaking them up," in which a worker called
from his job would be escorted between two servicemen, who
would bump him between them as they walked down the
aisle. In 1932, tool and die men who were considering joining a union had their tools smashed. Men were fired for no
reason, and there was no appeal. Workers could not smoke on
Ford property (a ban not lifted until the 1940s when Henry
Ford II, who smoked, ordered it rescinded). For years workers
were barred from speaking at lunch, a taboo, Sward says, that
led workers to talk out of the side of their mouths like con-
victs, a practice known as the "Ford whisper."

Under such conditions, the workers were bound to be
restless and rebellious. The "Henderson Report," written at
the direction of the National Recovery Administration, declared in 1935: "Labor unrest exists to a degree higher than
warranted by the Depression. The unrest flows from insecurity,
low annual earnings, unequitable hiring and rehiring methods,

espionage, speedups and displacement of workers at an extremely early age. . . . Unless something is done soon, they [the workers] intend to take things into their own hands."

Yet, there was no union to which workers could turn to correct management abuses. The American Federation of Labor, led by President William Green, opposed the idea of industrial organization, largely because the AFL's craft unions did not want to lose jurisdiction over the skilled tradesmen in the automobile industry. When the workers went on strikes anyway, and independent unions sprouted, the AFL relented, chartered an international auto union in August 1935, and appointed Francis Dillon, an old-line AFL organizer, president. But the AFL was discredited in the eyes of many workers: months before, Dillon had accepted a compromise that ended walkouts by some thirty thousand General Motors workers in Toledo, Cleveland and Norwood, Ohio, but won the workers no concessions. The AFL, many workers thought, was far too timid for their needs.

In October, John L. Lewis, angered by the AFL's failure to support industrial unions, which he said were necessary in the automobile, steel, and coal industries, withdrew his United Mine Workers from the federation and formed the Committee for Industrial Organization (later, the Congress of Industrial Organizations). In April 1936, at a convention in South Bend, Indiana, the young United Automobile Workers union, with thirty thousand members, won independence within the AFL. Homer Martin was elected president, Wyndham Mortimer first vice president, and George Addes secretary-treasurer. The UAW joined the CIO while maintaining its AFL ties. Lewis gave the union 100,000 dollars for organizing (after the union pledged to support Franklin Roosevelt in the 1936 presidential election), and soon a number of small locals from such organizations as the Mechanics Educational Society of America, the Automotive Industrial Workers Association, and the Associated Automobile Workers of America came over to the newly predominant auto union. Late that

summer, when the AFL ordered the union to sever its ties
with the CIO, the union refused and was expelled from the
Federation.

The UAW organizers knew that if they wanted to build
the union, they had to organize one of the Big Three. None of
the union leaders wanted to start with Ford, given the company's heavy reliance on violence; General Motors was chosen
over Chrysler because General Motors was the leader—the
policymaker—of the industry.

In the summer of 1936, UAW officers dispatched a number
of organizers—led by Mortimer, Walter's brother Roy Reuther,
Robert Travis, and Henry Kraus—to Flint, the heart of General
Motors. Mortimer had hoped to arrive in secret but moments
after he reached his hotel room, it is said, the phone rang
and a voice warned, "You better get the hell back where you
came from, you son of a bitch, or we'll take you out in a box."

Mortimer knew that General Motors would not deal with
the union unless forced to, which meant a strike. He and
other union leaders decided upon a strategy: General Motors
had only two sets of dies for its 1937 cars, one at the Fisher
Body Number One plant in Flint, the other at the Fisher Body
plant in Cleveland. If these plants were struck, the corporation would be paralyzed. But the organizers wanted to wait
until the first of the year, so that workers would not lose a
scheduled eighty dollar Christmas bonus and so that the
workers would not be on the streets, without jobs, without
money, over the most special American holiday. Moreover, a
new governor, Frank Murphy, the liberal ex-mayor of Detroit,
would take office January 1. The union thought Murphy would
be more sympathetic to its cause than his predecessor, Frank
Fitzgerald, and wanted him in office before the walkout.

Mortimer and his colleagues spent the last half of 1936
trying to build an organization. They could not hold open
meetings; General Motors would send spies and then fire the
union men who attended. Instead, they met in the workers'
homes, often in basements at night. President Roosevelt's re-

election in November gave them a psychological boost: the workers became braver, the union came out in the open, men started wearing union buttons in the plants. Momentum was gathering. At the end of November, workers staged a nine day sitdown at the General Motors Bendix plant in Detroit; five Ford and Chrysler plants were also shut down. In December, Walter Reuther, Victor Reuther, and Richard Frankensteen led the ten day strike at Kelsey-Hayes, and the company capitulated when Harry Bennett, who hated the union, but who hated a disruption in Ford's production even more, ordered Kelsey-Hayes to settle so that Ford could receive wheels and brake drums on schedule.

Early in December, in an address at Indianapolis, dedicating a new plant, William S. Knudsen, General Motors executive vice president, delivered a surprisingly conciliatory statement. "I think collective bargaining is here to stay," he said, "but I do think collective bargaining ought to take place before a shut-down rather than after." The union took Knudsen at his word. Union leaders sent a letter, over Homer Martin's signature, asking Knudsen to begin negotiations on matters of union recognition, the speedup, discrimination against union members, and piecework. Knudsen refused. Such matters, he said, were to be discussed between workers and plant managers at the local level.

On December 28, to the surprise of the union leadership, seven thousand workers at the Fisher Body plant in Cleveland left their jobs. In Flint, the night of December 30, Robert Travis received a call from a Fisher One worker saying that railroad cars were pulled up to the plant and General Motors was loading the dies for shipment to other plants. Travis, according to union legend, replied, "They're asking for it." He told the woman at the union office to switch on the red light at the union hall—the signal that there would be a meeting on the lunch break. "What do you want to do?" Travis asked the workers. "Shut her down," the men shouted. "Shut down the goddamn plant." Word was passed: *strike*. The men raced to the Fisher One plant. When the night whistle blew, nothing happened; the plant was silent. A worker opened a window on the third floor, Henry Kraus wrote, and cried, "She's ours."

Within days workers had seized Fisher Two in Flint, the Guide Lamp plant in Anderson, Indiana, and Cadillac and Fleetwood plants in Detroit. They walked out of the Chevrolet plant in Norwood, Ohio, the Chevrolet plant in Toledo, the Chevrolet and Fisher Body plants in Janesville, Wisconsin, and plants in St. Louis, Kansas City, and Atlanta. By January 7, General Motors—the industry giant—was shut down. More than 112,000 of the company's 150,000 production workers were on strike.

General Motors, stunned by the strikes, seeing them as a sign of revolution, seeing the union leaders as Bolsheviks and madmen, moved immediately to regain control of its plants. On December 31, the day after the Fisher One sitdown, the corporation issued a statement saying that the sitdowners were "trespassers" and "violators of the law of the land" and that the corporation would not bargain as long as the men stayed in its plants. On January 2, 1937, Judge Edward Black, a Genesee County circuit court judge, issued an injunction ordering evacuation of the plants and an end to picketing, meaning that the plants would be reopened. The union had no intention of complying. Lee Pressman, a CIO attorney assisting Maurice Sugar, the union's general counsel, wondered whether the judge, being a man of means, might not have a financial interest in the case. He telephoned a friend in New York and asked him to check whether Black owned General Motors stock. Not surprisingly, he did—3,365 shares, then worth some 220,000 dollars. The union gave the information to the press, Black was discredited, and the injunction was worthless.

Despite the company's belief that it was dealing with revolutionaries, the workers took excellent care of the property during their six week occupation. There was a daily clean-up period and regular striker patrols to guard against sabotage. Daily showers were mandatory. The management, Henry Kraus said, supplied brooms, paper towels, and toilet tissue. When the strike ended and a union leader saw file gougings on some car bodies, he declared angrily, "Only a stoolie would have done such a disgusting thing."

Only one real outburst of violence occurred during the strike: the "Battle of the Running Bulls," which came at the Fisher Two plant the night of January 11. Some one hundred union strikers were inside the plant, and when their food-bearers arrived with dinner, General Motors guards at the gates refused to allow them to enter. Heat in the plant was shut off even though it was bitterly cold—sixteen degrees below zero. Travis, in retaliation, ordered his men to seize the main gate, and some two dozen union men armed with homemade billy clubs descended the stairs, confronted the guards, and demanded keys to the gate. The chief guard refused. "Get the hell out of there," the strikers told the guards, and the guards retreated to the refuge of a ladies rest room. Soon the police arrived and began lobbing tear gas grenades at the strikers; the strikers in the plant turned high pressure water hoses on the police. The police retreated to the Flint River, regrouped, and attacked again. This time they were pelted by bottles and hinges. They retreated again, firing at the strikers as they marched away. Fourteen union men were wounded.*

---

* It was this incident that, in August 1970, moved a speaker at the National Student Association convention in St. Paul, Minnesota, to accuse Leonard Woodcock of hypocrisy. "Why is it the unions would use violence in the thirties," the student asked, "but are not willing to use violence in the 1970s?" Woodcock replied: "We seized the plants of the General Motors Corporation in 1936 and 1937 to get away from violence." He said, "Had we stayed in the streets, we would have been gunned down, ridden down. We seized those plants to get away from violence. The violence of 1937 was the Memorial Day Massacre in Chicago, when steel strikers were shot in the back. We didn't win our means by violence. We won our victories by the use of nonviolence. You can't win by violence. The odds are too much against you. But you can win the other way—and our existence has proven it."

The battle brought Governor Murphy to Flint the next day. At the request of the Flint mayor, he called out some 1,200 members of the Michigan National Guard, a contingent later increased to nearly 3,500, but he kept them at their billets at a school house. On January 14, at Murphy's request, General Motors and union representatives met with him at Lansing, the state capital. There, after a fifteen hour negotiation session, an agreement was announced—an oral agreement, because General Motors refused to enter into a written pact with the union—in which the union said it would evacuate its men from the plants and the corporation promised that it would not resume production or remove machinery. Bargaining on an agreement to end the strike was to begin January 18.

But the agreement fell apart. William H. Lawrence, the noted newsman then working for United Press, chanced by the Flint Alliance headquarters in the Durant Hotel, named after William Crapo Durant. The Alliance was a group of antiunion, procompany workers organized by a former Buick paymaster and a former mayor of Flint, with assistance from the corporation. At the headquarters, Lawrence saw a copy of a telegram from William Knudsen, informing the Alliance members that General Motors intended to deal with them, not with the UAW alone. Lawrence told John Brophy, a union leader, about the telegram, and the enraged Brophy telephoned UAW President Homer Martin: "Homer, this is a double-cross, one of the worst I've ever heard of." Martin ordered the men to stay in the plants.

Negotiations now moved to Washington. John L. Lewis took over for the inexperienced Martin and Frances Perkins, secretary of labor, served as President Roosevelt's emissary. She, and Governor Murphy, attempted to convince Lewis to order the plants cleared and to convince Alfred P. Sloan, Jr., the General Motors chairman, to negotiate with the union on its demand for recognition. But Lewis refused to evacuate the plants without a signed contract and Sloan refused to sign a contract. Miss Perkins persuaded Sloan to come to Washington on the conditions that the press not be informed of his trip and that Lewis not be present. Even then, Sloan was not happy to be there. On January 21, the day after Roosevelt's second inaugural, Lewis demanded that the Roosevelt Administration support the auto workers in "every reasonable and legal way" against their "rapacious enemy." Sloan seized upon this statement, saying that it made any conference worthless, and, with Knudsen and Donaldson Brown, company treasurer, took the train back to New York. He was relieved to be no longer dealing with the government, which he thought was almost as revolutionary as the strikers. For Sloan —this attitude prevailed at General Motors during the bitter 1945–6 strike and during the 1970 strike as well—it was a matter not only of wishing to avoid dealing with the union, but also of preserving the rights of the managers of the corporation to run it without interference and thereby of preserving free enterprise and, indeed, the American way of life.

A week later Sloan again rejected Miss Perkins' invitation to meet with her. "The question of the evacuation of the plants unlawfully held is not, in our view, an issue to be further negotiated," he explained. "We will bargain . . . as soon as our plants are evacuated and not before." Years later, in *My Years with General Motors,* Sloan wrote: "What made the prospect [of unionism] seem especially grim in those early years was the persistent union attempt to invade basic management prerogatives. Our rights to determine production schedules, to set work standards, and to discipline workers were all suddenly called into question. Add to this the recurrent tendency of the union to inject itself into pricing policies, and it is easy to understand why it seemed, to some corporate officials, as though the union might one day be virtually in control of our operations."

With Sloan's withdrawal, the Washington negotiations broke down. In Michigan, union men were beaten at Bay

City and Saginaw by mobs of men, some of them probably
General Motors foremen. On January 28, General Motors
sought another injunction for immediate evacuation of the
two Fisher Body plants.

The union leaders decided upon a daring strategy. The
Chevrolet Number Four plant, producing more than a million
engines a year, was considered the most important plant in
General Motors. If that were seized, union leaders agreed, it
would not only show the world how strong the union was, it
would also make the injunction to evacuate the Fisher plants
meaningless since the union would still control a plant essential
to General Motors operation.

Roy Reuther grabbed a shirt cardboard and outlined a
plan to capture Chevrolet Number Four. Travis then explained
to some thirty union men that the union had a bold plan
to bring victory, but said that the goal was to seize Chevrolet
Number Nine. He knew company spies would relay the
message to the corporation. At 3:20 p.m., February 1, workers
marched through the Chevrolet Number Nine plant, crying,
"Strike." The guards, alerted as Travis had known they would
be, marched into the plant. A wild fight ensued and the workers were defeated.

Meantime, a few selected union men had hid in the lavatories at Chevrolet Four. While the fight at Chevrolet Nine
was going on, they marched down the stairs, crying, "Shut
her down." Workers could not hear them above the factory
noise, so the union men retreated until reinforcements came
from Chevrolet Six. Shut off the machines, the workers were
told, and they did. The foremen were driven out. Chevrolet
Four belonged to the workers.

On February 2, the injunction to evacuate the two Fisher
plants was issued. The union defied it, Governor Murphy refused to use the National Guard to clear the plants, and the
White House continued to pressure the corporation to bargain.
Meanwhile, the sitdown was beginning to hurt General Motors
financially, since its competitors had not stopped producing

and selling cars. Additionally, capitalist solidarity against the unions seemed about to be broken: the United Steel Workers, buoyed by the actions of the auto strikers, were negotiating with U.S. Steel and it appeared Steel would grant recognition.

John L. Lewis came to Detroit and General Motors notified Murphy that it would negotiate. Lewis, who had become exasperated with Martin, ordered the UAW president out of town, saying, "Homer . . . get our story before the public . . . tour the country and hold mammoth meetings." Later, no one bothered to inform Martin when an agreement was reached. He was in Chicago, changing trains for a trip to the General Motors plant at Janesville, Wisconsin, and he read of the settlement in a newspaper. "They can't do that," he exclaimed. Ed Hall, the union secretary-treasurer, said, "Brother, they did it."

The negotiations between Lewis and John Thomas Smith, General Motors general counsel, were held in the Statler-Hilton Hotel in Detroit. Lewis, ill with a cold, was confined to his bed. Governor Murphy and a federal mediator, James Dewey, sat on Lewis' bed. The settlement came at 2:35 a.m., February 11—ten days after the seizure of Chevrolet Number Four, forty-four days since the beginning of the sitdown at Fisher One. Lewis, as he recounted the incident to biographer Saul Alinsky, asked, "Mr. Smith, do you want your plants reopened?" Smith replied, "Of course." Lewis said, "Well, then, it's six months"—meaning that the corporation would agree not to bargain or enter into agreements with any other labor union for half a year, which was tantamount to giving the UAW exclusive representation. The union agreed to evacuate the plants, and General Motors recognized the union as spokesman for its forty thousand members—but only for its members, not the entire work force—in the seventeen plants that had been shut by the strike. All strikers would be rehired. General Motors also agreed, unilaterally, to raise workers' pay five cents.

The agreement, one of sixteen national agreements that

have been signed between General Motors and the United
Automobile Workers, consisted of a single page of nine
paragraphs. Today, these documents run more than two
hundred pages, and more than a thousand paragraphs. When
the agreement was signed, Smith said, "Well, Mr. Lewis, you
beat us, but I'm not going to forget it. I just want to tell you
that one of these days we'll come back and give you the kind
of whipping that you and your people will never forget." Lewis
said, "Now I can get some sleep." Knudsen, the GM executive
vice president, asked, "Let us have peace and make cars." The
union said, "Let us make cars and build the union."

But the union was plunged into factional disputes that
would plague it for ten years. In August 1937, Homer Martin
conceded to General Motors the right to fire wildcat strikers;
rank-and-file pressure then forced him to withdraw this concession. He next sought to consolidate his fragile power by
limiting the autonomy of the local unions. He was resisted.
The Communists called him a company man; he accused
them of being strike-happy. Lewis engineered a fragile compromise at the union's Milwaukee convention in August 1937,
with Martin, nominal head of the Progressive Caucus, remaining president. Members of the rival Unity Caucus, composed largely of Socialists and Communists and led by Wyndham Mortimer, received two vice presidencies.

After the convention, in a continuing attempt to strengthen
his position, Martin named Richard Frankensteen to head
the union's organization drive, stalled largely because of the
internal fighting. Frankensteen, along with Walter Reuther,
had been beaten bloody by Ford servicemen at the famous
"Battle of the Overpass" at the Ford Rouge in May 1937,
as union organizers distributed handbills. Frankensteen was
then a Martin man, and Martin reasoned that if Frankensteen
was successful in organizing Ford, he—Martin—would emerge
supreme over the Unity Caucus men, particularly the rising
Walter Reuther. But Frankensteen coveted the union presidency himself, and in May 1938, when he called for an end to

factionalism, Martin fired him from the Ford drive. Frankensteen then joined the Unity Caucus. In June, with Martin
away from Detroit, Frankensteen announced that the anti-
Martin forces had control of the union. Martin returned and
suspended Frankensteen, Mortimer, George Addes, Ed Hall,
and Walter Wells, leaving only himself and R. J. Thomas, a
vice president, as officers. The board was thus controlled by
Martin once again, and it expelled Frankensteen, Mortimer,
and Hall.

With his wild penchant for suspensions and expulsions,
Martin destroyed himself. Lewis lost whatever patience he
had left for Martin, and he sent Sidney Hillman and Philip
Murray, his top troubleshooters, to Detroit to work out another compromise. The two placed the union into what
amounted to a receivership. All expelled and suspended officers
were reinstated, and a four member committee of Murray,
Hillman, Martin, and Thomas was set up to run the union.

Martin's career was almost over. In October 1938, the
union learned he had been bargaining secretly with Harry
Bennett, perhaps in an attempt by Ford to convince Martin, in
exchange for union recognition, to lead the auto union back
into the more conservative American Federation of Labor. The
discovery killed whatever strength Martin still possessed. In
January 1939, he denounced the union's agreement with the
CIO. The union board, in return, named R. J. Thomas acting
president. Martin resigned from the CIO executive board.

Now there were what amounted to two unions: Martin's
small faction and the UAW–CIO. Each side called a convention. At his convention, Martin received permission to affiliate
his union with whatever parent organization the board chose,
and in April he took his union into the American Federation of
Labor. The UAW–CIO, with Murray and Hillman working
out yet another compromise, elected Thomas president and
Addes secretary-treasurer. Vice-presidential offices were eliminated. As part of that compromise, although little notice
was paid to it, Walter Reuther, in exchange for support of

Thomas, had himself named director of the General Motors
Department, the largest department in the union. In National
Labor Relations Board elections across the country in the
next few months, the UAW–CIO won in plant after plant; the
UAW–AFL hung on for some years, mostly in small towns,
and then died.

Bennett and Ford, out of sympathy for Martin, and realizing that they had some responsibility for his downfall, gave
him a house which, some time later, he traded for a farm.
"This business of giving people homes became quite a thing
for us," Bennett wrote. "We built over 60 houses for people,
after the Wagner Act was passed."

Many men in the union were not particularly happy with
Thomas. He enjoyed cigars, beer, and poker—and has thus
been unfairly characterized all these years as a cigar-smoking,
beer-drinking, poker-playing man. Yet while he was likable,
honest, and hard-working, he was not a skilled leader. A man
from the ranks, he had, B. J. Widick and Irving Howe wrote
in *The U.A.W. and Walter Reuther*, the ranks' virtues and
limitations. In the 1960s, a union officer looking back at those
years said, "They respect Walter, but they considered R. J.
one of their own."

Under Thomas, however, the union became sufficiently
united to concentrate on unionizing the Ford Motor Company,
the remaining bastion of the open shop (Chrysler had settled
with the union shortly after GM). The "Battle of the Overpass" had made labor heroes of Reuther and Frankensteen, but
the defeat, along with the union's factionalism and the continuing Depression, had kept the union from Ford. A fence
had been built around the Rouge complex and more tough
men had been recruited for the Ford Service Department.
Then, in October 1940, a Dearborn ordinance prohibiting
leafleting—which Ford had pushed through the company-run
city council—was declared unconstitutional, and in December
a company appeal was rejected. The courts forced the company to post notices of compliance with NLRB statutes giving

workers the right to organize. Thousands of Rouge workers
showed up at the plant wearing union buttons.

In March 1941, about three thousand Rouge workers
staged a one hour sitdown strike, the first in the company's
history, which forced the company to rehire a number of shop
stewards Bennett had fired. A rash of sitdowns followed but
Bennett was not intimidated. On April 1, he fired eight Rouge
workers who made up the Local 600 grievance committee.
"They can bargain until Christmas," Bennett said, "but we
won't put those eight men back to work." That afternoon,
without union orders, the men stopped working. It was a
historic moment: the Rouge was down. Thousands of strikers
seized the main gates. At 12:35 a.m., April 2, the union sent
a message to leaders in the plant: "You are officially on strike."
Men paraded in the darkness from the plant to the union hall
a mile away. "It was like seeing men who had been half dead
suddenly come to life," Emil Mazey said of the union rally.
"That night you really understood what the union could mean
to men."

The two main issues were representation and wages. Ever
since the five dollar day was implemented in 1914, the Ford
company had enjoyed a reputation for paying high wages.
But the five dollar day was, in large part, a myth. It was
instituted in large measure to combat labor insurrection stirred
up by the Industrial Workers of the World. The IWW had
organizers in Ford's Highland Park plant in 1913 and it was
rumored they were going to call a strike the next year. Ford
made his announcement, with great fanfare, in January 1914.
What was not announced was that not everyone qualified for
the five dollars—it did not go to women workers, unmarried
men under twenty-two, workers with less than six months'
seniority, married men having family troubles, or anyone Ford
felt was "living unworthily." Two and a half years later, 30
per cent of the Ford work force was earning less than five
dollars a day. Still, the company's reputation for high pay continued, and even Henry Ford believed it. In 1941, Ford wages

were far below industry levels, but Ford insisted to Bennett that he paid the same as the other manufacturers did. When Bennett presented figures that demonstrated he was incorrect, Ford, Bennett wrote, exclaimed, "By God, Harry, we ought to be able to pay more than General Motors or Chrysler. They've got stockholders to settle with, and we've only got the family." With that, Bennett went to CIO headquarters in Washington and offered to raise Ford wages above those paid by Chrysler and General Motors. The union men, he wrote, were astonished and momentarily speechless, but, as he moved to leave, a lawyer whispered, "Don't let him out of the room." Whatever the truth in this story, the Ford company did yield, and this set the stage for settlement.

On April 11, the union men agreed to go back to work and Ford agreed to hold a union election and bargain with the workers' chosen representatives. In May, Ford workers voted overwhelmingly to join the UAW–CIO. On June 21, the contract was announced, the largest contract the union had won: some 52 million dollars in total wages, a dues checkoff, time and a half for overtime, two hours call-in pay. All plant protection men, including the servicemen, were required to wear uniforms or badges. Bennett said that all employees would be required to join the union and that the company would deduct union dues from the paycheck. Nowhere else had the UAW won the union shop or the checkoff. Bennett wrote in *We Never Called Him Henry:* "Mr. Ford told me, 'Give 'em everything—it won't work.' He then explained that he felt if we gave the union just a little, then they'd be right back at us for more. But if we gave them 'everything,' he thought, then they would fall to fighting and bickering among themselves. The way he said it, it was a case of 'enough rope.'" Ford seemed to find particular delight in giving the union the checkoff. Bennett said Ford told him, "That will make us their bankers, won't it? Then they can't get along without us. They'll need us just as bad as we need them." His suggestion that the union could become tremendously dependent on the

company had remarkable foresight. But Ford was still saddened by having to recognize the union; he thought a part of
the company had slipped away from him and, according to
Charles Sorensen, his long-time, tough production boss, he
talked of closing down the company—or of letting the union
take it over.

Major organizing was over for the union—and the war
was upon it. In these years it was Reuther, director of the
General Motors Department, not Thomas, the president, who
emerged as a national figure.

Reuther was born September 1, 1907, the eve of Labor
Day, in Wheeling, West Virginia, the son of Valentine Reuther,
a beer wagon driver, a trade unionist, a candidate for Congress
on the Socialist ticket. An unforgettable memory of his childhood, Reuther later recalled, was the day during World War
I when his father took him to visit Eugene V. Debs, the
Socialist leader, who was in federal prison at Moundsville,
West Virginia, having been convicted of sedition. At sixteen,
Reuther quit school and obtained a job as an apprentice tool
and die maker at Wheeling Steel, where he was to lose a toe
when a four hundred pound die fell on his foot. At nineteen,
hearing of better wages, he went to Detroit, like so many other
young men, and obtained a job at 85 cents an hour on the
night shift at Briggs Manufacturing. Seeking higher pay, he
went to Ford in Highland Park as a tool and die maker for
1.10 dollars an hour. He worked nights, attending high school
and Detroit City College, now Wayne State University, by
day. He became a foreman, bossing some forty men. In 1932,
he festooned his Ford car with NORMAN THOMAS FOR PRESIDENT
stickers and stumped the state for the Socialist candidate.
Either for the campaigning or for his union activity, he was
fired—and he never worked in an American factory again.

The day before the 1933 bank holiday, Walter and Victor
withdrew some nine hundred dollars in savings from the bank

and, after issuing a press release about their plans, embarked
on a tour of the world—a trip the Reuther brothers called a
"tour of social engineering." They traveled in ten European
countries in eleven months. They bicycled to Berlin, arriving
the day after the Reichstag fire. One day, Reuther later
said, he was caught in a crowd and pushed against a Mercedes-
Benz carrying Adolf Hitler. "I often thought I should have
had more than a camera," Reuther said.

The brothers then went to Russia and worked sixteen
months at the new Russian auto plant at Gorki on the Volga
River. Then they traveled through China and Japan, caught a
freighter back to America and took a bus across the country
to visit their parents. Late in 1935, Walter hitchhiked from
West Virginia to Detroit. With the passage of the National
Recovery Act (Section 7a gave employees the right to organize
and bargain collectively) the men in the auto plants were
trying to build a union. Walter wanted to help build the union,
and he became an organizer.

In April 1936, with the last five dollars from his local
union's treasury, Reuther hitchhiked to the UAW's second
convention at South Bend. He said he was an employee at
the Detroit Ternstedt plant and when delegates replied they
had never heard of him, he said he was on the black list and
had worked under an assumed name. The story was not true.
He later told biographers Frank Cormier and William J. Eaton,
"I might say that my credentials were highly in question . . .
I never did work at Ternstedt. . . . We just made a tactical
decision that I would be associated with Ternstedt." George
Addes says: "He wasn't a member. We fixed up a membership
card. I was secretary-treasurer; it was a simple matter to make
a member out of him." Reuther was elected to the UAW
executive board.

Reuther returned to Detroit, borrowed three hundred dollars from the UAW, and, working without a salary, set up
an organizing office at 35th and Michigan Avenue, a corner
where thousands of Ford workers caught the streetcar to go

to the Ford Rouge plant. His wife, May, whom he had married that March, worked as his fifteen-dollar-a-week secretary. They lived in a small apartment on LaSalle Boulevard, now in the heart of the city's black ghetto, with his wife's parents. "I never knew people to eat less," his wife said. "I was so thin the mattress hurt my hips."

Reuther knew he needed a strong operating base if he was to be effective, so he amalgamated several small locals, including the Ternstedt local, into UAW Local 174, the Westside local. Within six months, membership rose to 2,400. In December 1936, he and Victor led the Kelsey-Hayes sitdown strike, and after five days, defeated the company, winning a 65 cent minimum wage. Membership soared to 30,000. Reuther was on his way—almost, observers have said, as if his rise was ordained.

By the late 1930s, because of his beating at the Overpass and the strategy strike he led against General Motors in 1937, Reuther was already one of the best-known figures in American labor.

In 1940, Reuther emerged on front pages across the country with his famous five-hundred-planes-a-day plan, a proposal for converting unused automobile factories to wartime airplane production. He submitted the proposal to the Office of Production Management and in 1942 defended it for five hours in a celebrated debate with Charles E. Wilson, General Motors president. The plan was never adopted; the only thing wrong with it, said Secretary of the Treasury Henry Morgenthau, "was the wrong man proposed it."

Reuther was not deterred. Plan followed plan. With his friend, Secretary of the Interior Harold Ickes, Reuther devised a scheme to raise the liner *Normandie,* which had burned and fallen on its side in the New York harbor. To boost the national campaign to save scrap metal for the war effort, Reuther proposed that the iron fence around the White House be taken down and used for scrap. He proposed to President Roosevelt the creation of an independent war labor board

charged with mobilizing labor resources for the war, and he
suggested that the government create public corporations for
the manufacture of railroad cars and prefabricated housing.
At war's end, he was working on a plan for a portable foxhole.
Walter, it was said, even had a plan for licking his wounds.

Within the union, while Thomas was calling for sublimat-
ing UAW goals for the war effort, the ambitious Reuther, as
shrewd a tactician in politics as he was in bargaining, was
bolstering his stature with the rank-and-file. In 1942, Reuther
and most other leaders supported a no-strike policy. Many
rank-and-filers opposed that plan, but in 1943 Reuther found
a way to win back support. The Communists announced their
support for piecework, a means of incentive pay. Reuther,
sensing that the rank-and-file was against piecework, which
would tend to speed up the work rate, announced that he
opposed the plan, and at the union convention at Buffalo in
1943, his proposal against piecework was passed. Opposing
the Communists, Reuther was learning, could be a good
political tool.

Even though a rank-and-file caucus opposed to the no-
strike pledge arose at the 1944 union convention in Grand
Rapids, Michigan, and the workers rejected Reuther's plan
to retain the no-strike pledge for plants engaged in war production, Reuther emerged from the war years with his reputation
as a militant intact. He sensed, as the war ended, as prices
were going up, that the workers were squeezed, that they were
ready for wage increases, that they were willing to strike
for those increases.

On August 18, 1945, Reuther asked General Motors for
a 30 per cent wage increase—without a price increase. The
company waited six weeks to reply, then rejected the offer.
Negotiations began October 19, with neither side, as a matter
of principle, ready to concede any points. On November 21,
with talks stalled, some 180,000 General Motors workers across
the country went on strike. Both sides were adamant; the
bitter struggle dragged on for 113 days before Reuther was

undercut by the leftist United Electrical Workers, which accepted General Motors' offer of 18.5 cents, and by the steel workers, who settled with the steel industry for the same amount. He accepted the management proposal of 18.5 cents —a figure that he had scorned earlier in the strike. But while Reuther lost at the bargaining table, he won in the union. By showing he was unafraid of General Motors, by leading the restless workers, he was able to build the support necessary to oust R. J. Thomas from the union presidency, the prize he had been seeking for perhaps a decade.

The 1946 convention in Atlantic City was a riotous affair, so characteristic of an auto workers convention in those years, with the delegates behaving like legionnaires. Members fought in the hotels, in the bars, and on the boardwalk. Once, two Reuther gangs, each mistaking the other for a Thomas gang, came to blows in the Ambassador Hotel. In *Union Guy*, a remembrance, Clayton Fountain said that the Communists brought "glamorous female comrades" to provide sexual pleasures, free, in exchange for promises of Thomas support. It is not clear how the arrangement was policed, once the pleasures had been sampled; indeed, Fountain said, some Reuther men sampled and then, political if not familial loyalists, voted for Reuther anyway. Delegates dropped water-filled bags from hotel windows, yelling "timber" as they fell; they broke furniture and discharged firecrackers. George Addes told the delegates such hijinks must stop. Objects dropped from the hotel windows, he said, could injure or kill a "delegate or a human being."

The pro-Thomas people denounced Reuther for what one called "sacrificing the GM workers in a long, unnecessary strike" to win support from union militants. Thomas asked the convention, "What did he win in the strike, I ask any American?" No Communist himself, Thomas willingly accepted their support in the union; it was not, he said, a "question of right or left in this union—it's whether you're for or against Reuther." He said, "I don't know much about the class struggle.

I'm interested in wages, hours, and working conditions." There is an old union expression that members used in explaining how to identify a Communist: if he walks like a duck and quacks like a duck, he must be a duck. When leftist speakers arose in support of Thomas, great quacking noises came from the Reuther delegates.

The support of Philip Murray, who had succeeded Lewis as president of the Congress of Industrial Organizations, was sought by both sides. He had been a staunch Thomas supporter—more accurately, a Reuther hater—but in the past weeks, sensing a Reuther surge, had become friendly with Reuther. Murray was the convention's main speaker, and Thomas had named a committee to escort him into the convention hall, pointedly excluding Reuther. When Murray left his hotel, Reuther was there anyway, and he followed along, walking quickly. When Murray entered the hall, Reuther was at his side, holding onto his left arm. "Jeez," Thomas said. "You would have thought he had slept with Phil the night before." Once on the platform, Murray's only reference to Thomas came near the end of his speech, when he turned toward Thomas and referred to him as "this great big guy for whom I have a distinct fondness, the president of your union." This was interpreted by the Thomas faction as an endorsement, but it was a lukewarm endorsement at best. That morning, in fact, Murray had sat at breakfast with Reuther when Reuther offered George Addes a deal: if Addes would switch his support from Thomas, Reuther said, he would support Addes for secretary-treasurer, dumping his candidate, Emil Mazey. Addes refused.

Reuther challenged Thomas to a debate "at a night session of the convention with the press and public excluded so that no punches need be pulled." It was a ploy, for both Reuther and Thomas were already speaking of each other in the harshest of terms. But Thomas refused, and that gave Reuther extra support. Then came the balloting, hours long, punctuated at times by fist fights on the floor. Reuther won by 112

votes. Thomas wept as he left the stage. "Maybe I didn't
do a good enough job," he said, "but believe me, I tried."
Reuther conducted a press conference. "There is much work
to be done in the world," he said. "We won the war. The task
is now to win the peace. We have the job of mobilizing America, the labor and progressive forces, so that we can be certain
that there will be just as determined a fight on the home
front to make the peace secure as was demonstrated by our
boys on the battlefront to make victory possible."

Reuther was president, but he was not in control of the
union. He and his followers, in concentrating on the presidency, had neglected the other union offices. The delegates
elected Thomas to a vice presidency and Richard T. Leonard,
a Thomas ally, to the second vice presidency. All but one of
the incumbents were returned to office, giving the Thomas-
Addes forces a majority. The exception was Emil Mazey, who
was elected to the board. He was in the Army at the time,
confined to a remote island in the Pacific because he had led
a demonstration of soldiers who wanted to be shipped back
to America immediately after the war ended; his mail was cut
off by the Army and a friend gave him the news: "Hey, I've
heard you've been elected to a job with the union."

The Thomas-Addes faction controlled the board, fourteen
to eight, and a fight as bitter as those in the prewar days
raged within the union. Addes put through a resolution re-
pudiating most of Reuther's economic and political philosophy.
He also refused to allow Reuther to examine the union's
financial records, but Reuther, discovering that the president's
signature must appear on all union checks, told Addes that
unless he was given access to the records, he would sign no
payroll checks. He was given access to the records. "Those
fellows hated my guts," Reuther told William Manchester
in *Holiday*. "But they loved their checks."

In those days, after an election, the UAW leaders met and
traded off the chairmanships of the various departments. In
a shrewd action, Reuther exchanged the directorship of the
competitive shops department for the education and pub-

licity departments. He appointed Victor Reuther head of the
education department and a long-time ally, Frank Winn,
publicity director; all UAW publicity took on a pro-Reuther
tone. Thomas believed that the competitive shops department,
the union's organizing arm, was a plum. But he was unable
to organize the shops effectively—as Reuther pointed out to
delegates at the next convention.

In fighting his enemies in the union, Reuther found it
useful to lump them with his other opponents, the Communists. A Communist-led strike at the Allis-Chalmers plant in
Wisconsin turned into a failure, lasting more than three hundred days. Reuther and John Brophy went to Milwaukee and
settled with the company. When enemies charged they had
made a secret deal with management, Reuther responded,
"Our failure at Allis-Chalmers was the result of the open interference on the part of the Communist Party in the affairs of
the local union involved. This Communist Party interference
served to destroy the confidence and loyalty of the workers
in the local strike leadership. It gave the vicious management
. . . an all-too-effective weapon to exploit in breaking the
strike." At the CIO convention in November 1946, Murray
followed Reuther's lead in opposing the Communists by passing a resolution declaring that CIO members "resent and reject
efforts of the Communist Party or other political parties [to
interfere] in the affairs of the CIO."

In the spring of 1947, the Thomas-Addes faction attempted
to bring the Farm Equipment Workers Union, with some
35,000 members, supposedly Communist-influenced, into the
UAW. Under the plan, the equipment workers would have
been given five hundred votes at the coming convention,
enough, perhaps, to ensure Reuther's defeat. The Reuther
caucus pushed through an amendment requiring a referendum
on the plan, and then spread across the country, debating and
beating the plan's supporters. The Thomas-Addes proposal was
rejected two to one.

Reuther's enemies distributed in the shops a thirty-five-
page book, "The Bosses' Boy," picturing him as a tool of the

manufacturers. Reuther said this was a "distortion, fabrication, and forgery," a Communist plot to dishonor him. In September 1947, Reuther issued a report strongly critical of the "mechanical majority" on the UAW board, criticizing the Thomas-Addes faction for wasting funds and for incompetent administration. The Communist Party, the report charged, was influencing the Thomas-Addes faction. When Thomas replied in newspapers, Reuther condemned him for using the "reactionary anti-labor press." Noting that Reuther was attacking him in the same papers, Thomas said, "He is like a guy delivering a lecture on temperance in the middle of his second bottle of whiskey." Thomas said, "Reuther wants unity of applause for Walter, Victor, and Roy Reuther, and, by God, anybody who doesn't go along with the program is a disrupter."

Reuther was too astute for his opponents. At the UAW convention in Atlantic City in November 1947, he seized nearly total control of the union, giving it what it had never had before: control at the top. No major candidate ran against Reuther, and his caucus won eighteen of twenty-two board seats, including one for Leonard Woodcock. Mazey defeated Addes for secretary-treasurer, receiving just 760 votes less than Reuther.

Many reporters and editorialists saw the Reuther victory as a victory for rightwing forces. Reuther declared, "If the editorial writers . . . are inclined to write that the UAW and the leadership of this convention are drifting toward a more conservative policy, I say to those editorial writers they are wrong, because this convention and its leadership is committed to the kind of militant, fighting trade-union program that will mobilize not only our union but the people in America in support of an aggressive, over-all economic, social, and political program." He said: "We are the vanguard in America, in that great crusade to build a better world. We are the architects of the future, and we are going to fashion the weapons with which we will work and fight and build."

Now that he had won the power and control he had sought
for so long, Reuther dismissed more than one hundred UAW
staff members who, he said, were Communists or fellow-
travelers. Many—including some of the union's strongest
leaders—were clearly just his enemies. "They never had the
guts to call you a Communist," Addes, one of those dismissed,
said. "They called you a fellow-traveler."

The other old opponents also left or were ousted. Richard
Frankensteen, once Reuther's ally, was discharged; he later
became a management representative, on occasion negotiating across the table from Leonard Woodcock. R. J. Thomas
left the union, accepted a staff job with the Congress of Industrial Organizations, and died in the 1960s. Reuther fired
Maurice Sugar, who had been outside counsel to the UAW
since the Flint sitdown strike, telling the executive board that
if Sugar was not a Communist, then the Communists were
being duped out of their dues. Sugar and his wife retired to
live in a handsome log lodge on the shores of Black Lake,
Michigan, less than six hundred yards from where the UAW
years later would locate its educational center. Reuther never
stopped by to say hello, and, says Sugar resentfully, when the
people of the nearby town were invited to tour the center
in a good will gesture, everyone, "every goddamned person
in the county," was invited—except the Sugars.

The total UAW membership in the late 1940s was about
500,000 and, it has been said, about 500 of them were Communists. Reuther, who rallied his support with the slogan,
"Against Outside Interference," wrote in *Collier's* Magazine
in February 1948: "We have beaten the Communists in the
United Automobile Workers. . . . We have beaten them. The
story of how we did it reads almost like the report of an ex-
periment in creative democracy. . . ." The Communists, he
said, had "prospered in our midst until recently, because they
so skillfully cultivated persons who could be made, in some
degree, to serve their purposes." He said, "Working through
such strategically placed victims, the Communists captured

the leadership of a number of local unions and could count on assistance from members of the regional and international union staffs."

Noting the popularity and power Reuther was gaining with his Communist purge, Philip Murray picked it up and applied it to the CIO. He fired Lee Pressman, general counsel, after hearing reports that Pressman had been at Communist headquarters discussing CIO affairs. At the CIO convention in 1949, the United Electrical Workers and the Farm Equipment Workers, who, Murray charged, were Communist-dominated, were expelled. In 1950, nine more unions were expelled for what the CIO said were Communist ties. "It shouldn't be called McCarthyism," says an old union man, an opponent of Reuther in those days. "It should be called Reutherism."

Reuther was perhaps the greatest moralist and idealist in the labor movement, a man who showed great personal courage when shot by a would-be assassin in April 1948. But internally he often acted like a commissar. Reuther's attitude toward his critics, says a labor journalist of that era, was, "he chopped them off as ruthlessly as Jimmy Hoffa at [Teamster Local] 299." George Addes says that when he thinks of Reuther, he thinks of the scene in Mafia stories in which one Don comes to tell another, yes, I killed your son, but I am sure you will come to understand that it was business, not a personal matter.

Reuther was a strange, complex man, vain, intelligent, exasperatingly self-righteous, ambitious, hypocritical. "He was unquestionably a gifted leader of men," says a former staff member, "but sometimes I've been on a plane and he was the biggest fucking bore in the free world." Reuther, laughs a long-time friend, was the kind of man who would take a look when a good-looking woman entered a room, like most men. Other men would admit this, but Reuther, the friend says, would not.

Mazey recalls the time when the UAW executive board was discussing whether to observe the union's twentieth anniversary in August 1955 or in April 1956, using as the

founding date either August 1935, when it was chartered by
the American Federation of Labor, or April 1936, the date of
the South Bend, Indiana, convention, when the union
joined with the CIO. Reuther favored the South Bend date,
since, Mazey says, he had not been active in the UAW in
1935, but had been at South Bend. Mazey argued that the
correct date was the union's founding as an AFL union. He
lost. Mazey recalls: "I told him, 'Goddammit, Walter, the
Russians aren't the only ones who rewrite history.' "

In a ceremony at Flint in 1961, when the union commemo-
rated the 1936–7 sitdown strike, Reuther was at the podium
telling about that historic struggle, while his brothers, Roy
and Victor, who played far greater roles in the sitdown than
Walter, sat in the audience. And at the UAW's 1966 convention at Long Beach, California, Wyndham Mortimer, a leftist
who had been one of the union's leaders in its early days, the
first of the organizers sent to Flint, sat in the balcony each
day. As the convention neared its end, another old union
leader went to the platform and asked Reuther to introduce
Mortimer to the delegates. Reuther refused. The delegate was
incensed. He returned to the floor, rose on a point of privilege,
and pointed to Mortimer in the balcony. The delegates rose
in applause. Reuther glared from the platform. "Other people
have made contributions to this union," he said.

And although Reuther was a member of the Socialist
Party for perhaps as long as five years in the 1930s, as late as
October 1937 there was no mention of this in his UAW biog-
raphy. Mazey, who never hid his own membership, and who
remained a Socialist for years, says, "I often told Walter,
'Walter, what the hell are you ashamed of your past for?' "

To many of the old people who formed the union with
him, Reuther was a hypocrite and a traitor. He did not, they
believe, live up to the promises, the excitement, the challenges
of his early union days.

Reuther, as Murray Kempton wrote in *Part of Our Time*,
was "rather conservative and unexpectedly normal in his lack
of the impulse to destruction." Kempton said, "Those made

timid and those exalted by his image could wake together in
the fifties to find that Walter Reuther was not a barnburner
after all. Valentine Reuther did not bring his boys up to burn
barns. . . . So much has happened to the Reuther boys—some
of it tragic, some of it almost tragic, all of it rather fantastic—
that it is surprising how little it has done to them. They have
had adventures, but they were not raised to be adventurers.
They were raised to follow a trade and be a credit to their
home. . . ."

The UAW, as the years passed under Reuther, emerged
with the problems of what it had become, an institution, a big
business. Unions are never very democratic, and while the
UAW is perhaps the most democratic large union, Reuther's
idea of democracy was a guided democracy. A Socialist critic,
Martin Glaberman, says that Reuther was "a statist, the plan-
ner, ready to nationalize but not ready to relinquish control.
It is all for the good of the workers, of course, but it has to
be done for them, not by them."

Reuther, *Time* reported, would often end disputes among
his officials by saying, "I think I know the feeling of the workers." Yet, surrounded by people who adored him and protected
by his public relations men, Reuther became vain and isolated.
He had fashioned the union staff in his own image, giving the
union his qualities. He hired college-trained technicians, like
Nat Weinberg and Jack Conway; they made up perhaps the
most intelligent, knowledgeable staff of any union in the
country, and they were fiercely loyal to Reuther. Once a reporter listened for fifteen minutes as a UAW staff member
told stories of Reuther's large ego and how he constantly
nourished it. "Walter certainly takes himself seriously," the
reporter said. The staff member replied coldly, "Walter has
reason to take himself seriously." And Roy Wilkins, the Negro
leader, called Reuther "the most inaccessible man in the
United States."

In the last year of his life, Reuther devoted much time to what was to be a memorial to himself, the UAW's sumptuous recreation and education center at Black Lake—his destination on the flight that took his life.

The project, originally budgeted at 5 million dollars, spreads for 850 acres along the shore of a beautiful, 10,000 acre lake. The site was purchased in 1967 from the Detroit advertising magnate, Lou Maxon, who made millions hawking Fords, Packards, Heinz pickles, Gillette razors, and Mohawk tires. Maxon used to invite auto executives, among others, to visit him. Once a bargaining session at Ford was delayed while Harry Bennett visited Maxon's lodge; when Bennett returned, as Reuther told the story, he raved about Maxon's place and showed pictures to the union men. "After the revolution," Reuther told Bennett, "we'll own that place."

Reuther demanded that the project be perfect. He would sit up late at night, poring over plans for the center. He charged about the grounds in a green velour Alpine hat, personally marking the trees he wanted kept, touring the facilities with one of the construction men. The man would say, Walter, here's the stairs we just finished. Reuther would look at it, say nothing for a time, then say, I don't like it. The construction man would say nothing. I can't live with it, Reuther would say. But Walter, the construction man would say, it's finished. It's completed. I can't live with it, Reuther would say. Men would tear the stairs out, and new stairs that Reuther liked would be built.

Without approval from the executive board—not to mention the membership—Reuther poured a constant stream of money into the project until it cost more than 23 million dollars and placed the union in grave financial difficulties. By that time, it was hard to find a union official who had approved of the project. It was Walter's doing, they said—a comment on Reuther's influence or on the officials' desire to pass off the responsibility.

The buildings, connected by elevated causeways, are made

of birch, cedar, teak, Douglas fir and glass; the roof on a
strikingly handsome gymnasium is made of bronze, the bronze
to turn green as it ages. Huge bronze gargoyles made in the
Michelucci foundry in Pistoia, Italy, hang over the gymnasium
roof, and there was fear, unnecessary as it turned out, that
the roof could not stand the heavy Michigan snows.

As a gift to Reuther, Oskar Stonorov, his architect friend,
imported bronze and Venetian glass plaques representing the
exact arrangement of the heavens at the moment of Reuther's
birth and installed them in a central foyer around a modernistic
fireplace. Reuther, it is said, was displeased.

The center can accommodate about 250 people for each
training period. Its purpose is the instruction and indoctrina-
tion of lower level union officials. The delegates are selected
by the local unions, meaning dissidents do not usually attend.
A union man says that when the first group arrived an instructor welcomed them by saying Black Lake was their
center, "treat it as you would your homes." Another official
whispered, "I've seen their homes. Don't tell them that."

During the 1970 negotiations, the chief company negotiators and their aides were invited by the union to visit Black
Lake. The union was asking that the companies allocate one-
quarter of a cent per worker per hour for Black Lake in order
to assist in the training of union shop stewards and committeemen, a proposal the union did not win. The company executives went, enjoyed themselves and thanked the union men
for the hospitality. When they left, they laughed that the
union should possess such an extravagant center. Free enterprise and private property, they said, are not dead.

The UAW reached its peak in the early 1960s. It had
been effective in marshaling support for John F. Kennedy in
his 1960 presidential race (after sitting out the 1948 elections,
Reuther had strenuously supported each succeeding Democratic presidential candidate, through Hubert Humphrey in

1968); staff members still were relatively young, bright, ex-
uberant; the future appeared shining. Then problems came.
In 1966, Victor Reuther charged that the AFL, under George
Meany, had been funneling money from the Central Intelligence Agency to help counter Communist infiltration of labor
unions in Latin America. The charges were never proved.
Then Thomas W. Braden, the columnist, revealed that, acting
for the CIA, he had delivered 50,000 in 50-dollar bills to
Walter Reuther at UAW headquarters in Detroit. The money,
he said, was spent by Victor Reuther to bolster labor unions
in Europe, mostly in West Germany. Walter Reuther acknowledged the funds had been received but, characteristically,
found reasons for his action. It was an "emergency situation,"
he said, because the weak European labor unions were "especially vulnerable to Communist subversion."

Victor Reuther's charge against the AFL-CIO deepened
the existing rift between Walter Reuther and Meany. Reuther
had been president of the CIO when it merged with the
AFL in December 1955; he expected, logically, to succeed
Meany as president of the merged union. But Meany considered Reuther a blowhard, a man who did not follow through
on the many plans he announced with such drum-beating,
and refused to step down. The two men clashed in personality, in desire for social action, in ambition. Before the AFL-
CIO convention of December 1967, Reuther announced that
he would lead the fight for a more militant labor movement.
But he failed to appear at the convention, saying that critical
negotiations with General Motors made it necessary for him
to remain in Detroit. On July 1, 1968, Reuther led the UAW
out of the AFL-CIO. About a month later he formed—with
the Teamsters, of all unions, a seamy partner for a professed
idealist—the Alliance for Labor Action, an alliance that was
little more than a paper organization.

When the issues of the 1960s and early 1970s arose—the
Vietnam war, the black riots, automobile safety, pollution,
consumerism—the union seemed out-of-touch, old-fashioned,

old-hat. There are a handful of liberals on the executive board, but most members are conservatives. The UAW became a right-of-center union with a left-of-center reputation. It was for others to lead the campaigns; the union was not out in front, nor, at times, even in the parade. Reuther marched with civil rights workers in Selma, Alabama, and with garbage workers in Memphis, Tennessee, with hospital workers in Charleston, South Carolina; he supported Cesar Chavez in organizing the grape pickers in Great Central Valley, California. Trying desperately to recover the image he once had as a dedicated civil rights advocate, he was, says a man who worked for him, "hysterically seeking the front row in a parade that had passed him by." The man says, "He was up to his ass in all sorts of things, the Urban Coalition, things like that. He was good friends with the President of the United States, and he knew senators and bankers and people like Walker Cisler [chairman of Detroit Edison Company]. But he wasn't doing a fucking thing. Certainly the union wasn't—except servicing its members, which was great, of course. But I don't think that's quite enough—not for the UAW."

Today, the UAW does little to attack the many problems that workers face in American society: racism, the tax system, sex discrimination, highway safety, factory safety, housing, environmental pollution. It was the sons of the working class that were being claimed by the war in Vietnam, but the UAW did not attack the war until attacking the war was acceptable, even popular. Freeways are axing through the neighborhoods of the working class, not the rich or the well-to-do, but the UAW has not attacked freeways.

For years the UAW has said that housing was a major problem in America, but after the Korean war, when new homes were urgently needed, the union insisted that the scarce steel supplies go to build automobiles, not houses; it has done little to demand that good housing be brought within the range of the working class (Reuther pledged the UAW to a low-cost housing effort in Detroit, but this ended up a failure) or to urge the automobile companies, with their sophisticated technology, to enter the mass production housing industry. Nor has it urged them to direct their productive genius toward mass transportation programs. The union's recreation program—the lack of recreation space being a major problem for working people—is understaffed and in-effective; it does little about urban parks; its idea of recrea-tion is to conduct bowling and golf tournaments. Its legal de-partment has made some effort in behalf of housing integra-tion, but remains largely unimaginative and unaggressive. Its industrial safety department is much too small and is not effective.

Workers in America are no less, and no more, racist than any other group, but the UAW has refused to discuss with its members the nature of racism, refused to explain to them that many of America's problems are class, not racial problems, refused to demonstrate to them how working class whites and blacks are confronted by the same enemies.

When the busing issue exploded in the North, and blue-collar workers, including many UAW members, became frightened by the specter of blacks being bused to their neighborhoods and their children being bused to black neigh-borhoods, the UAW refused to take a stand. When liberal Democratic congressmen the UAW had long supported rushed to the conservative side, saying they were opposed to busing, the UAW leadership privately condemned them; publicly the leaders said nothing. For a time, there was talk within the Democratic Party that Douglas Fraser, the UAW vice presi-dent, should seek the Democratic nomination for senator; Fraser, who would have confronted the membership on the busing issue, refused, bowing to counsel of the union leader-ship that it would harm the union to challenge the workers. But by refusing to challenge the workers, by refusing to at-tempt to point out the effect of shoddy inner-city schools on black children, by refusing to go to the membership and say that because of housing patterns busing is the only way to

bring about integration, by refusing to ask workers to try to
act without emotion and to give careful thought to the matter—by refusing to do all this—the UAW has treated blue-
collar workers in the demeaning fashion it has condemned
when this treatment has come from others. By refusing to take
a stand, the leadership, like others, has helped to appeal to
the rank-and-file's most emotional and darkest instincts, despite
the leadership's talk for years of the dignity and intelligence
possessed by working people.

Union lessons have been forgotten. In 1937, Arnold Lenz,
head of production at Chevrolet, told Roy Reuther, "The
trouble with you, Reuther, and all you fellows, is that you're
still young and full of piss and vinegar." Most UAW leaders
were then in their twenties and thirties. Now, most of the
union leaders are in their fifties and sixties. Assumedly, young
people today have the same—or perhaps more—piss and
vinegar that was so much a part of the makeup of the men
who built the union. But they have little power in the union,
even though 40 per cent of the UAW is less than thirty years
of age. At a youth conference at Solidarity House a year before his death, Reuther told fifty young UAW members, "The
future of this union and of the world is in the hands of your
generation." But a young local president from Shreveport,
Louisiana, complained, "Young people have trouble getting
elected to local union offices. In some locals it takes ten or
twenty years."

While 14 per cent of the workers in the automobile plants
are women, there are no more than a handful of women foremen, and most of them work in cut-and-sew departments,
where most employees are women. Few women are active in
leadership roles in the UAW. One woman, Olga Madar, serves
on the international executive board; she was added in 1966
in a gesture of male solidarity with women workers and was
later named a vice president.

While about 30 per cent of the UAW's members are black,
and blacks make up 60 to 70 per cent of the workers on many

urban assembly lines, only about 125 of the union's 925 or so staff members are black. Moreover, the Negroes in high places in the UAW—the few who make it—are moderate men looked upon by many black workers as Uncle Toms. There are two blacks, Nelson Jack Edwards and Marcellius Ivory, on the UAW's executive board, and both were hand-picked.

"When our union was structured 35 years ago, it was structured basically with a white membership," Edwards says. "And from that white membership, we extracted the leadership. They took the rein back at that time—and some of them are still around. And that kind of structure will not sustain the union today against the forces in the shop that demand change." Blacks who rise to high positions, like Edwards, have always been carefully selected in the UAW. Blacks who could have fought, critics say, became too fond of their salaries and positions to fight; they had little education and if they did not have their high union staff jobs, they would be forced to take jobs at far less money—perhaps even return to the factories. Becoming a union staff man in the early days gave Negroes great status in the Negro community. One black active in the union at that time recalls the black international representatives who "would swagger through the valley"— the celebrated Paradise Valley, Detroit's old black honky-tonk area—"and people would say, 'who's that?' and someone would say, 'that's an international representative.'" Yet this man says he never blamed the union for the lack of blacks in positions of prominence. He blamed the blacks: blacks did not create power bases, he says, and thus could be ignored by the whites.

At the union's 1941 Buffalo convention, Reuther successfully fought leftists and blacks who wanted to guarantee two spots on the executive board for Negroes. Reuther said that this would be adopting a quota system, and so was as unfair as adopting a quota for whites on the board.

Just before the 1945–6 strike against General Motors ended, George Crockett, Jr.,—a black man, now a criminal court judge in Detroit, who headed the UAW's fair employment practices office during World War II and for a short time after—telephoned Reuther and asked whether, as Crockett says Reuther had promised, the new contract would contain a fair employment practices clause. Reuther said he did not believe so—the strike had lasted too long to hold out for a demand like that. Crockett swore at Reuther, but Reuther did not change his mind. At the March 1946 convention, the one at which Reuther was elected president, Reuther spoke before a black caucus, telling them that he was an advocate of desegregation. Crockett listened, then stood and attacked Reuther, saying that Reuther had sold out in the General Motors contract. A few days after Reuther's election, Crockett received a "Dear George" letter saying that because the two were so opposed, Reuther believed Crockett should leave the union. Crockett stayed for a while, working for R. J. Thomas, and then left. Crockett says of Reuther, "I think he put the trade union into the big time, and that's the best way to say it."

Many young blacks in the plants today believe that the UAW is no different from General Motors, Ford, or Chrysler when it comes to aiding blacks. "We're still on the plantation," says a black Ford worker. "That's what the plant is—short for plantation." Another black Ford worker says, "Nobody does anything for us—not the companies, not the union."

The thirties, the time of the beginning of the union, have been largely forgotten. Few workers learn the words to "Solidarity Forever," the union anthem. A union official, chiding young members who, he said, had forgotten the suffering that their fathers had gone through, was dismayed that these young members could not even identify the Battle of the Underpass [sic]!

In 1967, as he trooped the line of pickets during the sixty-seven day Ford strike, Reuther asked a local union official where the pickets, warming themselves over fires, obtained their coal. They probably stole it from the company as workers did in the old days, Reuther said. No, the local man said, the coal came from the company. Mr. Ford had agreed to give it to them. A truck was sent through the picket line to pick it up. And the oil drums in which they built their fires? Reuther asked. They probably stole them from the company, like the union men did in the old days. No, Walter, the local union man said. The union and the company had an agreement: the company provided the barrels. After a long pause, Reuther spoke: "Karl Marx," he declared, "would never believe this."

In March 1971, after the UAW had concluded its contracts with the auto companies, some four hundred members of the UAW secretarial and janitorial staff at Solidarity House walked off their jobs in a three week strike, demanding a 10.85 dollar weekly raise. Woodcock said that the union was embarrassed. The union's position, he said, cracking a small joke, was firm but inflexible. A number of executives at Solidarity House did something they would never do at General Motors or another corporation—they crossed the picket lines. If they did not wish to cross the lines, UAW leaders told them, they could take time off, without pay, until the strike ended. Emil Mazey said that the union's 8.05 dollar weekly wage offer was all the union intended to offer—a position, one could say, not a proposal. But the real issue was not wages, it was paternalism. The workers were tired of being treated, one said, "as pea-brained women." When the strike went on, Mazey said the janitorial and secretarial employees were "greedy and selfish," and Woodcock said they were attempting to "blackmail" the union. Mazey, dressed in a fine overcoat and hat one cold morning, lost his temper talking to the strikers. Why, he said, he had built the union before these people were born. The women, Mazey said, were "little bitches."

For the workers, the ordinary union members if not the leadership, working in the shop is in large part the same as it has been for years. In negotiation after negotiation, while

Reuther and other union leaders won many victories, they did not bring about any fundamental change in the work place. The changes that have come about are largely the result of improved technology that was due not to corporate concern for the working man, nor even to the ability of the UAW to blackjack the company, but mostly to the corporation's desire to improve productivity.

For all the UAW's liberalism—for all Reuther's rhetoric—the assembly lines remain plodding, monotonous places. A long-time aide to Reuther: "I think a lot of conditions would have changed anyway, with technology and so on. So it's hard to say what the direct result of the presence of the union is and what isn't." A member of the revolutionary Congress of Black Workers: "Woodcock is a model man, compared to Meany. But that doesn't mean anything in terms of real problems people run into in the shops." He says, "These fuckers, man, they got a nice position on the war, nice position on civil liberties, blah, blah, blah. It ain't got a goddamned thing to do with the conditions that's kicking the ass out of the motherfucker out there in Department 78, Department 25. On the question of conditions, the company ain't done a mother-fucking thing about it, and the union don't do nothing." One must realize, a UAW vice president says, that as long as men build automobiles, as long as the assembly line exists, shop conditions probably will not change in any fundamental way. He says one must realize that "in negotiations, you can't get into this." This is unfortunate, he says, but true.

Chapter 5

"Keep quiet...
you are all wound up"

The automobile negotiations, occurring every three years, are an intriguing American drama, the nation's most ambitious, upright union confronting those quintessential corporations, those most American of businesses, the automobile companies—pitting enterprises devoted to the profit system against an institution that came into existence to protest the excesses of that system.

A mediator says he always states for the record that unions enable a corporation to maintain dialogue with its workers and that the negotiations, by allowing the two sides in most cases to achieve a peaceful settlement, provide stability and predictability for an industry. All this is true. But if one wishes to know the truth, the mediator says, "An outfit like GM puts up with the union because it would be expensive and a bitch to bust them."

Time has altered the relationship of the automobile companies and the union. Years ago, Harry Anderson, then the General Motors chief negotiator, was asked in an appearance before the La Follette Investigating Committee how he kept informed on union matters. Anderson said he read books, although he could not recall the names of any. He said he believed, however, that he had read a two volume history of the American Federation of Labor. "Could I," a senator asked, "find out how to organize a good labor union from that book?" Anderson replied, "I don't know about a good labor union."

After thirty-five years, relations are much more amicable, much more civilized, since, as Earl Bramblett declared the day the 1970 talks opened at General Motors, the two sides have many common interests, many common goals.

Early in the 1970 talks, the UAW complained to General Motors that while an atmosphere of mutual respect had come to exist between the parties, the corporation has "never accepted the union in the full sense of the term." General Motors denied this, noting that in 1969 alone, it had paid in its plants more than 13 million dollars to union committeemen— men who do not work on assembly lines or at machines, but who represent union members in disputes with management —13 million dollars for no work whatsoever. "There can be no question," the corporation said, "that the role of the UAW as representative of the employees has been firmly established and firmly accepted in General Motors."

General Motors, like most companies, sees itself as the model employer, believing that most, if not all, gains that have been made in the plants would have come without the unions. "They always say 'we blackjacked them out of this or that,'" Bramblett says. "That's a lot of malarkey. Progress is made, union or not."

What the companies desire—and receive—from the union is predictability in labor relations. Forced to deal with unions, they want to deal with one union, one set of leaders, and thus they have great interest in stability within the UAW and in a continuation of union leadership. They also want to have the limits of the bargaining clearly understood and subscribed to. "GM's position has always been, give the union the money, the least possible, but give them what it takes," says a former negotiator. "But don't let them take the business away from us." The union has come to accept this philosophy as the basis of its relationship with the companies: it will get money, some changes in work procedures, usually nothing more. "We make collective bargaining agreements," Reuther once declared, "not revolutions." Both the union and the companies, a mediator says, have one major goal: "They want to make cars at a profit."

The events that preceded the 1970 strike were remarkably similar to those which preceded the 1945–6 strike, the strike that had set the guidelines for all negotiations to come. Both times the country had been waging war for several years. Both times price increases had raced past wage gains.

In 1945, working hours had been slashed as the nation converted to peacetime production. Lower pay scales had been established and jobs downgraded. The cost of living had risen an estimated 30 to 40 per cent, but wages were prohibited by the Little Steel Formula from rising more than 15 per cent above the wages of 1941. Food costs, even by conservative estimates, had increased 50 per cent since 1939. Clothing costs had risen 18 per cent.

On August 16, 1945, two days before V-J Day, President Truman issued an executive order permitting wage increases so long as they did not result in price increases—in effect, scrapping the Little Steel Formula. This was what Reuther needed, and on August 18 he submitted his brief to General Motors demanding a 30 per cent wage increase, and demanding that the union be allowed to examine the corporation's books to determine whether the demands could be met. The union made the same demands of the Ford Motor Company and Chrysler Corporation.

In September, Reuther sold a new strategy to the union's executive board: the famous "one-at-a-time" strategy that the union follows today. Reuther's arguments were based upon the tenets of free enterprise and his knowledge of the automobile companies. In such a competitive industry as the postwar automobile industry, he reasoned, it made sense to single out one company as the strike target; the other companies, he said, unwilling to lose production and sales at such a critical juncture, would continue business as usual or even increase production to take advantage of a struck company. Desire for profits, Reuther argued, would outweigh the companies' dislike of the union.

In October, after waiting six weeks as a sign of his disdain for the union, Charles E. Wilson, the General Motors president, issued a statement rejecting Reuther's demands in the strongest, clearest terms. Wilson wrote Reuther: "We shall resist the monopolistic power of your union to force this 30 per cent increase in basic wages. Such an increase in our plants would soon spread to the plants of all our suppliers and would affect all elements of cost. Automobiles would shortly cost 30 percent more to produce. Prices to consumers would have to be raised 30 percent. If wage raises in automobile plants forced such increases in car prices, the market for automobiles would be restricted. Fewer cars would be sold; fewer people would be able to afford and enjoy them; and fewer workers would be employed in making them." What was needed if America was to gain a high level of peacetime production, Wilson said, was not higher wages, but more work, harder work, and to the union's dumfoundedness, he proposed a 5 to 8 per cent wage rise—but with an increase in the work week from 40 to 45 hours. When Wilson defended the 45 hour week proposal before the National Labor Relations Board, Maurice Sugar, UAW attorney, asked why, if he favored the 45 hour week, he did not favor a 50 or 60 hour week. "I have worked 60, even 80 hours a week," Wilson replied. "But that's too long. My insteps broke down and as a result I have to wear steel braces in my shoes."

Negotiations began October 19 at the General Motors Building. The General Motors people were new at bargaining; autocratic men, they were used to telling what a policy would be, how it would be carried out, and by when; they issued instructions, they did not negotiate. In this new situation, they were surprised and often made to look foolish, for Reuther was savvy and cunning, and, an assistant to him at the time recalls, it was "amazing how Walter out-thought, out-fought, out-foxed the company men."

The first day of negotiations, Reuther told his public relations director, Frank Winn, to invite the dozen or so reporters present to come into the negotiation room and, in an unprecedented action, sit in on the talks. When the General Motors executives, led by Harry Anderson, arrived, they found the reporters, sitting silently, grins on their faces. The executives were incensed. This was an outrage, they said, and stalked from the room. Goddammit, they said, there was no way in hell they were going to negotiate a contract in front of the goddamned reporters. They noted that in 1942, when General Motors suggested that the talks be opened to the public since the war made the talks of public importance, Reuther, having nothing to gain, had refused.

As a compromise, the company and the union agreed that stenographers, one for the company, one for the union, would make transcripts of the negotiations. Either side could make statements off the record, but the company men often became so enraged at Reuther and other union men that they often launched into long, angry, profane speeches without stipulating that what they were about to say should not be transcribed. A. L. Zwerdling, an assistant to Reuther, and Victor Reuther would read the transcript to the reporters, emphasizing the passages that enhanced the union's position and embarrassed the corporation.

Once Victor stopped as he read a passage, almost like a heroine in a silent movie, and insisted that the next section was too indelicate, that Zwerdling must read it. Zwerdling did —a passage in which Anderson, incensed at Walter Reuther, said, goddammit, he wasn't going to talk with Reuther any longer, goddammit, he wasn't going to do it, because his father had always warned him not to get into a pissing match with a skunk.

The transcripts of the talks are extremely valuable, for they provide insights into the men themselves and into the relationships that existed between the two sides, between men equal in arrogance and combativeness.

REUTHER: I think when monopolies like the aluminum industry, owned 85 percent nowadays, and magnesium, when the monopolies jeopardize the safety of the country, they can no longer be trusted in private hands to use them for a profit. That is my private philosophy. It hasn't got a damn thing to do with automobiles or industries operating on a non-monopolistic basis. And it has nothing to do with the question of wages in this case.

COEN [Harry Coen, assistant director of personnel for General Motors]: It all colors your thinking. . . . Do you believe we have to learn to live 50 percent better, or do you believe first we have to learn how to create that much more wealth? What has that got to do with dividing up the profits and reducing the salaries of the people in the corporation?

REUTHER: Because unless we get a more realistic distribution of America's wealth, we don't get enough to keep this machine going.

COEN: There it is again. You can't talk about this thing without exposing your socialist desires.

REUTHER: If fighting for a more equal and equitable distribution of the wealth of this country is socialistic, I stand guilty of being a socialist.

COEN: I think you are convicted.

REUTHER: I plead guilty.

. . .

COEN: There is nothing sincere in your approach. There hasn't been yet, so far as requesting a public meeting. It is just another chance for you to get up on the soapbox before more people. You know we are all worn out on this thing. It is no news to your people. And you just get a few more people in here to listen to it.

REUTHER: Harry, if it was . . .

COEN: Keep quiet, will you? You are all wound up. Relax. I have been away hunting for a week. I am in good shape. I can look at this thing in its true perspective and I know it is all horseshit. . . .

.   .   .

COEN: Is the UAW fighting the fight of the whole world?

REUTHER: We have been fighting to hold prices and increase purchasing power. We are making our little contribution in that respect.

COEN: Why don't you get down to your size and get down to the type of job you are supposed to be doing as a trade-union leader, and talk about money you would like to have for your people and let that labor statesmanship go to hell for a while. . . .

CORBIN [Edwin Corbin, a union negotiator]: Do you mean if we came in here with a 30 percent wage demand and offered to join you in going before OPA for a 30 percent increase in the price of your cars, you would talk business?

COEN: We don't ask you to join with us on the price of cars. It is none of your damned business what GM does about prices.

CORBIN: The hell it isn't. I intend to buy a car.

.   .   .

REUTHER: We have said to the corporation, and I repeat, that if we can't prove, based upon the facts, or if the corporation can disprove our facts that we can get a 30 percent wage increase without price increases, then we don't want 30 percent.

ANDERSON: Who are you going to prove it to, Walter?

REUTHER: Harry, bring out the facts.

ANDERSON: Who are you going to prove it to?

REUTHER: We will prove it to anybody. We will prove it.

ANDERSON: So what?

REUTHER: The point is, if we prove it to you, will you give it to us?

ANDERSON: If you can prove it. Like George Romney's talk [Romney was general manager of the Automobile Manufacturers Association]; George Romney asked you the question point blank, could you settle your demands for less than 30 percent? What was your answer?

REUTHER: I will answer that. Let me give you the answer now on the record. We are prepared to settle this demand for less than 30 percent, providing you can disprove our contention that wages can be increased 30 percent without increasing prices and you can still make a profit. If you can prove we can't get 30 percent, hold prices, and still make a nice profit, we will settle for less than 30 percent.

.   .   .

ANDERSON: Walter, you must want a strike.

REUTHER: Harry, goddamn it, the way you are going about it, you are forcing us to strike.

ANDERSON: I will tell you why you want to make a strike. . . .

REUTHER: Tell us.

ANDERSON: Because you have got the boys pretty well stirred up that you want a strike. In addition to that, before you had the first meeting with us, you petitioned the National Labor Relations Board for a strike vote, before you were even in the room.

REUTHER: Harry, that is the damn law you had passed.

ANDERSON: That we had passed?

REUTHER: Sure.

ANDERSON: Horse manure. . . .

.   .   .

ANDERSON: That is really up to us to decide, Walter— whether we are willing to pay it or not.

REUTHER: Your position is that your ability to pay is not a factor?

ANDERSON: That is right.

In a brief to the corporation, later published as the pamphlet "Purchasing Power for Prosperity" and broadsided across the country, Reuther argued that General Motors could pay the 30 per cent the union was demanding, maintain 1942 prices, and still earn an after-tax profit of 187 million dollars. Increased volume, Reuther said, would compensate for the drop in profit per unit.

On November 7, General Motors offered a 10 per cent wage increase, with the provision that the Office of Price Administration authorize a price increase. The union rejected the offer. Reuther suggested that the two sides submit their dispute to arbitration, provided the arbitration begin within twenty-four hours. He still insisted that the union be allowed to inspect the company's books to determine for itself—and for the public—whether General Motors could afford to pay the 30 per cent increase. As Reuther knew would happen, the company rejected his proposal, saying that the union was attempting to take away the fundamental management right of setting prices which it believed to be fair and which the market supported. Reuther's offer of arbitration, the company said, was a "demand for abdication." General Motors, Wilson said, would not "relinquish its rights to manage its business." The stage was set. On November 21, some 180,000 General Motors workers in 96 plants across the country walked off their jobs. They joined some 140,000 workers idled by the changeover from war to peacetime production, and who were waiting to be called back to work when General Motors began producing automobiles.

John Thomas Smith, the corporation's general counsel, had told John L. Lewis in the Statler Hotel eight years before that the corporation would give the union a thrashing and now, GM believed, the time for that thrashing was at hand. Believing that it was defending the American free enterprise system from radical onslaught, believing that it was the corporation's responsibility to make that defense, General Motors announced it was breaking off negotiations until the union was prepared to modify its wage demands and "abandon its attempt to negotiate wages on the basis of our past profits, assumed future profits and our selling prices." In advertisements in newspapers across the country, the corporation asked, "Is the Union Seeking Facts of New Economic Power?" Did the union want "a look at the books or a Finger in the Pie?"

In December, President Truman asked the union to end the strike, which he called a "major obstacle holding up our reconversion program." The president announced he was appointing a fact-finding board to investigate the strike. The union rejected the president's plea, Reuther saying that the workers would not be "human guinea pigs." If the workers went back to their jobs without an agreement, he said, they might not even get the 13.5 cent increase that General Motors had offered early that month. The corporation said only that it was studying the president's request.

Meantime, in a typically Reutherian move, the UAW invited fifteen prominent citizens, favorably disposed toward the union, to listen to transcripts of the talks, to take testimony, and to recommend a settlement. The committee included Walter White, of the National Association for the Advancement of Colored People; Leon Henderson, a New Dealer and author of the "Henderson Report," a 1930s study critical of the automobile industry; Harry Overstreet, a psychology professor at City College of New York; Dr. Henry Hitt Crane, pastor of Detroit's Central Methodist Church, a church Reuther often attended. After two days of public hearings and study of the transcripts, on December 9, the committee issued a report supporting the union. It said it had found "no convincing evidence that the UAW's 30 percent wage demand could not be met." In words Reuther could have written himself, the committee said: "The union in its refusal to accept a wage increase that implies price increases has lifted the whole matter of collective bargaining to a new high. . . ." The committee asked that the president's fact-finding panel determine "what increase in wages can be given on the basis of the corporation's ability to pay without an increase in prices."

The president's fact-finding panel—composed of Lloyd Garrison, chairman of the War Labor Board, Dr. Milton Eisenhower, president of Kansas State University, and Walter P. Stacy, a North Carolina state supreme court justice—met with both parties on December 20. General Motors warned that if its ability to pay was an issue, it would not participate in the proceedings. Minutes later, a telegram arrived from President Truman and Garrison read it aloud. The panel, the president said, had the authority to inquire into the corporation's ability to pay and had the right to examine General Motors' books. The General Motors delegation immediately walked out of the room.

The corporation's attorney, Walter Gordon Merritt, a noted antilabor lawyer who had represented employers in the famous Danbury Hatters case early in the century, said that the question was not whether the union, or the panel, possessed the right to examine the corporation's books, but whether the corporation would yield to the union's "revolutionary ideology." To yield, Merritt said, "would mean the end of free enterprise."

A company pamphlet, "Here is the Issue," elaborated on the corporation's argument. "A 'look at the books,'" the pamphlet said, "is a clever phrase intended as an opening wedge whereby the unions hope to pry their way into the whole field of management. It leads surely to the day when union bosses, under threat of strike, will seek to tell us *what* we can make, *when* we can make it." Wilson, the corporation president, added, "Is America to continue as a democratic nation, based on free competition, with government the servant of the people—or is it to become a socialistic nation with all activities controlled and regimented, and with the people the servants of the government?"

A Detroit executive recalls dining with Wilson in Washington the night that General Motors withdrew from the hearings before the president's panel. What, Wilson asked, would the withdrawal mean for the corporation? The executive told him it meant that General Motors' public relations would be damaged, but, he said, this would make little difference since the firm's public relations were poor already. Yes, said Wilson, that was true. Yes, the company's public relations would be damaged, yes, this would make little difference. The decision stood.

The fact-finding panel went ahead in its work without General Motors. On January 10, Truman announced its recommendations: a wage increase of 17.5 per cent, or 19.5 cents—without an increase in prices. Earlier, Reuther had told Eisenhower that 19.5 cents was too small an increase; the strikers, Reuther said, "would have to work for years to recover the losses incurred by the strike." Now he announced his elation, saying that although the panel had cut his demand almost in half, the decision was a "complete endorsement" of the union's position and a "historic step in the fight to establish full production." The corporation, still unalterably opposed to government intervention in the negotiations, rejected the proposal. Reuther decried the action as a "defiance of public responsibility" and a refusal by the corporation to "meet the obligations to the men and women who work for it."

As strikers walked picket lines in the cold weather, Reuther established what he called the National Committee of Citizens to Aid GM Strikers (there were no strike benefits in this long strike), a diverse group that included old friends from war days like Mrs. Roosevelt, Harold Ickes, and Henry Morgenthau; and others like Henry Luce, the publisher, Helen Gahagan Douglas, the California congresswoman, and Senator Wayne Morse. Not only did the committee bring the union a great deal of favorable publicity, but it also raised more than one million dollars.

But while Reuther held out, he was undercut, struck by one blow after another. The union's departments bargained separately in those days, and in late January, first the Chrysler and then the Ford Department settled, both for 18 cents or 15.1 per cent. Neither contract prohibited a price increase.

Reuther insisted that the courage shown by the General Motors strikers had forced higher settlements than otherwise would have been achieved, but, aware that the other settlements might make General Motors more resistant and the strikers less determined, Reuther reduced his demand to the 19.5 cents recommended by the fact-finding committee—still insisting, however, that there be no price increase.

To Reuther's dismay, the Truman Administration retreated from its opposition to price increases in an attempt to end the steel walkout. The steel strikers subsequently settled for 18.5 cents; the companies were granted a price increase of some 6 dollars a ton, and this was followed by further increases. On February 12, the left-dominated United Electrical Workers, representing some 30,000 General Motors employees, settled with General Motors for 18.5 cents. The union, led by James Matles, wished to sabotage Reuther, who was sure to seek the UAW presidency. It was a betrayal, the UAW fumed, adding that it had not known that the electrical workers and General Motors had been negotiating. The UAW, said R. J. Thomas, was in an "awful spot."

Reuther was enraged. "I won't be made a damn fool of forever," he declared. "The President's offer of 19.5 cents was a compromise of our demand, and I will be God-damned if I will compromise a compromise. We are not going to take less than this, and this is all horseshit about going back to work."

Horseshit, perhaps, but Reuther was defeated. The day General Motors settled with the electrical workers it made an 18.5 cent offer to the UAW. Reuther stomped from the negotiations, but the pattern for settlement was set. All he could do was maneuver to achieve the appearance of victory. He offered to settle for 18.5 cents if the corporation would put an additional cent into a wage equalization fund. No, the corporation said. He then suggested that the union and the corporation arbitrate the disputed penny. No, the corporation said. What the union was seeking, the corporation said, was a "third party to assume the responsibility" of settling the strike. It proposed that the workers be polled to see whether they wished to return to work. Reuther rejected the proposal, proposing in return that the workers be allowed to choose between General Motors' offer of 18.5 cents and his proposal of 18.5 cents with the disputed penny to be arbitrated. Surely, the corporation said, he was jesting. "Who," the corporation asked, "would not vote to accept the increased wages and other favorable proposals made by the company if they could still retain the opportunity for further gains?"

Finally, on March 13, Philip Murray, president of the CIO, and Charles E. Wilson, General Motors president, reached an agreement: a wage increase of 18.5 cents, plus some additional benefits, largely in the areas of vacation and overtime, which, Reuther claimed, raised the package beyond 19.5 cents. Reuther, who was not present at the final meeting, claimed victory. (A Reuther aide of the era recalls: "I thought it was a victory. I was young, and to me Walter Reuther was Jesus Christ.") Yet the union had not received the money it had asked for. Reuther had not, as he had declared was necessary in December, smashed "the arrogance of great wealth of General Motors"; he had not won the union victory that he said would be the framework on which "to build an America of new economic and political freedom." Should the union lose, he had said, "it would be 1919 and the twenties all over again. . . . If we do not hold prices while increasing wages, we do nothing more than put workers on an economic treadmill." Within two months of the settlement, the Office of Price Administration authorized General Motors to raise its prices up to eighty dollars, and by the end of the summer, the OPA had granted three more price increases to the automobile industry.

Nonetheless, to many workers—automobile workers and other industrial workers as well—the UAW and especially Reuther had won a smashing victory. The union had taken on the world's most powerful corporation, and had not backed down. The strike invigorated the UAW; enthusiasm and excitement were at their highest since the sitdown strikes ten years before. On March 27, fourteen days after the strike ended, Reuther, now thirty-eight, was hoisted on the shoulders of his supporters and marched to the podium of the convention hall in Atlantic City. He had won the union presidency.

(In 1970, chatting about the UAW's strike against General Motors, then several weeks old, a company negotiator said: "A lesson of the 1945–1946 strike was that you could win politically by a strike, and I don't think this was lost on the UAW leadership over the years. I think there was a large element of this in this year's strike—by that I mean that Woodcock and the union leadership went into GM and came out on top.")

But General Motors actually won the 1945–6 strike by beating the union back on its wage demand and by winning on the matter of principle, which it considered even more important. For General Motors, it was not a matter of the penny; General Motors could have given the union the penny —or two or three or five pennies. What was important to Sloan and to Wilson and to the other executives was who would run General Motors, the corporation or the union. In a special message to stockholders after the strike, Sloan wrote that the union's demands, "if granted, would have constituted an impractical pattern for management-labor relationships and a deeply significant step toward the socialization of American industry." In the 1960s, more than fifteen years later, many General Motors executives still talked of how the corporation had confronted the union in the 1945–6 strike and how, because of that confrontation, General Motors would never be struck again.

The bitterness, hostility, and lost production caused by the 1945–6 strike, however, deeply disturbed Sloan and Wilson. They were determined to avoid further work stoppages and to put wage increases on a predictable basis. In 1948, seven days before the contract deadline, Wilson proposed his personal solution: wages would vary according to increases or decreases in the cost-of-living and other wage increases would be tied to increases in productivity. Reuther was opposed to cost-of-living allowances, but he lay recovering in Grace Hospital from the assassination attempt and Mazey° was leading the union for the time. The two sides reached an agreement incorporating both of Wilson's proposals, along with a 2 per cent—or 6 per cent an hour—wage increase in each of the two years of the contract.

The corporation was immensely pleased by the 1948 contract, for it meant stability in labor relations, and in 1950 Wilson proposed that the two formulas be incorporated into a five year contract. The UAW was surprised by the offer—it did not know whether it should commit itself for so long a time. But after much discussion the union leadership accepted the proposal, and General Motors was convinced it had bought labor peace.

Fortune, leading the applause from the American business community, called the contract "the treaty of Detroit," saying, "G.M. may have paid a billion for peace [but] it got a bargain." The article continued: "General Motors has regained control over one of the crucial management functions . . . long-range scheduling of production, model changes, and tool and plant investment. It has been so long since any big U.S. manufacturer could plan with confidence in its labor relations that industry has almost forgotten what it felt like. The full consequence of such a liberation of engineering and production talent can as yet only be guessed at, but one estimate from Detroit is that in planning freedom alone the contract is worth 15 cents per man per hour to the corporation."

The magazine said that the union, by agreeing in the contract to the "principle that advances in real wages are to be gained only through advances in productivity" had given "unequivocal acceptance" to the productivity clause that it had

---

° Mazey is somewhat piqued that his role in the talks has been obscured. "These people around here," he says of the UAW today, "act as if I never negotiated a contract."

accepted with "no particular enthusiasm" in 1948. Moreover, the magazine said, "The U.A.W. has acquired a vested interest in the proposition that General Motors is a good employer. Were Mr. Reuther six months from now" to attempt to reopen what seemed an ironclad agreement, he would not only "impugn the good faith of the corporation" but also "his own judgment in signing a five-year contract."

But neither General Motors, the American business community, nor *Fortune* reckoned with Reuther's amazing ability to adapt to changing situations and to wrap himself in righteousness as he did so. For in 1953, when the Korean war brought inflation and workers demanded higher wages, Reuther asked that the corporations reopen the five year contracts. They were not contracts, Reuther insisted, but rather "living documents" that could—must—be changed when circumstances called for change.

To force the companies to reopen the contracts, the international union permitted local unions to stage small strikes over issues that the international would normally have ordered peacefully resolved. There were a number of wildcat walkouts. To end the harassment and accommodate the international—management is as disturbed by worker dissatisfaction as the union—the companies opened negotiations. In May 1953, Reuther signed a two year agreement with General Motors, giving GM production workers a 10 cent wage increase, with an additional 10 cents for skilled workers. The cost-of-living formula was revised to give each worker a penny for each .6 increase in the Consumer Price Index, instead of a penny for each 1.14, as had been agreed in 1948; the annual improvement (productivity) increase, which had been 3 cents per hour each year in 1948 and 4 cents in 1950, was raised to 5 cents. Similar contracts were signed with Ford and Chrysler.

Reuther then settled on his policy of avoiding General Motors and taking on Ford, Chrysler, or American Motors. In 1955, he selected Ford as the target in the landmark negotia-

tions that secured for the automobile workers the beginnings of one of the dreams of the union: the guaranteed annual wage.

Workers in the automobile industry had always been plagued by layoffs brought about each year when the companies shut down or curtailed operations to retool for new models. "The fear of being laid off," a church publication said in the late 1930s, attempting to explain why auto workers had seized the plants during the sitdown strike at Flint, "hangs over the head of every worker. He does not know when the sword will fall." During the Depression, the Automobile Manufacturers Association agreed to introduce new models in the fall instead of the first of the year, the long-time practice, in an attempt to increase demand for cars during the otherwise sluggish fourth quarter. This had helped stabilize employment, but workers still were laid off for what was usually six to eight weeks in the late summer as the manufacturers retooled for new models.

In 1951, Reuther had begun laying the groundwork for a guaranteed annual wage—establishing a study committee, working the topic into speeches, articles and debates, and appointing a public advisory committee of economists to consider the matter. The companies were as adamant in their opposition to the idea as the union was in its determination to win it. In the 1955 talks, when Reuther first formally mentioned the plan to John Bugas, Ford vice president and successor to Harry Bennett as the head of Ford's labor relations operations, Bugas declared, "This is something that we will never, never do." Reuther said, "Never say never, John."

To counter the idea, General Motors offered to help finance a stock purchase program for blue-collar workers much like its program for many white-collar workers. Reuther rejected that offer. "Hell, that's for the provident," he told Louis G. Seaton, General Motors vice president for labor relations. "I'm interested in the folks who can't take care of themselves." He was also interested in negotiating a plan he proposed, not one proposed by General Motors. Two weeks later,

Ford indicated it would make an offer on the guaranteed annual wage. When the day came, Bugas arrived in the meeting
room, sat down, and proceeded to read, word for word, the
stock-sharing plan General Motors proposed two weeks before. Reuther was enraged. "How the hell," he demanded, "do
you get a Chevy on a Ford assembly line?"

Bugas insisted that the guaranteed annual wage was not a
popular issue with the workers. Workers wanted higher wages,
he said, as workers always do. Reuther later described the
tactics he used with Bugas: "I never really enjoyed doing this
to John, because I never really felt he was playing in our
league on this tactical stuff.° That didn't stop me from doing
it. . . . I said to John, 'Will you agree to have a referendum
vote of Ford workers? . . . If they vote for yours, we'll sign
a contract containing your proposal. If they vote for ours,
we'll sign a contract with that. Since you say they want yours
by nine to one, you're not taking any chances.' Poor John. I
thought he'd die." The ploy worked. On May 31, with the
Ford workers scheduled to walk out at noon and the union
ready with a 25 million dollar strike fund, Reuther and Bugas
reached agreement after a twenty-six hour bargaining session
in a Detroit hotel; the two men were standing wearily for a
break, staring at each other, when Reuther said, "You've got
a deal, Johnny." The settlement did not provide a guaranteed
annual wage, but a guaranteed semiannual wage: a guarantee
of four weeks' pay at 65 per cent normal wages, including state
unemployment benefits, plus twenty-two more weeks at 60
per cent pay. A Ford executive paraphrasing Voltaire's description of the Holy Roman Empire, scoffed at the importance
of the agreement by saying that what the union had won was
"neither guaranteed nor annual nor a wage." Nevertheless,
it was a historic breakthrough.

° Henry Ford II came to believe Bugas was not in *his* league either. Bugas
had been a well-known FBI man when Bennett persuaded him to join the
company during World War II. Ford guided Bugas out of the company and
a friend says today, "Henry and Johnny hardly ever speak."

Reuther then turned to General Motors to attempt to win the same contract, and, as he reconstructed the scene years later, he confronted Seaton:

> GENERAL MOTORS: We're against what you have done.
>
> REUTHER: You're not telling me anything new. You not only said "no" here, but you said "no" at the Ford table. I think it's pretty scandalous when General Motors is able to dictate the collective bargaining posture of its major competitor. . . .
>
> GM: We know that the ballgame is changed. But we can give you trouble by taking that SUB [supplemental unemployment benefits] nickel and putting it on the wages. Your membership doesn't understand yet what you're doing. If we put another nickel on there, they just might run over the top of you.
>
> REUTHER: Why don't you do it?
>
> GM: We don't think we can get away with it.

Finally, after a week of intense negotiations, Seaton, wearily, told Reuther the corporation would accept the Ford package, Chinese copy and all.

What, a puzzled Reuther asked, was a Chinese copy?

A Chinese copy, Seaton explained, was what a sea captain was given when he went to a Chinese tailor and ordered a new pair of trousers—but an exact copy, the sea captain insisted, of the trousers he was wearing. When he returned, the sea captain found that the tailor had indeed made an exact copy of his trousers, including a duplicate of the patch on the old trousers. General Motors was accepting the Ford package, Seaton said, including its flaws—its patches.

General Motors did not wish to yield, but it had to do so, for this was the rule of the negotiations. Particularly upset was Frederic Donner, the flinty, straight-laced executive and a man of the old school, who believed that workers should receive no money for time they did not work, a logical if unenlightened argument.

Before the 1958 negotiations—three year contracts now

being standard—Reuther talked of bargaining for a short work week. The union adopted a resolution saying that the short work week would be the major demand in the talks. Like the 30-and-out demand of 1970, the demand for a short work week arose with the rank-and-file, and Reuther skillfully adopted it as his own.

However, in the face of the nationwide recession that, coupled with the boom in foreign cars, had reduced profits, it was obvious that the industry would adamantly resist a short work week. Reuther simply refused to strike, even though the contracts expired without a settlement. Leonard Woodcock, then head of the General Motors Department, said, "We are going to rock and roll all summer."

At one point in the negotiations, Reuther declared that if the companies would reduce their car prices by one hundred dollars, the union would scale down its demands. Chrysler Corporation contended it would be ruined by such a reduction, and Chrysler Chairman L. L. Colbert asked, "Would it not be just as logical for the automobile industry to ask members of the UAW to take an immediate and sizeable wage cut, which the companies would then 'take into consideration' in pricing their 1958 automobiles?"

Reuther eventually changed goals again, announcing that what the union really sought in the talks was a profit-sharing system, even though he had historically been opposed to profit-sharing. But this goal was purely for display; when the companies and the union finally settled in October, the gains were largely limited to improvements in fringe benefits. Reuther considered every contract magnificent, each one a milestone in labor negotiations, and pronounced the 1958 version a success: "It is a good settlement," he said, "good not only for General Motors and its workers but for everyone, since it is a non-inflationary settlement." Many workers did not agree. There was a widespread rash of wildcat strikes.

In 1961, American Motors was the target for the first time and Reuther, settling without a strike, agreed to a profit-sharing plan, long a favorite concept of AMC Chairman George Romney. The settlements at the other companies were somewhat different, American Motors not sharing in the reciprocity arrangement of the Big Three: at Ford, GM, and Chrysler, the settlements dealt mainly with fringe benefits. At General Motors there was a large-scale walkout called "the toilet strike" before the corporation agreed to twenty-four minutes a day of personal relief time on the assembly line.

Oddly, Reuther never pushed profit-sharing at other corporations, although he estimated in 1963 that if General Motors and the Ford Motor Company had instituted an AMC-type profit-sharing plan, then, based on 1962 profit figures, General Motors workers that year would have received an additional 915 dollars in wages and Ford workers, 845 dollars. "If we could get the profit-sharing from GM," Leonard Woodcock said, "it would be like getting the keys to Ft. Knox after somebody had shot the guards." The big companies were adamantly opposed to profit-sharing—which they felt would interfere with the rights and responsibilities of management—and Reuther did not wish to evangelize for profit-sharing to the membership, perhaps because profit-sharing would bring virtually guaranteed wage increases, destroying this role for the international union.

In 1964 Reuther went to Chrysler Corporation for the pattern, and won a 100 dollar a month early retirement program, which was then matched by General Motors and Ford; three years later, after a sixty-seven day strike at the Ford Motor Company, a strike Henry Ford II said was "totally unjustified," and prolonged because "we would not accede to the unconscionable demands of a powerful union," Reuther won the guaranteed annual wage he had sought so long. Under the plan, workers are guaranteed 95 per cent of take-home pay, including state unemployment benefits, for up to fifty-two weeks, minus 7.50 dollars commuting and lunch fees.

. . .

came from the company side: the
...vement wage increase, the cost-of-living formula,
...ring. The union rarely, if ever, acknowledged this.
...d, Reuther, whose stature was equaled by his self-
...teousness, took credit for the cost-of-living formula just
...month before he died, telling delegates at the UAW convention in April 1970, "I was kicked around inside of this union and inside of the American labor movement" for the cost-of-living provision. Louis G. Seaton, assistant to Harry Anderson at the 1948 negotiations, told Reuther biographers, "After it got signed, it became a union proposal. And we don't fight about it."

During all these years, the company men developed a kind of fondness for Reuther, even though they, like the editorialists, seldom gave him the praise in life they gave him in death. In the early days, as *Fortune* said in 1945, management saw Reuther "not as an *enfant terrible* but as something quite serious—even a menace." But in a quarter-century of dealing with him they had come to realize that, like them, and despite his bluster and braggadocio, Reuther was a capitalist and a businessman. "In his own way, Walter is the head of a corporation, you know," the late Rabbi Morris Adler, Reuther's friend and head of the union's public review board, said in *Holiday:* "I think Charles E. Wilson understood that." Reuther railed against excessive profits and high executive salaries, and for a time was fond of calling the automobile plants "gold-plated sweatshops," meaning that while workers made high salaries for industrial workers and had lucrative fringe benefits, the plants, like English mills, were dirty, monotonous, oppressive places. But basically Reuther accepted the corporate system. "Walter would make noises about price control and what not," says a mediator, "but I don't think he ever really meant it."

When Wilson was president of General Motors, he often asked a friend, "What does Reuther want?" In the 1940s, to each other well, developing a liking for e... passed, often chatting on the phone or in Wilso... No other relationship between Reuther and automobile e... tives was nearly as cordial, but even Henry Ford II,* would often become exasperated with him, felt that when th... two talked directly, they could reach an understanding and Reuther would follow through.

Still, the companies never came to trust him completely, especially after 1953, when he forced them to reopen the five year contracts. And they were forever in the dark about what drove Reuther, what produced his strange Calvinism. But while they were puzzled by Walter—this was how he was known to both company executives and union members, *Walter*—they had come to recognize the essential truth: Reuther and the other union leaders and the union men were not madmen; the union leaders and many members believed that what was good for the companies was good for the workers. As one automobile executive said to *Look*, "Thank God for Walter Reuther."

As skilled a public relations man as he was a tactician, Reuther deserves credit for establishing the ritual of the negotiations, beginning his drum-beating months before the talks began, listing the broad goals the union intended to achieve, why the demands were due them, how the corpora-

* This did not stop the UAW from criticizing Wilson, the criticism becoming especially virulent in 1949, when Wilson, a gentleman farmer, discovered that his prize bull was ill. General Electric, at no expense to Wilson, flew a 140,000-volt x-ray machine to Wilson's farm at Metamora, Michigan, to x-ray the bull, and Detroit Edison company ran a special line to the farm so the machine could be run. Then Wilson flew in a number of medical specialists. The bull eventually recovered in full. Reuther asked workers at a UAW conference in Milwaukee, "Why did C. E. Wilson's bull get the best of medical care while millions of these kids all over America are not getting that kind of care? It is because C. E. Wilson's bull cost $16,000 and you get boys and workers for free. . . ."

tions could easily afford to meet the demands. Unlike 1970, when he gave his support to many specific demands and became boxed in, Reuther was usually careful not to back himself into a corner, not to say he would win *this* or *that*, a wage increase of so many cents, a pension benefit of so many dollars, time-off periods of so many minutes, for he knew if he declared publicly what he intended to win, and did not achieve these goals, he would be embarrassed and would have to go to the membership for ratification of a settlement that was not as rich or extensive as the settlement he had promised. Always, he stressed to his officers, a union leadership must be "sufficiently irresponsible" in its dealings with the corporations; it must talk loud and talk of strikes, it must be prepared to strike, this to ensure that the corporations would not know what the union would do. Had the military been Reuther's calling, he would have been a commander of armor, not of infantry.

During the opening week of the triennial talks, two months before the expiration of the contracts, Reuther, accompanied by three or four dozen subordinates, would troop first to General Motors, then to Ford, and then Chrysler, making long, blustery speeches for two or three hours without stopping, saying they would stop at nothing short of victory, that there was no sacrifice the workers would not make to win their goals. Across the table, the company men would sit patiently, smoking their cigarettes, letting Reuther talk, since they knew Reuther enjoyed this. When Reuther stepped before the microphones and cameras and made the same speech for the press, the company men said little in reply, stating their own arguments quickly and unemotionally. This was, they knew, Walter's show, let Walter have it.

A company negotiator: "Walter, if he had a big table meeting with lots of people there, would sometimes say things to put on a show. If he was meeting with a smaller group, say three, four, five people, there was very little of that. . . . I don't recall we ever had a blow-up other than for purposes we realized he was putting on a show for the committee."

Harry Coen, a tough General Motors negotiator of the 1930s and 1940s,° once said of Reuther: "There are two kinds of Walter Reuthers, the Reuther we deal with, and a second Reuther who's out throwing punches before the public."

After the opening session, Reuther would usually stay away from the talks for several weeks, leaving his lieutenants in charge. As the date for the expiration of contracts approached, Reuther would return, often at the critical point when he could resolve an issue or two and win a settlement, other times when he could rant at management and call a strike—in either case, the precise time when his entrance would be the most effective and the most dramatic. "When Walter comes back, then you know he's getting serious," said a Chrysler negotiator in 1967. Once, at Ford, Reuther was asked by a newsman whether he had come prepared to work out a settlement. Reuther reached into his briefcase, produced a toothbrush and held it up for the reporters. From then on, Reuther would be asked whether he had his toothbrush; if he had, it was a signal that the bargaining was in a crucial phase.

Reuther's birthday was often spent in negotiations. And in 1955, on his forty-eighth birthday, Louis Seaton presented Reuther with a cake; moments later, the reporters gave him a second cake—larger than Seaton's. "Like the GM offer," Reuther said, "Mr. Seaton's cake was inadequate."

One year at Ford, when the settlement was reached, Reuther announced that he was moving to General Motors. Reporters had given him a birthday cake, and now, when asked whether he intended to achieve more at General Motors than he had at Ford, Reuther said: "We got the cake at Ford and we'll get the à la mode at General Motors." From then on the phrases "cake" and "à la mode" became part of the negotiation

° Coen had worked for the railroads in his younger days and, at critical points in the talks, used to reach into his pocket, pull out his railroad brotherhood membership card, and say, Don't tell me about the union, I belonged to a union for years.

lexicon. *Do you expect to get any frosting on the cake at GM, Walter? Do you expect to get à la mode at Ford? Walter, do you think there will be any frosting at Chrysler? Leonard, do you think there will be any so-called à la mode at Ford?*

Still, while the union established the ritual of the talks and makes the headlines—the company has the power. The union goes to the companies and the union makes the demands; the companies provide the money to pay for the demands. The union is led by its president, the corporation by vice presidents. It is better that way, for corporation chairmen and presidents are businessmen not bargainers; if they came to the bargaining table they would probably make fools of themselves, and the union men, the elected negotiators, would rag them unmercifully. But the difference in rank adds to the atmosphere of inequality. Always, it is the union that is the villain, for, as A. J. Liebling pointed out in *The Press,* it is always said that the union is demanding so much more from the company, never that the company is demanding that the union work for so much less.

The union can shut a company down, but only the company can provide what brings a settlement: money.

At the union convention in April 1970, Reuther declared: "We are not just about economics. This union was not born just because of the struggle for another dollar in the pay envelope. This union was born out of the struggle against inhuman exploitation of the speed-up in the automobile industry. . . . In 1970 let us never forget that fighting to improve working conditions, to provide dignity on the job, always has to be an important item on our agenda." Yet, in automobile negotiations, as in most labor negotiations, the first items that are forgotten are the demands for improvement in working conditions, demands that would change the nature of the relationship between union and corporation.*

A labor journalist states: "These guys—Reuther, certainly

* Admittedly, there are considerable negotiations on the local level concerning plant-by-plant working conditions.

Woodcock to a considerable extent, and Doug Fraser much less so—they can enunciate these conditions, how shitty it is, but their commitment to changing these conditions is a good deal less than total. And even the GM national negotiating committee—their commitment is a good deal less than total. . . . First of all there is the fact of estrangement. Even the negotiating committee does not work in the plant. . . . They don't know what a shitting, fucking bitch it is hanging doors. They know, but they are equally conscious of having themselves escaped that. . . . Labor leaders define their situations as guys who have gotten away from this kind of shit.

"And beyond this is that the guys in the plants—the workers—they don't put this at the top of their lists. They've had this shit all their working lives, and they are so brainwashed that while they bitch about it, they are conditioned to believe that this is the way life is, and will be, and ought to be for shit-heads like themselves. The sense of self-esteem of the average automobile worker is damn near non-existent. . . . You take a guy and you beat him down the way you get beat down in an auto plant, and you burden him with the kind of consumer goodies and time-payments that a guy gets involved in, and he really is trapped. And if you say to him—especially in a bad year like 1970 was—what do you want? Money? Or do you want job security or do you want improvement in your working conditions? He is going to go for money. . . . So you have this phenomenon every time of working conditions being terribly important when they go into negotiations, when the conventions are held, but they just kind of leach out because they are really not a priority item for anybody—and because they attack, directly, the auto company's prerogative of running the company itself."

Chapter 6

"He only called them an octopus"

On October 1, 1970, a pleasant fall day, Leonard Woodcock left his apartment in downtown Detroit and, meeting Pat Greathouse, a union vice president and director of the agricultural implement division, was driven out on the Edsel Ford Freeway to Detroit Metropolitan Airport. The two were on their way to Peoria, Illinois, some 150 miles southwest of Chicago, a bleak factory midlands town that is the home of the Caterpillar Tractor Company, one of the nation's largest farm machinery and farm implement manufacturers. For several weeks, simultaneously with its talks with General Motors, the United Automobile Workers had been negotiating with Caterpillar; the contract would expire at midnight and a strike was scheduled. But the union had devised a scheme, which, if it worked, would not only keep Caterpillar's thirty thousand workers on their jobs but also bring pressure on the General Motors Corporation. It was a businesslike proposition: if Caterpillar would grant the union unlimited cost-of-living, computed quarterly, the union would guarantee the company would not be struck.

Normally, there would be no reason for Woodcock to appear at the Caterpillar negotiations; Greathouse is a shrewd, skilled man. It was Greathouse who helped assure the union presidency for Woodcock, taking himself out of the contest and, it is said, helping to persuade a powerful executive board member, Robert Johnson of Chicago, to vote for Woodcock. Greathouse is, moreover, perhaps the union's most imaginative bargainer, perhaps as creative as Reuther himself, often winning items in the small agricultural division before they are won in the large automobile industry: a 100 dollar vacation bonus, five weeks of vacation instead of four, a week's holiday between Christmas and New Year's. Wages are as high, and sometimes higher, in the agricultural machine and implement industry as in the automobile industry.

But the union wanted Woodcock at the talks for political reasons, so that—if the cost-of-living ploy succeeded—Woodcock could quickly take credit for the settlement and use it as a weapon in the General Motors negotiations. "We had him come down there because we wanted to get him involved," Greathouse says. "It was important for the auto negotiations that he be involved. Certainly if we could move back the cost-of-living at Caterpillar, it would do two things: it would strengthen the resolution of our members to get it in auto, and it would put a certain amount of pressure on General Motors. Obviously we weren't about to go down there and settle that and come up here and settle for less. That's not the way the system works."

Three years before, in accordance with the pattern established at Ford Motor Company, an 8-cent-a-year ceiling had been placed on cost-of-living increases at Caterpillar. But in 1968, Local 851 of the International Association of Machinists, representing some 5,000 non-UAW workers at the Caterpillar plant in Joliet, Illinois, had gone on strike demanding a return to the old cost-of-living formula. The strike lasted 56 days. Before settling it, Caterpillar went to Greathouse and told him it was planning to give in. Greathouse understood the corporation's dilemma and agreed that the UAW would make no issue of the fact that the machinists would have a better contract than the auto workers. Go ahead and settle, he said.

But now the fact that the machinists had unlimited cost-of-living was a wedge for the union, and Woodcock and Greathouse intended to use it to win cost-of-living guarantees for the UAW.

The two men arrived in Peoria about noon and were driven downtown to meet with Caterpillar executives. At eight that night, after four hours of negotiations, four hours before the strike was scheduled to begin, Caterpillar Vice President C. N. Hathaway, the company's chief negotiator, stepped before microphones in the mirrored, chandeliered LaSalle Room of the Pere Marquette Hotel and announced that an agreement had been reached. One of the terms of settlement: the corporation agreed to remove the ceiling on cost-of-living increases. There would be no strike at Caterpillar.

Next morning, Woodcock returned to Detroit, conducting a press conference at Metropolitan Airport. Yes, he said, the union had won cost-of-living at Caterpillar; yes, it was an important victory. He hoped, he said, that the fact that Caterpillar, a far smaller, less profitable company than General Motors, could afford to grant unlimited cost-of-living would be "an incentive to the auto industry." He said: "I would think it would have an impact on GM." Then Woodcock put forth a proposal: if the company would remove the cost-of-living ceiling, the union would abandon its demand that cost-of-living be computed on each three-tenths of a point change in the Consumer Price Index. Instead, Woodcock said, the union would continue with the formula of computing the cost-of-living at one cent for each four-tenths of a point increase in the price index. Over a typical year, with the cost of living increasing about 4 per cent, the new union proposal would, the union said, save the corporation some 35 million dollars a year that the three-tenths formula would consume.

Later that day at the General Motors Building, Earl Bramblett insisted that the Caterpillar settlement would have no effect on the General Motors negotiations. "Caterpillar bargains for Caterpillar," Bramblett said. "GM bargains for GM." However, Bramblett said, the corporation, as it always does, would examine all proposals the union put forth. Woodcock returned to the negotiations and, smiling slightly, said to Bramblett, Well, Earl, I suppose you read in the newspapers about Caterpillar lifting the lid on cost-of-living. Yes, Bramblett said, he was aware of what the union had won at Caterpillar. But he said that the General Motors Corporation was in the business of building automobiles, not farm equipment; the Caterpillar contract would have no effect on General Motors. Yet, Bramblett's language was muted, his response subdued, and this told the union men they had scored a point: the corporation understood that the union had established a precedent that would be most difficult to ignore. This was an enjoyable moment for the union leaders, for they believed, and thought General Motors believed, that the corporation had been had —that the corporation knew it would have to give the union the unlimited cost-of-living won at Caterpillar. Woodcock: "When Mr. Bramblett made it [the corporation's position] public, he did say, yes, that's Caterpillar's business. But the way he said it, it made it clear to me that *this* we were going to get. It was just a question of time."

The strike at General Motors was a strike of stupendous size. The night it began, more than 340,000 General Motors employees walked out; now, two weeks later, the number on strike or sent home by the corporation had climbed to nearly 400,000. (Some 15 plants remained open to manufacture parts which GM sells to Ford, Chrysler and AMC. These companies could not stay open without the parts from their arch-competitor. The UAW did not want these companies to close. GM accommodated these firms—and the union.) Thousands of other workers in supplier plants had been laid off as suppliers curtailed or suspended operations. By mid-October, the number of workers on strike or idled by the strike would rise to more than 500,000. General Motors said that it was losing 90 million dollars a day in sales, suppliers were losing 40 million dollars a day, local, state, and national governments were losing 20 million dollars a day in taxes.

As yet, however, the strike was having no real impact on the men and women most directly concerned—the strikers themselves. Pay checks for time already worked had continued for the first week of the strike. Now they were receiving 30 to 40 dollars a week in strike benefits, 30 for a single worker, 35 for a married worker, 40 for a married worker with children. This was considerably less than the average of 175 dollars a week in gross pay, 135 dollars a week take-home. Still, in the first few weeks there was a euphoria, a carefree attitude among the workers, and the strike was much like a vacation: workers slept late, raked leaves, washed cars, worked on their houses, went pheasant hunting.

Ray Serensky, a worker at the Cadillac Fleetwood plant in Detroit, says, "At first it was great. You're off; you don't have to go to work. Then you realize that the check won't be coming every week, and then it's bad." But the strike benefits and food stamps, he says, enabled his family to get by without hardship; Serensky spent his time playing hockey with co-workers and friends at a local rink.

George Bufford, who works at the Chevrolet Engineering Center at the General Motors Technical Center, says, "I got by very well because of the strike fund. I didn't get behind at all." He walked the picket line twice a week and spent time fishing at a lake near his home in Brighton, Michigan.

John Hajdino, a local union official at the Fisher Two plant in Flint, states: "I heard a lot of guys say they got along just as well on strike as when they were working."

Liquor sales in Michigan, where 170,000 strikers lived, climbed 4 per cent in the first week of the strike. "The history of major strikes," the manager of the state Liquor Control Commission told the Detroit *Free Press*, "seems to be that right at the start the men get paint and materials to fix their houses and buy a few extra jugs. . . . It's probably just an expression of relief from the daily grind." A Columbia University professor, B. J. Widick, who has worked in automobile factories and studied and written about auto workers and the United Automobile Workers, explains, "Nothing is better than a strike after you've been working a couple of years overtime, or just when you've been working hard for a long time. It's just a pleasure to be out of there for a month." A labor mediator: "Only middle-class workers on a salary look at blue-collar workers and think they look at a strike in terms of how much wages they're going to lose. His wife worries about that, not the worker. The worker, he takes on the boss."

The union had been well prepared for the strike. Thousands of picket signs were printed before the strike deadline and distributed to local union halls. The night the strike began, workers poured from the plants, some simply going home, some grabbing the signs and setting up picket lines, making remarks to their buddies: See you after Christmas. Get your deer rifle oiled up.

But times change. The union has changed. This was the 1970s, not the 1930s. There was not in this strike the fervor, the excitement that might have been expected in a strike against this huge corporation, this old enemy.

An old Flint, sitdown striker still in the plant says: "In the first strike there was far more enthusiasm and a far more emotional response to these issues. If there was an action by the corporation there was a counter-action quickly by a large number of workers." This time, he says, "There was not any real solidarity between say the workers of Pontiac and the workers of Lansing and the workers of Detroit. There was not even the inter-participation between locals in the same city."

Picket lines often were made up of only a handful of men, especially after the excitement of the first days of the strike had ended. Strikes may still be a weapon in labor relations, but not picketing. "Picketing an empty plant is an obsolete exercise," says Emil Mazey. The union used mass picketing in the old days to ensure that the companies would not operate the plants; today, the companies would not consider operating the plants. Besides, Mazey says, picket lines can bring problems: the picketers start drinking and harass the management men going through the gate. "The picketing we do now," Mazey says, "is to maintain tradition and let people passing by know we are on strike. We have no mass picketing today."

As an alternative to picketing as a means for building and maintaining enthusiasm, the union runs strike schools. Once-weekly attendance is usually mandatory if workers are to receive strike benefits. The workers troop to the cement block and brick union halls, squeezing their cars into every possible space, sitting on the wooden or metal chairs to listen to what are often long, wearisome declamations on the history of the union, the importance of the strike, brotherhood, and solidarity. Usually instructors from the union's education department conduct the classes, and they stress the important gains the union has won in its many years of struggle: higher wages, pensions, health and life insurance, holidays, supplemental unemployment benefits. Sometimes movies about Walter Reuther or the history of the trade union movement are shown. Sometimes the workers stand—this being an excellent opportunity, one of the few occasions many union members attend a union meeting—hand over heart, to recite the union's oath, which pledges the worker to observe the union constitution, to divulge no union secrets, and to "bear true and faithful allegiance" to the UAW. Sometimes, too, the workers sing "Solidarity Forever," the union anthem dating to the fabled days of the Depression and the sitdown strikes, the romantic, heroic words sounding strange in these unromantic, unheroic times:

> They have taken untold millions that they
> never toiled to earn,
> But without our brain and muscle not a single
> wheel can turn.
> We can break their haughty power, gain our
> freedom when we learn
> That the union makes us strong.

Solidarity forever,
Solidarity forever,
Solidarity forever
For the union makes us strong.

In 1970, all locals participated in the schools, and attendance, depending on the size of the local, might range from a
dozen to several thousand. Often the sessions served little
purpose; the union ran them, it seemed, almost because there
was little else to do with the workers—surely they could not
stay home—almost out of a vestigial notion that when strikes
occur there must be strike schools. One day in Lansing,
Michigan, the *Wall Street Journal* reported, when a union
education department instructor asked the workers why the
union conducted the schools, why they were there—expecting
to hear that they were there to learn to understand and ap-
preciate the union—a worker replied, "So we can get our
forty bucks."

In these early days of this strike, the union was taking
a sharply antagonistic stance toward the corporation, with
Woodcock often denouncing General Motors bitterly, condemning it for arrogance and imperiousness. On several occasions he said that the corporation acted as if it were God.
On the American Broadcasting Company's *Issues and Answers,*
he condemned the corporation for its "SDS, North Vietnam
non-negotiation position." Another time, walking from the
bargaining room in the General Motors Building, he said
angrily, "If the name of the game is for one side to sound
retreat, this is going to be one hell of a long strike."

Irving Bluestone, according to United Press International,
told New Jersey union leaders in September that the union
was determined to teach General Motors a lesson it would
not forget. "The UAW struck General Motors in 1945 and
taught them a lesson," he said. "Now, 25 years later, we're

going to teach them another lesson." Bluestone later said he
had been misquoted, although he did not convince the other
union leaders.

But suddenly, in early October, the union deliberately
ended its caustic attacks. "We were on the wrong track,"
Mazey says. "I counselled in our leadership meetings that we
had to stop sending messages to the General Motors Corporation that we wanted a long strike, and that the more statements there were about a long strike, the chances were the
General Motors Corporation might think it could buy another
thirty years of peace by giving us a long strike—another 1945–
1946. If we were sending messages to General Motors by
what we said, then the General Motors people might have
thought, 'Hell, these people don't mind a long strike, and there
isn't any point of making a move at the bargaining table to
try to find a reasonable settlement.' "

Woodcock, an honest man, says he had erred. "I had
forgotten some of my early organizing experience," he says.
"And that is, when you indulge in inflammatory rhetoric, you
delight the people who are with you in the first place; you
don't do much to the people who are in the middle; the people
who are against you anyway you offend, and you also tend
to alienate *some* of those in the middle whom you have to convince in order to win." Woodcock says he learned from this
mistake. By October 5, when the two sides met to bargain
about national issues for the first time since the strike began,
he could say with a straight face that he had "nothing but the
kindest feelings" for the General Motors Corporation.

The union and the corporation had not intended to return
to bargaining on national money issues until they had made
substantial progress in settling the 155 local negotiations
which, with the national contract, had to be concluded before
the strike could end. The first three weeks of the strike were
devoted to reaching local agreements; still, by October 1, only
nine locals had settled. The corporation places a huge "negotiation thermometer" in the bargaining room, and as the num-

ber of local settlements rises, the corporation men raise the
level of the mercury in the thermometer. Over the weekend
of October 3–4, six more settlements were added on the
thermometer, one, the agreement at the important Detroit
Allison Diesel plant, which allowed some 6,300 workers to
return to their jobs making diesel engines for Ford, Chrysler,
and Caterpillar Tractor. Yet 15 settlements out of 155 do not
represent much progress, and it was clear that the local negotiations would drag on interminably if there were no pressure
toward settlement—and this pressure could only come with
progress in the national negotiations.

The local negotiations constitute a vexing problem to the
corporation and the union. The right of local unions to bargain
with plant executives was conceived by the union years ago
to help meet dissatisfaction at the local level. The industry
had become so large, the automobile plants spread so far
from Detroit, that the local unions often felt neglected
and unimportant. Some of the locals—like the 16,000-
member Buick local in Flint—are larger than some international unions. The national negotiators could not give substantial attention to local disputes, although issues stemming
from local working conditions are often as important to the
workers as the national issues of wages, health and insurance
benefits, and retirement. It was Leonard Woodcock who placed
importance on the right of the local unions to bargain with
General Motors at the plant level—with authorization from the
international union to strike if their demands are not met—and
this is noted by union biographers as one of Woodcock's major
achievements.

The union leadership says that giving the local unions the
right to bargain is a classic exercise in worker democracy.
They bargain over such issues as production standards, seniority, protective clothing, plant safety, plant environment, paving
of parking lots, cafeteria menus. "The local demands are
directed toward real problems confronting the workers," says
Irving Bluestone. "They are designed to alleviate poor working

conditions and to improve the lot of the worker at the work place where he spends so much of his day." The local talks demonstrate, the leadership says, that the union is a union *of* the membership—not just *for* the membership.

To the General Motors executives, the talks represent what GM Chairman Roche calls "the biggest single problem" in their labor negotiations. It is these local talks, says Earl R. Bramblett, "which determine the length of the strike. . . . This thing is growing; it gets worse every time." Since 1958, General Motors says, when local contracts were first nego-tiated, the corporation has lost more than 100 million man-hours of work due to the local demands, including 43 million hours during the 1964 talks. "The results from the local issues, in some cases," says Roche, "have been almost as bad as if we had a full-blown economic strike."

The number of local demands grows each bargaining year. In 1958, the union submitted 11,000 local demands to the General Motors Corporation; in 1970, there were more than 38,000. The UAW, the corporation complains, has no method for ensuring that only meaningful demands are submitted. Many of the demands, the corporation says, represent griev-ances that ought to be resolved through the normal four-step grievance procedure. The union does not deny Bramblett's description of the way the demands are often formulated: the locals, Bramblett says, "hold department meetings and say, 'Anybody got anything you want? Put it in the hopper.' And then they simply type them up." Roche: "I think it is perfectly obvious that if we have 38,000 real grievances in General Motors plants, we wouldn't be operating."

"Admittedly," Bluestone concedes, "many of the local de-mands are frivolous" and "the UAW could no doubt do a better job in screening the demands." The point, however, Bluestone says, is that "if the companies were really con-cerned with plant conditions, the demands would be taken care of without a strike." The fact is that mops, gloves, fans, cleaning compound—all these cost money, and local plant officials are judged by how they save money, not how they spend it. Bluestone says, "We've said to the corporation, 'Why is it necessary for people to walk the bricks in order to get decent working conditions and have health and safety matters taken care of?' These things should be taken care of as they arise."

In 1970, the local demands seemed more far-reaching than ever before. There were the standard demands, which usually appear in all negotiations: requests for protective gloves, aprons, parkas, sweatbands, plastic sleeves, knee pads; for correction of defective breaks on in-plant vehicles, installation of antiskid materials on plant stairways, prohibitions against requiring workers to cross over assembly lines; for insect and rodent control, installation of fans, cleaner restrooms, removal of oil slicks on the floor, improved lighting; for more vending machines, more soap in the washrooms, for special relief time for hot and smoky jobs. But there were other larger, somewhat extraordinary demands: for free lunches and free legal advice; for free service on workers' cars, for day-care centers near plants. At UAW Local 22, a large Cadillac local on Detroit's west side, the membership demanded that the corporation install more toilets; the local president, Frank Runnels, says, "There are executives with more johns in their homes than we have in some of our departments." The local also demanded more fans, more water coolers, and the establishment of banking facilities in the plants so that workers could enjoy the white-collar amenity of cashing their checks during the day on corporation time. A major demand at the Oldsmobile plant in Lansing, Michigan, was that the corporation hire more guards for the parking lots to protect workers' automobiles. The workers also wanted the corporation to clean the parking lots more frequently, especially during second shifts when beer and whisky bottles accumulate in the lots. "That's one we didn't have to worry about 30 years ago," Emil Mazey remarked, "because no one had cars." Once in negotiations, the workers at one local demanded that the corporation paint their cars; the demand seemed outrageous, but upon investigation, plant officials discovered that when a wire fence around the workers' parking lot had been painted, no shield had been placed between the fence and the cars, and the chain link design had been sprayed onto each car. UAW Local 150, the Cadillac Fleetwood local, asked to have prime rib added to the menu in the plant cafeteria and to have hand cream and mirrors placed in the lavatories. The Fisher Body local in Willow Run, Michigan, outside Detroit, fought with General Motors management over a demand that workers be allowed to eat chicken and pizza in the plants. The corporation contended that chicken and pizza lured rats, although it did not make the same claim in the case of tuna fish or peanut butter and jelly sandwiches.

What the local demands illustrate is the double standard that exists in American labor. Most of them represent benefits that are given to white-collar workers without thought, and become frivolous only when blue-collar workers seek them. The most important and most publicized local dispute of the 1970 negotiations grew out of this double standard and illustrated, additionally, much about the United Automobile Workers, the General Motors Corporation, and the nature of the relationship between these two institutions.

In late September, GM routinely announced that the UAW had agreed to allow several hundred specialists in safety and antipollution research to return to their jobs. Many of the specialists worked at the General Motors Technical Center, a handsome, 330-acre research facility in Warren, Michigan, a working class suburb north of Detroit. Conceived by Alfred P. Sloan, Jr., who wished to consolidate the corporation's extensive research activities, the center was built in the 1940s at a cost of more than 50 million dollars. The corporation's research director, Charles F. Kettering, insisted to Sloan that the facility be a monument to modern design, and

GM commissioned Eero Saarinen, the famous architect, to
lay out the center and design the buildings. The goal, Saarinen
said, was to create "a beautiful and human environment in
which men can give free rein to their intelligence and skills."
The center is a tribute to Saarinen's genius. Some 30 buildings
are clustered amidst 13,000 trees around a 22-acre manmade
lake. Two fountains pump, it is claimed, more water than the
fountains at Versailles. The buildings have clean, straight
lines; they are of glass and steel, with the end walls of bricks
glazed in crimson, scarlet, orange, lemon, royal blue, char-
treuse, and sky blue in the fashion of the palaces of the Assyrian
kings. The floors in many buildings are constructed of large
maple blocks. Few work places in America surpass the technical center in style and beauty.

UAW Local 160 represents the five thousand union workers, one-fourth of the work force, at the technical center, most
of them skilled workers and thus among the most highly paid
members of the union. The technical center workers do not
face the drudgery, the monotony, the noise, odor, and meaninglessness of the assembly line, the heat or back-breaking
labor of the foundries. There is not the violence, the black-
white tension, the heroin, or the guns that trouble many plants
—these problems caused mostly by blacks from the ghetto
streets, and there are few blacks in the skilled trades. They
have been kept out, and neither the union nor the companies
have effectively fought this practice. The technical center
workers are considered the blue-collar elite; many are literally
not blue-collar workers at all, for, like salaried workers, they
wear white collars (the difference is that blue-collar workers
are paid an hourly wage while white-collar workers are paid a
weekly or monthly salary and the groups are covered by different work rules). It is these technical-professional workers who,
some economists say, will compose such a large block of the
labor force of the future. It is contended that these workers will
not be confronted by the problems of alienation and meaninglessness in work, that they will have no class consciousness or
militancy.

Yet despite the special status of the Tech Center workers, Local 160 is one of the most rebellious locals in the UAW, and during the 1970 strike its militance embarrassed the union and angered the corporation. After General Motors and the international union agreed that the safety and antipollution workers could return to their jobs, the Local 160 leadership unexpectedly declared that none of these specialists would be allowed to cross the local's picket lines. It was a stunning rebuff to the corporation and to the international, whose motto for thirty-five years has been: Solidarity.

No other local refused to allow the specialists to cross picket lines, and the international union advised Local 160 that it should reverse its decision. The local refused. William Carr, its president, said he would put the matter to a vote of the membership, but would recommend that the workers ignore the international directive. Carr explained that he felt GM, which had spent so much money and effort fighting proposed government antipollution standards, was being duplicitous for the benefit of public relations.

The international was in a difficult position. Not only was the leadership being challenged by a local union, always a bothersome situation, but also the union found itself in a position that seemed similar to the one for which Carr had criticized GM: the UAW still had antipollution demands before the corporation, and now, the union's concern for combating plant and automobile pollution could appear counterfeit.

Woodcock dispatched Bluestone to the Local 160 meeting at a National Guard Armory in northeast Detroit, near Warren. "I still think they should go back to work," Woodcock said, "but the decision is theirs." He apparently gave a different message to Bluestone, however, for Bluestone told the local leadership before the general meeting that he had come not to *ask* them but to *tell* them to let the safety and pollution experts return to work.

At the membership meeting, Bluestone told some 2,500 workers that "the image of the UAW" would suffer if the

situation continued; moreover, he said, the chances of the
union's winning its safety and pollution demands would be
impaired. The workers booed and hissed. "Go and get some
guts," one worker shouted. Carr told the workers, "There are
already 20,000 scabs in there leeching off us while we're on
strike" [the nonunion salaried employees who were reporting
to work and drawing regular salaries, and who would, after
the contract was settled, receive the same increases in pay
and benefits, since the corporation is intent on keeping the
white-collar workers ahead of the union men]. He said, "We
don't care to add another 300 scabs of our own." The local
voted overwhelmingly to refuse to allow the technical workers
to cross the picket lines. Bluestone, who played his emissary's
role, said the vote illustrated that the UAW was a democratically run organization, not one in which the leadership
dictated policy to its membership. But Bluestone had surely
tried.

General Motors, aware of public relations gains it could
make, took its case to the public. Bramblett declared that the
local's action was "deplorable and contrary to the public
interest." John Z. DeLorean, Chevrolet general manager, sent
letters to the striking technical center employees asking them
to reconsider: the research work, DeLorean said, was "most
critical to the company's future, [to] the program to combat
pollution and improve car safety, and to the nation as well."
On October 19, Harold Warner, General Motors executive
vice president, called a press conference to denounce the
local's action which, he said, if allowed to stand, would set
back the corporation's pollution and safety programs "for
years to come." Warner said the international seemed to have
"lost control of the local." Asked whether the corporation
intended to demonstrate this concern for the environment
and automobile safety by acceding to the union's demands
on pollution and safeguards, Warner replied he did not know,
he could not say. When, he was asked, would the corporation,
so concerned about safety, install energy-absorbing bumpers

or a safety hood latch on its automobiles? Warner said he did
not know.

Peter Kelly, vice president of Local 160, said Warner's
claims were "a lot of garbage." Carr said that General Motors
was using a "public relations gimmick" and that the international had taken the "easy way out" in agreeing to the corporation's request that the technical workers return to their
jobs. "You talk about pollution and safety," Carr said, "and
you're talking about motherhood and country."

The issue ended. The local did not allow the workers to
return to their jobs at the technical center. Despite the claims
of DeLorean and Warner, the corporation's safety and antipollution programs were not impaired.

The international union was happy to forget the incident.
Many men in the UAW look upon the members of Local 160
as greedy and, because there is perhaps a socialist element
in the local's leadership and membership, as rabble-rousers.
"The trouble with the guys at Local 160," says Robert Murphy,
a member of the union's GM national negotiating team, "is
they want everything." This is not true. The workers at Local
160 are discontented not because they want everything, for
they concede they have quite a bit, but because the one thing
they want most—to be treated like the other, white-collar
workers at the technical center—they cannot win.

Carr and Kelly argue that workers on the assembly line
and in the foundries have no time or energy to think about
the double standard of factory life. Long ago, moreover, most
brain power was taken from the factory to the air-conditioned
corporation offices. In the technical center, where blue-collar
and white-collar employees often work side by side, performing the same or similar tasks, the double standard is clearer.
The corporation, Carr says, "works hard at maintaining" the
double standard so that white-collar workers, receiving higher
wages, more benefits, and more amenities, will not succumb
to unionization.

In the Chevrolet engineering building at the technical

center, blue-collar workers who wish to go outside for lunch
must walk out designated doors; if they wish to stroll to the
lake, the door they must use makes their route a circuitous
one, and by the time they get to the lake their lunch hour
(a misnomer in factories, for it lasts half an hour) is almost
over. If a blue-collar man is walking down a corridor with a
white-collar friend they may come to an area, a lunch area or
a classified area, where the white-collar man may go, but
the blue-collar man may not. When the white-collar lunch
room overflows, the white-collar men may use the blue-collar
dining room; when the blue-collar dining room overflows, the
blue-collar workers cannot use the white-collar room. The
corporation provides uniforms for some of the blue-collar workers, saying that the uniforms protect the workers' private clothing and make for orderly operation; the workers say that the
color-coded uniforms are a way to make blue-collar workers
stand out from other employees. During a laundry strike that
lasted several months, the blue-collar workers wore their
regular clothes and the technical center was no less orderly.

The distinction between the two categories of workers
seems much like that between officers and enlisted men in the
armed services. "You figure all of you are in the same business,"
says Neal Madsen, a member of the union's General Motors
national bargaining team and a technical center employee,
"but these distinctions have a psychological effect on the
employees." An international union officer: "You walk through
the place, and you can't tell the trade unionist, the UAW
guy, from the salary guy. They're working side by side; they're
wearing the same shirt, the same tie, they're doing the same
work; you can't tell the difference. Yet there is the double
standard. And it's this thing, I think, that is most irritating to
those people." Carr says the union does little to combat the
double standard affecting white- and blue-collar workers:
"The union plays quite a role in restraining working people
in our society." There is, he insists, a "flow between the corporation and the international to keep the corporation running

—the international is a satellite of the corporation." He says, "Solidarity for the sake of solidarity doesn't serve the union at all."

Late in October, some 3,000 union retirees, men and women who remembered the suffering and the battles of the 1930s, converged on the General Motors Building in a massive demonstration, part of a force of some 200,000 retired workers who staged demonstrations in General Motors factory cities across the country. While an elderly retiree danced a jig to the quick, happy sounds of a German band and cried, "It's just like the old days"; while Leonard Woodcock, Irving Bluestone, Olga Madar, Ken Bannon, and other union officers donned the gray berets of the UAW retirees and marched with them; while Woodcock pledged that the union would once again win "equity for our retired workers"—on this fall afternoon some 3,200 members of Local 160, more than three-fifths of the membership, backed up traffic for ten miles from the technical center in an old-fashioned picket action, one of the few actions of this kind during the strike. Strikers—these workers of the future who supposedly will have no militancy or class consciousness—drove slowly around the technical center to stall traffic. They dumped roofing nails on the street in front of the center's entrances—as they had done a week before. They swore at the white-collar workers who tried to go to their jobs, stopping 60 per cent of them from going through union lines. Carr and Kelly were arrested for violation of the state strike law, although charges were later dropped. In all, twenty-two strikers were arrested by Warren police. Bramblett said: "I have no idea what these people hoped to gain."

When Woodcock announced the return to national bargaining in early October, he also called a special convention for October 24 to authorize an increase in dues for the union's rapidly emptying treasury. In the first three weeks of the strike, the 120 million dollar strike fund had dwindled to 84 million—enough for about five more weeks of strike benefits, with 14 million dollars a week going to workers and 23 million dollars a month due the General Motors Corporation for health and life insurance. But a unique arrangement worked out by the two antagonists stretched the strike fund: General Motors agreed to pay the 23 million dollars a month insurance costs and to hold off billing the union until after the first of the year, in effect floating the union a gigantic loan and helping to finance a strike against itself. This meant the strike fund would last eight weeks, until the end of November.

Bramblett says the arrangement with the union was not the same as advancing it strike money. The corporation, he says, had no other alternative. It could have canceled the insurance, or demanded that the union or the workers pay the premiums; however, to do so would have brought much criticism, for General Motors would have appeared to many people as the paradigm of the heartless employer—which many people consider it anyway—bringing hardship not only to strikers but also to their wives and children. This was a step no sane corporation could take if it wished to call itself an enlightened enterprise. "We have to live together," Bramblett says. After the first of the year, when the strike was over and most men and women back at their jobs, the union paid General Motors' 46 million dollar bill—at 5 per cent interest, the prevailing commercial rate. Because not all the strike fund had been in cash, Emil Mazey had borrowed 25 million dollars from the Teamsters, 10 million from the steel workers and 3 million from the rubber workers. Some banks, concerned about the union's financial difficulties with Black Lake—the union had borrowed 13 million dollars from the strike fund to help construct the retreat—turned down Mazey's request for loans, although he did receive a 500,000 dollar loan from the Manufacturers National Bank in Detroit. Of course, the union was not so desperate that it would take *any* handout. When the workers at the Russian auto complex at Gorki, in the Soviet Union (where Walter and Victor Reuther had worked several months as young men on their world tour), offered to send 50,000 rubles to assist the union, the message was ignored. But even with General Motors paying insurance costs and with loans from other unions, a dues increase, to be collected from those workers at the nonstruck companies, was necessary to shore up the strike fund—and to show rank-and-file determination to the corporation.

The union's special convention, held October 24 at Cobo Hall, had all the trappings of a war council: the rough-looking men in nylon jackets—a union tradition, many locals adopting a color for its delegates—some men and women wearing plastic boaters, a brass band playing "Happy Days Are Here Again."

Among the American unions, the United Automobile Workers, at least since Reuther took control in 1946 and 1947, has always had remarkably staid conventions, due perhaps to Reuther's puritanism and to the union's high-quality leadership which would allow no great hijinks. There is drinking, but there is always drinking at conventions, and Reuther could tolerate drinking; sometimes delegates will sneak a whore or two into hotel rooms, but one would never, for example, find the platoons of glassy-eyed hookers at a UAW convention that one would find at some other labor conventions. At the 1970 convention one prostitute complained that the UAW convention was lousy for business. An education and a clothing convention the weeks before had been much better, she said.

Reuther particularly disliked the AFL-CIO executive board meetings held in the winter in Miami. At one such board meeting, when he saw the large, luxurious room reserved for him, Reuther gave it to another board member, James Carey of the electrical workers, and moved to a smaller room down the hall. When reporters came to the room, hoping to interview Reuther, they found a smiling Carey who, when asked where Reuther was, said he was down the hall in a closet—probably squeezing his own orange juice.

In 1959, when the executive board met in San Juan, Puerto Rico, Reuther won endorsement for a plan to stage a march on Washington to protest high unemployment. When President Eisenhower was asked about the proposal, he noted that the labor leaders were meeting on the "sunny beaches" of Puerto Rico, far from the areas of unemployment. Reuther was distressed by the president's remark. He telegrammed Eisenhower: "Mr. President, I have spent no time on the sunny beaches of Puerto Rico nor have I been with you and your many big business friends on the golf course, the duck blinds, and the quail hunts."

Yet, while UAW conventions were different than most other labor meetings, the men working long hours, often conducting many night sessions, the outcome of the democratically run UAW conventions was usually no different from the outcome of autocratically run Teamster conventions. Even though the UAW delegates were allowed to talk at length, Reuther always thoroughly planned how proposals would be presented, always marshaled support. Men in the audience could be counted upon to step to microphones and endorse Reuther's proposals. There was, at UAW conventions, no more uncertainty as to how leadership proposals would fare than at Teamster conventions.

This time, although the delegates were called to Cobo Hall primarily to authorize the dues increase, it was Woodcock's fifteen minute, keynote address, not the vote to raise dues, that gave the convention its significance. The strike was five weeks old. Even with a dues increase, there would be strike benefits available for only a few more weeks. The workers had been out long enough; much of the enjoyment had already waned and soon, the union knew, the strike would become messy and bitter. It was time to deal, and the union selected the special convention as a forum to tell General Motors it had made this decision. It was time serious negotiations began.

The union leadership—Woodcock, Mazey, Bluestone, Bannon, Fraser—planned Woodcock's address carefully: he would state the union's position precisely; he would say nothing to antagonize the corporation.

"This strike is a fight against inflation," Woodcock told the delegates, "and it is a fight for sanity and reason in the setting of wages so that we do not have ever-rising and escalating costs." Thus, he said, the strike "has direct meaning for all our members and their families and for the working class—both in the United States and Canada."

General Motors, Woodcock said, was "hiding behind the local negotiations . . . dragging [its] feet." This was not surprising, he said, for although the strike had entered its forty-first day, the company "until just a few days ago" probably had felt no real pressure, since it had some 600,000 unsold cars in its inventory, a supply of seven or eight weeks, when the union walked out. Still, Woodcock said, to remove the local issues as a screen, the union leadership was asking the locals to redouble their efforts to gain local settlements. "Let's carry the fight to them at the bargaining table," Woodcock said, "and if it is they who are deliberately stalling the negotiations, let us make it absolutely clear where the fault lies."

Turning to the key issue, cost-of-living, Woodcock said that a few days before he had gone to his bookshelf and picked up a copy of Alfred P. Sloan, Jr.'s, book, *My Years with General Motors*. "Sure enough," Woodcock said, "on page three hundred ninety three, Mr. Sloan [had] these words: 'The natural inclination of unions in an inflationary period is to bargain for wage increases high enough to allow for future price increases, and in anticipating these high prices, the wage gains tend to push them up still higher.'" Sloan, Woodcock said, was explaining why the corporation agreed to give the union the cost-of-living formula in 1948; now, he said, the corporation was saying, "Oh, but we can't move back." Woodcock continued: "You know, they have the gall, General Motors has the gall, to say to us one day, 'You went to some other company [Ford] to ditch the General Motors formula. . . .' Well, we're back at General Motors to get it back. . . ."

The union, he said, sought "only an honorable settlement."

He said: "I would pray General Motors does not push this strike to the point where our strike fund is drained and we cannot pay any weekly benefits to the families of those on strike. There is nothing involved in this strike to justify the huge General Motors Corporation inflicting such cruelty and suffering on human beings. I hope the top management of this corporation is not so shielded from reality as not to be aware that if they create the bitterness which would flow from such a situation, it will hang over and plague the General Motors Corporation for years and years to come."

To assist the union if the strike should last a long time, Woodcock said, the union had put together—much like Walter Reuther had put together in 1945-6—what it called the National Committee to Aid GM Strikers, a group of seventy-eight well-known citizens headed by Paul H. Douglas, the former Illinois senator. Committee members were politicians, show business entertainers, writers, and university professors. Woodcock said that "the humane concern expressed by these prominent people and the potential involvement of millions of other decent Americans will go a long way towards assuring that striking GM workers will be able to pursue the merits of the dispute in the knowledge that bare minimum standards of living for their families will be maintained until the strike is concluded in an honorable way."*

---

* The committee was created as much for its public relations value as for its fund-raising or morale-raising potential. Almost every conceivable liberal was included: Congresswoman Bella Abzug, Senator Birch E. Bayh, actor and singer Theodore Bikel, Georgia State Representative Julian Bond, Cesar Chavez, Ramsey Clark, John Kenneth Galbraith, Mrs. Anna Roosevelt Halstead, Senator Philip A. Hart, Hubert H. Humphrey, George Meany, Mrs. Martin Luther King, Jr., Senator Edmund Muskie, Edward Bennett Williams. The committee never really moved into high gear, perhaps because negotiations began moving so quickly after the October 24 convention. Whereas the 1945-6 citizens' committee raised more than one million dollars, the 1970 committee raised 30,634.36 dollars, a "disappointingly small" sum, the committee conceded. The committee did, it reported, "focus public attention" on the needs of the strikers. It received 8 signed letters supporting the strike, 66 signed letters opposing the strike, and 178 unsigned letters expressing, "in vituperative and in some instances obscene language," opposition to the strike.

Woodcock took pains to reject the notion that the UAW intended to teach General Motors a lesson or that it sought to defeat the corporation. His most stinging use of invective was to call General Motors an octopus. "Hell," a union man said, "he only called them an octopus. GM calls itself that."

When Woodcock finished, he received enthusiastic, but not unrestrained, applause. The delegates took up the executive board's recommendation to raise the dues of nonstriking union members, and debate went so quickly that a journalist who stepped outside the hall to purchase a candy bar, expecting a long session, returned moments later to find the recommendation had been passed, the journalist falling victim to swift union democracy.

The new dues would bolster the strike fund by about 10 million dollars a month. Nonstriking workers at Ford, Chrysler, American Motors, and the farm implement firms were assessed an extra 20 dollars a month on top of the normal dues of 7 to 8 dollars a month; the dues for other union members not on strike or laid off were doubled to 15 to 16 dollars a month. The delegates rejected a proposal to raise dues even higher to support the strike indefinitely.

What Woodcock did not discuss at the convention was as much a part of his message to General Motors as what he did say. "I did not talk about dental care," he explains, "and at the point that dental care was not talked about, GM knew they didn't have to do that." What was of critical importance, Woodcock says, was to ensure that a wage settlement would provide an average increase of at least 51 cents an hour. To the leadership's mind, he says, 51 cents was the "magic figure" that would clinch a settlement and ratification. The average had to be 51 cents, he says, not 50, for many classes of workers

---

"In the writer's memory, not since the early days of the New Deal has there been such a paranoiac reaction to a plea for help," the committee secretary insisted. A man identified as a Philadelphia lawyer wrote, "I regret my inability to send anything; however, I have been unable to figure out how to package a tinker's dam."

receive a penny less than the average, and 49 cents would
not be enough for them; 50 cents, he says, would have a
special ring to the rank-and-file; it would sound better than,
say, 44 cents, which, according to the union, would have been
the settlement if the dental plan had been won, because the
union estimated that the dental plan would cost 6 cents a
worker. By informing the corporation that the union was no
longer insisting on the dental plan—that is, by not mentioning
the dental plan—Woodcock says, the corporation "knew
where our priorities were": the magic 50 cents.

At a press conference after the convention, Woodcock
relayed other signs to General Motors. He said it was not the
union that had suggested the strike might last past Christmas
and New Year's and into the first of the year; he said he
believed that the leaders of the corporation, Roche and Cole,
were gentlemanly, civilized men who would not force the
strike through the holidays and inflict serious burdens on the
strikers and their families.

All day, General Motors had kept a team of publicists on
the eleventh floor of the General Motors Building waiting to
draft a reply to what the corporation anticipated would be
a venomous attack from Woodcock. But there was no attack
and no reason for a reply. The publicists were sent home, a
pleasant Saturday wasted, but with the corporation happy,
for clearly Woodcock was ready to negotiate, clearly he
wanted the strike to end. If Reuther had been president, the
corporation men said, if Reuther had made the convention
speech, he would have torn the General Motors Corporation
a new asshole, and that speech alone, they agreed, perhaps
would have prolonged the strike another two or three weeks.
"A propaganda blast would have automatically demanded
a response" and thus "automatically used up several days,"
Bramblett says. "A very provocative sort of statement could
have pushed the strike into December."

Next morning, beginning at 10 a.m. at the General Motors
Building, Woodcock, Bluestone, and Ernest Moran, Woodcock's aide, met with Earl Bramblett and George Morris,

Bramblett's chief assistant, over coffee and breakfast rolls.°

Woodcock told Bramblett and Morris that the strike had run long enough and that both sides must begin putting a settlement together. Bramblett said that if the union was seriously interested in working for a settlement, the two sides ought to establish a deadline and bargain against the deadline. There were, he pointed out, the time-consuming mechanics of reaching an agreement, having it ratified, and getting the workers back on their jobs; it would take about three weeks, he added, to gear the corporation for reasonably full production, to get enough feeder plants into operation to provide the parts to operate the assembly lines. The union, both sides agreed, faced problems of its own: to ratify a settlement, it would have to summon its executive board and its General Motors council to Detroit to recommend ratification; then the contract would have to be submitted to the 394,000 General Motors workers across the country. The ratification process, the union said, would take about ten days.

The plan to concentrate on settling local disputes was clearly not working. Some six weeks had passed, and many local leaders were dragging their feet. Only 52 local agreements had been reached. General Motors had wanted to settle about 70 per cent, or 110, of its 155 local agreements before working at the national level, in an attempt to guard against repetition of the 1964 situation when it settled a ten day strike with the UAW but was troubled for several weeks by unsettled local disputes. In 1967, the national Ford strike was settled after five weeks, but unresolved local issues kept Ford shut down three more weeks.

Bramblett suggested to Woodcock and Bluestone that the

° General Motors provides coffee and doughnuts for both the company and union negotiators, a practice that dates from the 1950 bargaining session. Seaton had gone through a lengthy explanation of the company's viewpoint on a controversial union demand, zealously diagraming the company's position on a blackboard. When he finished, one union negotiator, to Seaton's distress, asked him to repeat. The union man had been out of the room fetching a cup of coffee. Gruffly, but patiently, Seaton again outlined his position—but he also ordered that coffee and doughnuts be delivered every morning to the company and union conference rooms.

two sides establish a November 10 deadline. He believed, he said, that if both sides worked diligently, local and national settlements could be reached by that time. An agreement by the tenth, he said, would allow the corporation to resume production before Thanksgiving, and mean that most General Motors employees would be back at work, receiving pay-checks, before Christmas. Bramblett proposed that the two sides publicly announce the deadline, so that the locals would be aware of the date by which they should be settled.

Woodcock, Bluestone, and Moran left the room to caucus. When they returned, Woodcock told Bramblett that his pro-posal would not work. It would be a mistake to announce a deadline publicly. A dozen or more plants were fairly close to settlement, he said, and if the local leaders knew they had until November 10 to reach agreement, they might hold back until the last moment, hoping to extract a larger settlement and to win political victories by appearing to local members as courageous leaders willing to confront the corporation until it gave in. Further, local plant executives also might stall, for they know that once a national contract is reached, pres-sure on the local union from the international and from many workers will mount, making it difficult for the local to hold out for a larger contract. Bramblett saw logic in Woodcock's argument, and both sides agreed to keep the target date secret.

Woodcock and Bluestone, in return, proposed that the size of the bargaining committee be reduced so that only the top negotiators could explore contested areas. By cutting the size of the bargaining committee, Woodcock and Bluestone argued, both sides could probe more comfortably than they could if many men were present. Bramblett regarded this proposal as constructive, and it was accepted.

Limiting negotiations to key people when the negotiations enter the critical phase is an old practice. "Anybody who has done any bargaining at all," says George Morris, "will tell you that at some point you've got to get down to a small group."

The large negotiation sessions with General Motors consist
of some sixty to seventy men, thirty or more to each side,
all crowded around the polished walnut table, and microphones are used so everyone can hear. They are, Morris explains, "not a very good forum for settling things. When you
get down to the fine points, it's got to be done in a delicate
manner. You can't do it in any town hall setting."

Each side must be able to deal with the other with frank-
ness and the knowledge that what is said will remain confidential. Much sparring goes on: one side may offer to swap
one item for another, the trade may not work, and the proposal will be withdrawn; one side may explain precisely and
frankly why it needs to win a demand, or why it cannot give
in. The corporation may explain that it cannot yield on a
certain demand, that it is under intense pressure from the
federal administration or from other firms or industries; the
union may say it needs one particular item—cost-of-living,
for example—or it has no hope of winning ratification from
the membership.

By proposing the special probing committee, the union
was agreeing to bar the twelve members of the union's General Motors national negotiating team, the men elected by
their regions to represent the workers in the negotiations.
The negotiators, by approving the proposal, agreed to bar
themselves. Bluestone concedes it is a "fair question" why at
least some of the elected negotiators—say just one, perhaps
the chairman—should not be included in a special committee.
But, he says, after thorough discussion it was decided to limit
the committee to top officers and members of the union staff.
The corporation, he says, is "more comfortable" with these
men, because it has dealt with them many times in the past.
In truth, these are also the only people the *union* wants
present. Morris: "I think Irving could have said that he and
his people feel more comfortable in that kind of environment,
too."

The members of the negotiating team are, most of them,

unsophisticated, sometimes crude men. It is easy to distinguish them from corporation executives, or even from union executives, because of the difference in dress. They wear much less expensive clothing, shiny suits or perhaps sport coats with slacks and, perhaps, white socks. Two union negotiators often wore dark glasses and sometimes returned from lunch or dinner with toothpicks in their mouths.

No one fully trusts the elected negotiators. They are ancillary figures at best, sounding boards for the union leadership. Woodcock and Bluestone and other union leaders may bounce proposals off them to gain readings on how the proposals might fare with the rank-and-file; the men also stay in touch with their regions and their locals, and they may provide the leadership with reports of attitudes in the ranks. But mostly they provide the image to give the negotiations the smell of democracy.

These men have never participated in such a publicity-centered, important event in their lives and, unless they return three years later, will not again. Some newsmen seek out the members of the negotiating team and ply them with beer and whisky, hoping they will give them bargaining secrets. They are sometimes valuable sources, especially in the early going, but in the crucial moments they are not privy to the top-level negotiations and can reveal nothing of importance. Talking with members of the committee, suggests Emil Mazey, the secretary-treasurer, is a waste of time. Mazey explains: "The basic decisions were not made by the committee; we make the decisions, the top leaders of the union. And the decisions are conveyed to the committee and they agree." Told that Mazey had suggested the negotiators have no importance, a union executive board member stopped, surprised, and asked, "Emil said that?" There was a pause. He laughed. "Of course, he's right."

A company negotiator believes one reason the union establishes subcommittees during the talks is "to give the committee members something to do." A labor scholar says

that when negotiations enter the critical phase, the committee
members are excluded because "nobody wants them around,
and I mean nobody, nobody on either side. You could never
close the door and say 'This is important' and 'This isn't important.' Or 'We want this but we don't want this.' The elected
guys would kick and raise hell. Why, if the committee knew
what went on in these sessions, they'd be surprised as hell.
They'd say, 'Who the hell gave you guys the right to drop
anything?' If the committee was there, Oh, God, they'd die."

Bramblett says that creating small probing teams is necessary because negotiators must deal with "people that you
have confidence in so that if the thing blows up, you're not
caught with a lot of things you said in a big crowd." It is
true, finally, that elected negotiators are intensely political
men, intensely ambitious; some would not be above attempting to torpedo settlements at the last moment, demanding
something that obviously the corporation was not going to
give, for personal political gain. A union any more democratic
perhaps could not get a settlement.

On October 26, the day after the breakfast meeting with
Woodcock, Bluestone, and Moran, Bramblett called a press
conference ostensibly to reply to Woodcock's charges that
General Motors was delaying a settlement by stalling local
negotiations. He also wanted a forum to warn that unless an
agreement was concluded within the next two weeks, the strike
might last into December—and that once it lasted into December, it might drag past the first of the year. As he had
agreed with Woodcock and Bluestone, he did not announce
the establishment of the November 10 deadline nor the creation of the special probing committee. Bramblett said, "Any
suggestion we're dragging our feet is utter nonsense. We're
very much concerned about the loss of wages to our employees
and the impact upon the economy. . . . General Motors is
losing $90 million a day in sales. We want a settlement as
quick as we can get it. And that is the only notion we have
had. We are working as hard as we know how to work."

Next day, as if to underscore Bramblett's statement that
General Motors was concerned about lost sales, the corporation released its third-quarter report: it was shocking. The
General Motors Corporation, the symbol of American capital-
istic success, had lost 77 million dollars, its first loss since the
initial quarter of 1946, when it was shut down by the 113-day
strike and lost 36.1 million dollars, and only the second time
the corporation had lost money since 1921, just after it had
been reorganized by Pierre S. du Pont and Alfred P. Sloan, Jr.

The corporation's figures must, however, be accepted with
caution. General Motors had been on strike only the last two
weeks of the quarter. Included in the third-quarter report
were extensive costs for retooling for new models, and perhaps
part of the large expenditure that the corporation incurred
in automating and remodeling the Lordstown, Ohio, plant
to bring out the Vega subcompact. It is likely that the corporation charged all possible expenditures to the third quarter so
that it could show a large loss, for the report of a profit
certainly would have been awkward in the negotiations. "What
could the company have done then?" the Detroit *News* was
asked. "Tell the union it didn't have enough money for higher
wages?"

Both sides had intended to use this week to see whether
they could arrive at a basis for settlement. All week, negotiators for the union and the company quietly explored grounds
for agreement; they chatted in the halls of the negotiation
suite; they telephoned each other at their homes late at
night. The union believed there was an excellent possibility
for settlement. Still, the deadline had not been announced.
Ernest Moran: "We did not want to say that we're setting up
a synthetic deadline and have it blow up. We knew that at
the point it blew up, we were good until Christmas."

The corporation had hoped for more progress on local
negotiations, but at midweek the number of local agreements
stood at fifty-two, the same as on Sunday. Woodcock: "This
business of putting the pressure on the locals we had been

feeling for some time would not work. You set a synthetic date—say November 10—that the locals must be settled by or else. Or else what? Or else they won't be settled." Woodcock went to Bramblett and convinced him that if there was to be progress at the local level, there must be progress toward a national contract. "Something meaningful" had to happen in the national talks, Woodcock says, "because as long as nothing was settled nationally, they were going to just keep dragging locally."

Bramblett agreed to the union's proposal, and on Thursday, October 29, the special probing committee, consisting of Woodcock, Bluestone, Moran, Bramblett, Morris, and some trusted assistants on both sides, met for the first time to begin discussions toward a national agreement. At the union's suggestion, the two sides instituted a news blackout, in accordance with the long-standing philosophy that secrecy must prevail during the crucial stage of negotiations. On October 30, the United Automobile Workers released a three paragraph statement:

> With the unanimous approval of the UAW–GM national negotiating committee, and by mutual agreement between the parties, the UAW and General Motors Corp. have agreed to establish a special subcommittee to undertake intensive probing sessions to fully explore and discuss national issues that now separate the parties. . . .
>
> The parties have agreed that, during the period that these probing sessions are under way, there will be no public comment concerning the progress of these discussions.
>
> We plan to meet throughout the weekend and are urging our local unions to intensify bargaining on local issues during the same period.

Moments later, General Motors released a statement:

> We welcome this probing of all the outstanding national issues. We are prepared to meet as many hours as neces-

sary to do this. We are urging our plant managements to further intensify local negotiations in an effort to conclude local settlements.

Later that morning, Woodcock and Bramblett met, separately, with J. Curtis Counts, director of the Federal Mediation and Conciliation Service, who had arrived in Detroit from Washington. Counts saw Woodcock, Bluestone, and Moran in Woodcock's office at Solidarity House, and then he was driven to the General Motors Building where he met with Bramblett and Morris in Bramblett's office on the fourteenth floor, then lunched with Bramblett in the corporation dining room. Counts expressed to both sides President Nixon's concern over the length of the strike; he made it clear that if the strike were not settled quickly, he intended to send in mediators to assist in negotiations.

The union and the companies have historically been opposed to government intervention in automobile negotiations, and the government, perhaps because it is aware of this, has stayed clear of the automobile talks since 1945–6. Now Counts clearly posed the possibility of government intervention. "We are," he said, "monitoring the negotiations on a daily basis and if progress ceases, we will get into it actively." The announcement of the news blackout and the probing committee, he said, were "hopeful" indications of efforts needed "to produce the movement necessary to agreement." As Counts suspected, the union had timed its announcement of creation of the special committee to undercut him by dispelling any notion that he had flown to Detroit and quickly made arrangements that would lead toward a settlement. The off-year election was four days away, and a major effect of the strike was that it added to the Democratic issue of a depressed economy that was outweighing the Republican issue of law and order. Across the country many Republican candidates were in trouble, especially in the Midwest where General Motors workers were concentrated. Any hint that the Nixon

Administration had played even a small role in moving the corporation and the union toward a settlement might have
swung voters the other way.

Bargaining is a matter of timing, and Bramblett, a
master at timing, was waiting the union out, for he wanted
to make his move at the proper moment: if he made it too
soon, the union might come back and demand more. Bramblett rarely shows any emotion, and this was one of the things
his predecessor, Louis Seaton, liked about him; Seaton asked
Bramblett to join the labor relations staff after watching him
on the golf course and being impressed with his coolness and
confidence in a pressure situation. James Ogden, an assistant to
Woodcock, says, "Bramblett is one of the best poker players
I've ever seen in bargaining."

Bramblett denies that General Motors would stall negotiations: "We weren't trying to take advantage of them. . . .
We told them that. It didn't matter to us whether they had
$120 million in strike funds or were broke. We were trying
to reach an agreement that we could live with and it wasn't
in our interests to have them broke. . . . We were losing $90
million [a day] in sales. You think we would do that to see
their strike fund run out? That's absolutely ridiculous. Some
people get fancy ideas about strategy and all that. I don't
know anything about strategy. We only had one object, and
that was to reach an agreement that we could live with, that
we could manage, that would not hurt the country. That was
our sole objective from start to finish. That was our number
one and only objective."

The union leaders, concerned about the lack of movement
by the corporation, held an officers' meeting at Solidarity
House. Why wasn't anything happening? they asked. What
could the union do? Mazey said he was not convinced that
Roche, the corporation chairman, understood that the union
was prepared to settle, understood precisely the contract

the union needed to take to the rank-and-file. It was important, he said, that Roche be made directly aware of the situation. He says, "To have a major conflict of this kind without the top officials of the corporation and the union having an opportunity to converse . . . without their [the corporation leaders] being made aware of what the objects were, could prolong a strike. . . . It was important to have Roche and Ed Cole know precisely what we were seeking. . . ."

The union officials believed that Bramblett, attempting to force as tough a settlement as he could upon the union, was not communicating to Roche and other top corporation executives the intensity and firmness that the union had attached to its demands—particularly cost-of-living and 30-and-out. Douglas Fraser explains that the responsibility of the corporation negotiators is "to take our position and relay it to the top executives." Sometimes, Fraser says, the necessity of working through a middle man creates a communications gap between labor negotiators and corporation leaders. "You can't really transmit the union message second-hand," he says.

Mazey: "One of the major problems you have in bargaining is trying to find where the power structure is and who makes decisions." He has participated in negotiations, he says, in which "the company man has sometimes taken me aside and said, 'Look, I've gone as far as I'm able to go. Why don't you try to have a top meeting with corporation officials?'" According to Mazey, "You can never be sure that the company spokesman at the bargaining table accurately represents what you say. Because Earl Bramblett is not a policy maker. He is a policy carry-outer. He carries out a decision that has already been made by somebody else. Somebody else makes the spitballs and he comes in to throw them. That is his role. . . . Bramblett is merely the conveyor of the message."

The union officers made a decision: Woodcock must take the union case to the highest level; he must see Roche.

Chapter 7

The workers

The line, the goddamn line. Fifty-five cars an hour, 440 cars a shift . . . two shifts a day, 4,400 cars a week . . . 44 assembly plants, 9 million cars a year . . . lights, machinery, noise . . . hundreds of hustling workers, arms moving, legs moving . . . tightening bolts, fastening cables . . . using big electric wrenches and drills, the hoses stretched out behind them . . . and the colors, the brilliant colors: aqua, grabber lime, pewter, pinto red, sassy grass green, rosewood, ascot blue, Nevada silver, cottonwood green, in-violet, curious yellow, burgundy fire, glacial blue, Tor-Red, amber sherwood, formal black, sunflower, sandalwood, cranberry, snow white, Bahama yellow, true blue, rally red, yellow gold. . . . The Workers, 700,000 of them across the country, 200,000 of them in the Detroit area . . . men and women, whites and blacks . . . big blacks with Afros and young dudes with processes, paunchy whites, paunchy blacks, rednecks, fathers, husbands, suburbanites . . . women, tight-skinned, almost never pretty, with hair teased in the fashion of ten years ago . . . 8 hours a day, not counting half an hour off for lunch . . . 46 minutes of relief time, when a worker can sit down or use the toilet or get a Coke or a Mallo-Cup . . . workers sanding gray metal and rough spots on painted metal after the cars have come from the bake oven . . . taking windshields from a pile, slopping glue on and attaching a rubber sleeve . . . a worker attaching the windshield to a hydraulic lift with suction cups and swinging it onto the line . . . workers swinging the rear axle in and laying the rear springs on the line . . . the body now automatically dropped over the rear axle, the springs, the drive shaft . . . tires inflated by machine and workers taking them off conveyors and putting them on the axles . . . workers bolting the wheels down . . . workers in the pits underneath the assembly line, like slit trenches, standing all day at Ford or GM, sitting at Chrysler . . . installing wires, fastening bolts, 8 hours a day, their arms over their heads . . . workers beating on latches with rubber mallets to make the hoods fit . . . 8 hours a day, 48 weeks a year, 9,000 or so dollars a year, 130 to 150 dollars a week in take-home pay . . . THE LINE, THE FINEST PRODUCT OF AMERICAN INVENTIVENESS . . . 350 models to choose from . . . fascinating, absolutely fascinating, how the engines, tires, fenders, hoods are fed onto the line at the right time, a 429 CID V-8 or a 200 CID Six, the right size tires, the right color fenders and hood, the system run by teletype and computer . . . A WONDER OF THE WORLD . . . a few days from the time the iron ore is dug in the Mesabi Range in Minnesota, the coal in West Virginia, Pennsylvania, and Kentucky, the limestone in northern Michigan, the tires manufactured in Akron . . . the ore hauled to Gary, Cleveland, Pittsburgh, or Detroit, smelted into steel . . . rolled into sheet steel at 2,300 feet per minute . . . stamped into side panels, inner panels, outer panels, fenders, roofs, hoods, decks, floor pans . . . the iron cast into engines, steel forged into axles, rolled into frames . . . the body welded together . . . painted with zinc phosphate . . . painted with two coats of primer, wet-sanded, painted with three coats of acrylic enamel, baked for one hour at 250 degrees . . . dollied onto the line . . . the doors and deck hung . . . dropped over the engine and transmission . . . windshield, instrument panel, and upholstery installed . . . then down the final line . . . rear axle, rear springs, drive shaft, gas line, tires, fenders . . . six gallons of gasoline injected into the gas tank . . . battery hooked up . . . a worker

gets in, moving fast, turns the key, and this tremendous noise
. . . rrrrrRRRRRRRRRrrrrrRRRRR . . . the car starts up . . . Mustangs,
Cougars, Torinos, Dusters, Bonnevilles, GTOs, Firebirds,
Caprices, Mavericks, Pintos, Montereys, Imperials, Furys, El
Dorados, Galaxies, LTDs, Thunderbirds, Challengers, Darts,
Barracudas, Valiants, New Yorkers, Chevelles, Novas . . . off
the line . . . lights aligned, acceleration and brakes tested . . .
washed . . . waxed . . . and onto haul-away trucks or railroad
cars, fifteen to the car, and shipped across America.

In 1933, Diego Rivera, the Mexican painter, completed a
nine month project: an awesome set of murals in the garden
court of the Detroit Institute of Arts. The murals, in major
part depictions of life in the automobile plants, caused a furor.
For Rivera, a Communist, did not paint life in the plants as
the city fathers would have had it. He painted the workers
as grim-faced robots locked into dreary jobs, automatons.
The city was beside itself. Meetings were held. Letters poured
into the newspapers. Rivera was reviled. The Detroit *News*
and the Archdiocese of Detroit demanded that the murals
be whitewashed. Calmness prevailed, however, and the fres-
coes remain. So do the automobile plants that Rivera painted.
And now, nearly four decades later, this is clear: in many
cases, in many plants, life for the workers remains in large
part as monotonous and as full of drudgery as Rivera painted
it. It is preferable, for any number of them, to the mines, the
military, or clerical work. But for many of America's auto
workers—the very heart of the working class—life is dull,
brutish, weary, stuporous. Many workers hate their jobs;
many hate their lives.

There is much irony in this, for the automobile worker is
in a large sense the beneficiary of the best that America has
to offer. It is nothing less than the American Dream—the
promise that hard work will bring the good life—that brought
the automobile workers to Detroit. Murray Kempton, in *Part
of Our Time*, wrote of Detroit in the 1920s: "The workers
came there like pretty girls to Hollywood." Young men from

played-out lumber towns, the sand farms of northern Michigan and Ontario. White Southerners, from Tennessee, Kentucky, Alabama, Mississippi, Georgia—coming North to make big money in *Dee*-troit.° The immigrants: Italians, Swedes, Slavs, Hungarians, Scottish, Irish, Syrians, Germans, Bulgarians, Yugoslavs, Maltese, Greeks, Russians, English, Chinese, Mexicans. And, finally, first because they worked cheaply and often as scabs, and now because they provide a low-skill, close-at-hand labor force, the Negroes. Detroit's Negro population increased more than 600 per cent between 1910 and 1920. In the mid-1930s, the time of the great sitdowns, Detroit had more Poles than Poznan, more Ukrainians than all but two cities in the Ukraine, 75,000 Jews, 120,000 Negroes. "If there ever was a melting pot," says Leonard Woodcock, "I think it is the automobile industry."

Said the Guide Series of the Works Progress Administration: "Detroit had a special need for young men. The high-speed machines, in which auto parts were cut and shaped, and the throbbing conveyor belts, on which the finished cars were assembled, needed the suppleness of youthful fingers, the nervous alertness of youthful brains, and the stamina of youthful bodies. Detroit needed young men and the young men came."

Today, despite the fulfilled promise of jobs, despite the measure of economic security, despite the fact that the auto worker has reached a level of affluence—an accumulation of goods—unmatched in the history of the working class, many of the men and women employed in the nation's largest industry are unhappy, embittered. For them, the American Dream has failed.

In July 1970, the day that the UAW entered into negotia-

° The hillbillies, Louis Adamic wrote in *The Nation* in 1935, were recruited because they were "safer" than local labor, which was "poisoned by ideas of unionism and perhaps even more dangerous notions . . . To crash a job at a plant one man I know practiced up on the Southern dialect and drawl, then presented himself at the factory gates, and was hired as soon as he opened his mouth. Another good way for a man to get a job in Detroit, I am told, is to look and act stupid."

ons with the General Motors Corporation, the day Woodcock
old the corporation he hoped to avert a strike, that Vietnam
was the cause of the nation's inflation, the day that Bramblett
said both sides must work together for the nation's good—
the week that Woodcock would also go to Ford and Chrysler,
and make similar statements and get similar responses—that
day Bob Williams, a foundry worker, stood outside the Ford
Rouge plant, Albert Kahn's monument to industrial architec-
ture, the largest self-contained industrial complex in the
world, and said, "It don't change. It's still the same nasty old
plant."

Many people have become rich in the automobile
industry; scores if not hundreds of millionaires: Fords, Sloans,
Ketterings, Motts, Wilsons, Roches, Knudsens, Fishers. Thousands of middle and top level executives make excellent
money, as do many skilled tradesmen and foremen. Indeed,
most workers make salaries of 8,000, 9,000, and 10,000 dollars
a year—"decent money," in Earl Bramblett's words. He says
it is incorrect even to think of auto workers as *working class*.
Auto workers have achieved *affluence*, Bramblett says, and
"there is a big difference between affluence and the working
class." In a booklet that General Motors sent to its 400,000
production workers shortly before negotiations began in 1970
("How I hate that book," says a GM worker), the workers
were told they were "well up on the income ladder—the TOP
THIRD income group in the nation." Sidney McKenna, codirec-
tor of the Ford Motor Company negotiating team, says, "I
can scarcely believe that he [the auto worker] can be identified
as the working class poor." A woman at GM's Fisher Livonia
plant said, "We're different people than we were. I've worked
in the plant since 1928 . . . then we were just a bunch of blue-
collar workers who didn't amount to a hill of beans . . . Now,
well look, a lot of us can afford summer cottages, some of us
can afford boats, two cars, things like that."
Yet despite the phrases of the General Motors booklet,

despite contract gains, many of the workers in the shops are pressed to make ends meet. A worker at GM's Fisher Fleetwood plant says, "It takes *two* checks for a family to live comfortably in this day and age."

No one goes to work in the auto plants intending to stay there. This was true thirty-five or forty-five years ago, and it is true today. Always, the workers intended to stay a short time, a year or two, time to put some money away, and then get out. Many dreamed of going into business for themselves. Robert W. Dunn, in *Labor and Automobiles* (1929), wrote of the auto worker: "He is quite likely to regard his job as a temporary expedient, and to be dreaming about leaving the 'auto game' and opening a garage or a filling station on his own." But this fails and they stay in the plants. A Ford worker: "Once you get in, it's hard to get out, because you have a wife and a family and this is your means of support." A GM worker: "You get about ten or twelve years in, and you get to thinking about it. But like myself, I don't have any training for any other kind of job."

In *Man on the Assembly Line*, the classic study of automobile workers, published after World War II, Charles R. Walker and Robert Guest chronicled the despair of the men on the line. They concluded that the division of labor left workers merely shells of human beings. The system, said Daniel Bell in *Work and Its Discontents*, "draws all possible brain work away from the shop . . . [so that] the worker is divorced from any decision or modification about the product he is working on." And Ely Chinoy, in *Automobile Workers and the American Dream*, concluded that "non-skilled workers . . . can secure little significant experience of themselves as productive human beings." He said: "Automobile workers without education and training possess few opportunities for advancement . . . no matter how ambitious, capable, personable or hard-working they may be . . ."

Chinoy—his fine work was a study of the Oldsmobile plants in Lansing, Michigan—said that workers had not abandoned their belief in the American promise of opportunity despite the fact that it was closed to them. Auto workers, he said, grubbed on, staying in the shops only for the high wages. They want to get out, he wrote, but cannot.

Certainly the assembly line—the symbol of industrial America—has brought unparalleled production to America, some 250 million automobiles in the little more than half a century since Henry Ford introduced it in 1913–14. Other industries imitated the assembly line system, giving America uncounted toasters, television sets, automatic fry pans, radios, coffee pots, mixers, blenders, electric shavers. The standardization that it has brought has spread through the fabric of America, homogenizing our landscape, our culture, our lives. Douglas Fraser, the UAW vice president, says, "I don't think that anybody can argue that the assembly line is not the most efficient system." Yet, just as the automotive industry introduced this productive, efficient system, just as it has given to America a comfortable, private transportation system, it has brought a life for the workers that many speak of with hatred. Ken Bannon of the UAW says, "The most difficult job in the entire country—not just the auto industry—is fighting the assembly line. And it's not getting any easier."

A Cadillac worker tells: "You walk in the plant in the morning, and the *smell*. As soon as you get to the door, you say, 'What am I coming here for? I'm crazy.' " A fellow worker: "You follow that iron horse"—the assembly line—"all day, and your ass is dragging when you walk out." A supervisor at a GM Pontiac plant says of the assembly line worker: "You don't think . . . you're just an automated puppet." Another GM worker: "That's all I'm working for, my paycheck and retirement." Bannon, speaking of the assembly line: "It's a beast. It's an ugly, ugly beast." Frank Runnels, president of UAW Local 22, a Cadillac local: "A guy would have to be a freak to enjoy a life like this."

The huge plants are hot, clangorous places. Often there is smoke and stench. The work is difficult and dreary, not unlike the way Charles Chaplin represented it in *Modern Times*. Art Fox, a skilled tradesman at the Ford Rouge plant and a leader in the United Caucus, an antileadership group within the UAW, said, "It's an animal-like existence." There is, too, a saying among automobile workers that has been around for years, obviously not wholly true, but one that speaks to the brutishness of their lives. When they get home at night, the auto workers say, they are, many times, too tired to screw.

It is easy to forget what it takes to manufacture automobiles when one sees the products of the line, the sleek, handsomely painted, chrome-bumpered automobiles stacked on railroad cars, the cars stretching block after block through Detroit, Kansas City, Los Angeles, through the sprawling suburbs. Certainly too the auto plant work is not at all akin to that of a century ago in the steel mills or to the work in the mines. Earl Bramblett says, "It's not a job for a professor, it's not a job for a journalist. A journalist or a professor would come into a plant and find that it's a bad place, that the jobs are not good jobs, that the plant is no place to work. But, then, we don't offer any jobs for professors or journalists. A bishop might come in, look around, and find it intolerable, inhumane, not good. But a bishop would make a bad assembler."

Bramblett argues, "This notion you hear, that here's a guy that's put on eight bolts for thirty years, that's a myth. There isn't any such person. Jobs change every year—models change." But a UAW woman says, "It's a myth in that instead of turning *eight* bolts, you might have to turn a dozen or more." Even John Z. DeLorean, the handsomely tailored general manager of GM's Chevrolet Division, the swinger among General Motors executives, a man who, at forty-nine, married the ravishingly beautiful Kelly Harmon, age nineteen, a man who had his jaw lifted to be even more handsome—even he concedes the many unpleasant jobs in the plants: "One thing about those kind of jobs is that they just don't get done, obviously, and you can't blame a man for not doing it."

Hank Ghant, president of Chrysler's UAW Local 212—

a black man who sang "Joe Hill" at Walter Reuther's funeral —says, "You see, a guy goes into a shop, you punch your time clock, and you've got a certain route, same as in the Army. You do something at a specific time . . . you punch your time card, put your coveralls on, you know, and you go to your job. You have your lunch break, you go back to your job, and you punch out and go home." Grady Glenn, a black who heads the UAW unit at the Ford Frame plant in the Rouge complex, says, "You get up and go to work at five o'clock in the morning, and be at work at 6:30. You go home, clean up and eat, read the paper, and it's bedtime. It's gotta be, if you want to go back to work the next morning." A worker at Ford's Wayne, Michigan, assembly plant says, "When you get inside that plant, it's just like you are in jail."

Ford's McKenna, the company's number two negotiator, says, "I don't think that the work that people are required to do today is demeaning. I don't consider that a man loses his dignity by working for his wage." That, he says, "has always been a little difficult for me to believe." But Irving Bluestone, director of the UAW's GM Department, says, "I just can't imagine that a worker" on the assembly line "can take pride in what he's doing. Just putting on nuts and bolts, you know, what the hell kind of pride can you take in that?"

Bannon says of the assembly line, "You're fighting this iron tiger. You're handcuffed to it. You don't get a fair chance at it. And every so often the big man comes over with his key, and unhandcuffs you, and then you can go get a cup of coffee or have a little break." Bannon declares: "You're actually handcuffed there . . . when that car comes down you better be there; you can't be at the water fountain, you can't be on the john, you can't be having a snack. You are handcuffed to that line because when that product comes to you, brother, you better be there."

Bannon believes the assembly line can be changed. One day in August 1970, during the negotiations at Ford, he was chatting at the bargaining table with Malcolm Denise. Suddenly, Bannon said, here, I've got an idea. He stood up and walked to the blackboard, took a piece of chalk, and outlined a new method of operating an assembly line. He drew an assembly line and the cars on it and said, why not, instead of moving the car down the line and having each worker perform his tasks as the car passes him, why don't we assign a team of workers to each car. Each team, he said, would move down the assembly line with a car, and instead of each man performing the single tasks, the team would build the car in its entirety, from start to finish. This way, Bannon said, workers would gain greater satisfaction in their work; they could feel that they had constructed something themselves, he said —that they were not merely tightening bolts. The quality of workmanship would improve, he said, and absenteeism would fall.

The Ford negotiators were surprised by the proposal—a proposal so revolutionary that not only would the company not institute the idea, but neither side gave it serious thought. The proposal received a flurry of publicity the next day, a slow news day, but it never made news again.

An essential part of assembly line work is that the workers do not have to think about what they are doing since their jobs are mechanical and rote. A General Motors worker at the Flint Buick plant: "When you're working on the line, you're right across from the same guy every hour, every day, and after the first three months, you know all about him, and what you get to discuss after that is make-believe, and it just adds to the boredom of it." Runnels—president of UAW Local 22, a man who worked on the Cadillac assembly line for thirteen years—recalls his first year in the plant: "I was nineteen then, and when you are nineteen years old, you've got a lot of dreams. So you've got things to think about. But I'll tell you one thing, you don't dream about staying in the plants."

One man, a retiree, was asked if he was proud of the years he had put in the plants. He said, "Yes—proud that I pulled through."

In more than a hundred interviews with workers, most of

them group interviews with four, five, or more workers, I was saddened by this fact: no more than a handful said they enjoyed their jobs. I interviewed four workers at GM's Fisher Two plant in Flint, one of three Flint plants where UAW members staged their sitdown in the winter of 1936–7, winning recognition for the UAW. I asked a worker: "Do you enjoy going to work in the morning?"

He said, "Can I ask you a question: Do you enjoy going to work?"

"Sure," I answered, "for the most part."

The worker was shocked. He could not conceive of anyone who might be happy going to work. He said, "I guess there are jobs that guys like."

Behind me, another GM worker, a man who up to that point had said nothing, asked, "You never worked in a factory?"

"No," I said.

"You're pretty fortunate, aren't you?" he said. He was angry.

"Yes," I said.

There are, of course, the immense improvements in shop conditions that the UAW has worked out in its negotiations with the auto companies since the 1930s. There is seniority and job security. There are the 23 minutes of relief time in the first 4 hours of a shift, the 23 minutes in the second 4 hours, the cleaner plants, the toilets with doors, the fans for ventilation. There are, Bramblett boasts, more than 15,000 in-plant vending machines. There are the 4 hours' guaranteed daily wages, and the 95 per cent of weekly take-home pay guaranteed during the annual model change; there were, as of 1970, 11 paid holidays each year.

Automation has also brought many gains and eased some of the work. Irving Bluestone, who for years served as Reuther's intellectual-in-residence: "In the machine shops, the feeder plants, the stamping plants, you wouldn't recognize the difference over the past generation . . . because it is here where the major technological advances have taken place."

GM's Bramblett was lured to Detroit from Georgia by the promise of big money in the plants and worked on an engine assembly line at General Motors from 1928 to 1934, man-handling crankshafts into place, this in the days before lifting devices—he spent more time in the plants than Reuther or Woodcock. Bramblett says, "We have engineered out of existence a lot of disagreeable jobs. When I worked on the line we handled the crankshaft by hand, and in a six-cylinder engine that weighed sixty-five pounds. . . . We picked them up in our hands, moved them to a fixture for checking, and put them in. Nowadays all the cranks are handled with lifting devices, counterbalances. So you can tiptoe them around, and you don't really have to exert a lot of physical energy."

Bramblett continues: "Another thing that comes to mind is the polishing of paint on a finished car. You had a big rag wheel and an electric motor that was quite heavy . . . it turned, rotated. There was polish on it. This created wind, dust. It was quite a hard physical job. Modern day paint techniques do not require that anymore.

"I'm not suggesting that a factory is a lounge," Bramblett says. "It's a work place." But, he concludes, "I would say there are a lot of heavy lifting jobs, disagreeable jobs, nasty jobs, that have been . . . improved . . ."

Even Woodcock believes, "The modern foundry is a much better place to work in than the foundry of ten and twenty years ago. Take the shake-out operation. A guy used to shake out those molds, and breathe all that dust and suffer all that heat." Now the shake-out operation is automated, and that, Woodcock says, "is a god-send."

William Connolly, a member of UAW Local 696, the Fisher Two local at Flint, who participated in the 1936–7 sit-down strike, remembers: "We were spitting tacks. We used to take a handful of tacks, put them in our mouths to do our work with. And kids would come in there, breaking in, and whoops, they'd swallow a tack. And the first thing the old-timers would do is tell them, 'Take a handful of cotton and swallow it right away.' The theory was that the cotton would wrap itself around the head of the tack and protect the stomach. I don't know if it worked or not. But we used to do it anyhow." Now, he said, "We no longer spit tacks. It's all staples and hog-rings."

Windshields, which weigh about thirty pounds, are now moved into place on automatic lifting arms, the windshields attached to the arms by huge suction cups. Mechanical hoists are used for swinging seats onto the line for installation, and there are now mechanical roof loaders that place roof sections on top of the bodies for welding; mechanical door positioners; machines that place floor pans in position for welding to the underbody; and devices that transfer the completed underbody to what is called the "body build truck," the wheeled platform on which the body is constructed. Side frame fixtures, as large as half the side of a car, are moved into place mechanically. All these machines perform jobs previously done by hand or with hoists that still required much physical effort. In addition, automatic welders have eliminated many demanding welding jobs, and safety in the plants is remarkably improved. General Motors says that "the most hazardous thing an employee does is to leave the plant."

To many workers, however, automation is an enemy. Not, as it was once feared, because it has eliminated jobs, but because, they say, it has increased production and given workers more tasks. Van Brooks, a worker at Chrysler Corporation's Jefferson Avenue assembly plant, said, "I'll say up until 1958, when you got up in the morning—under the work standards and the system we were working under—it was a pleasure to come out here and go to work and meet the fellows and work. You didn't have to work under a strain. But after the recession, and they commenced to drive you and putting in automation . . . putting on so much pressure and adding so

many jobs to you, then when you got up in the morning—
when you get up in the morning now, you say, 'Oh man, I
wish I didn't have to go to the plant today.' "

The UAW's Fraser believes that many tasks that have
been eliminated required at least some degree of dexterity
which gave the worker some challenge. In many cases, the
jobs that had been left, Fraser said, are the most monotonous,
least demanding jobs. He said, "In an auto plant fifteen years
ago, there used to be some very fine jobs, what we called semi-
skills. The internal-external grinder, the trimmer, jobs like
this where you can use a little ingenuity and individuality and
some skill, and you could sort of beat the game by finding
short cuts. Now . . . I suspect when all these jobs were automated out of existence, some of the most interesting jobs
disappeared. And this has hurt the system."

There are ways a worker can improve his lot. If he
performs well and is nominated by his supervisors, he can be
promoted to foreman and earn a 25 per cent increase in pay.
He can apply to become a skilled tradesman, and earn the
skilled trades' higher wages. Yet few workers show interest in
becoming foremen, despite the fact that it seems a natural
goal. "The tension is too great," says Fraser. "The kids are
extremely difficult to discipline, if not impossible. They [the
foremen] are afraid of confrontation with the blacks . . .
there are all sorts of pressures." And the skilled trades are
often closed trades, especially to blacks.

The easiest and most frequently used way to get out of
the shops is to quit. There is another method of escape: staying
home, or at least off the line. Absenteeism, which traditionally
ran at a rate of about 2.5 per cent of the work force, has
soared in the last five years to a frightening 5 per cent or so.
GM's Bramblett says that on Fridays and Mondays, or on
Thursdays when Thursday is payday, "it's not wild to have
ten per cent of the people absent." It would seem that the ab-

senteeism rate would be highest in the most disagreeable jobs. But, in a Chrysler glass plant, a place that the UAW's Fraser called "scrupulously clean, very quiet, by the nature of the operation," the absenteeism rate stands at 8 to 9 per cent in the middle of the week and around 15 per cent on Fridays and Mondays. Before the statistics were known, Woodcock said, "I would have said, 'Oh, no, no, no, they [the glass plant figures] would be lower—assembly plants would be highest.'" He confesses, "It's all very puzzling."

Many of the workers who stay off the jobs are younger employees who feel they can make enough money in three or four days to meet their needs. A Chrysler worker says of the young workers, "They don't resist authority, but they don't like to be driven. And this is what most auto plants are trying to do today, drive." A surprising number of older workers sympathize with the young people on this point. "The younger generation is not going to take the crap that we had to take," said a retired UAW worker, and a friend added immediately, "They got more sense."

Black workers also contribute to the absenteeism rate: one can see them on Friday afternoon, after payday, sitting on car hoods in the parking lots behind a block-long string of bars across from Chrysler Corporation's Dodge main plant, drinking beer, whisky, and Boone's Farm Apple Wine. Often they do not return to work those Friday afternoons. Yet it is not shiftlessness; many workers, both young and old, black and white, stay home in rebellion. Grady Glenn, president of the Ford frame plant local: "Young people . . . won't accept the conditions their fathers accepted. It's much harder to tie young, black guys to the assembly line than it was thirty years ago."

In July 1970—days before the negotiations began—at 4:55 on a Wednesday afternoon shift, a thirty-six-year-old black employee of the Chrysler Corporation, James Johnson, Jr., walked into the Eldon Avenue axle plant, pulled an M-1 carbine from his pant leg, loaded it with a thirty-round banana clip, and went on a wild killing spree. "He's firing at everyone in white shirts," a worker cried. It is the foremen who wear white shirts. Within minutes, three men were dead: a foreman who had suspended Johnson for insubordination an hour before, plus another foreman, and a job setter. Johnson told the UAW committeeman who captured him, "They took me off the job I had held for two years and put a man with less seniority in my place."

That shooting made banner headlines, but was only one of several violent incidents in the plants. A man was killed in a shooting in another Chrysler plant the same month, and a teen-ager was shot dead in a General Motors plant. There have been other shootings, as well as many cases involving the display of weapons. According to James McGahey, president of the 23,000-member United Plant Guards, "There has been an extensive increase in incidents of assault with deadly weapons, the use of narcotics and a complete breakdown of respect for plant guards." He thinks—although the estimate is high—that probably as many as 60 per cent of the auto-mobile workers have guns on their person or in their cars or lockers.

Nelson Jack Edwards, a black UAW board member, says of the Johnson incident in heavy understatement, "We're not in sympathy with that kind of action." A majority of black workers agree with Edwards; they see themselves making progress and remain allied with the UAW. But other blacks see it differently. Glenn: "I can very easily see what provoked this guy James Johnson at Eldon." To the Congress of Black Workers, a coalition that is the enemy of both the companies and the UAW, Johnson was a hero. The revolutionary black newspaper, Detroit's *Inner-City Voice,* proclaimed in a red headline: ALL HAIL BROTHER JAMES JOHNSON.

The fact is that blacks are still making only small inroads into the skilled trades and foreman ranks. They tend to have the lowest paid, most disagreeable and difficult assembly line jobs. With no seniority they are the first laid off, as was demon-strated when hundreds of hard-core black "unemployables" hired in a well-publicized drive after the Detroit riot, were let go as the recession worsened in the summer and fall of 1970. A General Motors Pontiac plant has employed a crew of men to go into toilets to paint over racial slurs written on the walls. In lunchrooms, blacks usually sit with blacks, whites with whites. A UAW Chrysler committeeman says that for a black to obtain a supervisory position he must in most cases be friendly with a black who has already advanced, or he must ingratiate himself with white supervisors. Of discrimination, he said, "There's no question about it. . . . They're a little sneakier with it, but it still exists."

Negro workers band together, and this, Fraser believes, produces "some cases . . . where whites are discriminated against." Racial antagonisms on both sides run high. Foremen are often reluctant to discipline. Many insubordinate acts go unpunished. A UAW committeeman says, "You never know if a guy is going to pull out a gun and shoot you or what."

A militant black worker, member of the revolutionary movement, predicted, "The brothers aren't going to take this shit no more." Another militant: "The morning the *Free Press* came out with the front-page headline of the shooting in the Eldon plant, this blood came in that had been off for two days, see, and the foreman said to the blood, real tough, see, 'Come here. Where you been?' I took the front page of the fucking *Free Press* and I went over there and held it up to his fucking face. He turned his back."

Johnson's defense attorneys, members of a radical Detroit law firm, contended during a three week trial that the pressures of being a poor black from the rural South, combined with the strain of working on the assembly line, had made Johnson temporarily insane at the time of the shootings. The jury members, two of them factory workers and three of them the wives of factory workers, toured the plant, which had been cleaned and painted for the occasion. The jurors also heard testimony about harsh treatment of workers, violence, and poor working conditions at the Eldon Avenue plant. In May 1971, in a stunning decision, the jury found Johnson innocent because of temporary insanity and committed him to a state hospital. "Did you see the cement room in that plant?" one juror cried during deliberations. "Working there would drive anyone crazy."

In 1969, Malcolm Denise, vice president of labor relations for the Ford Motor Company, delivered a private address to a group of management executives. (The UAW pirated a copy of the speech and made it public during the 1970 talks.) Denise declared, "Employees in the seventies . . . will be even less willing [than they have been in recent years] to put up with dirty and uncomfortable working conditions, even less likely to accept the unvarying pace and functions on moving lines." He went on: "Large numbers of those we hire find factory life so distasteful that they quit after only a brief exposure."

Two questions come to mind: Must factories always be distasteful places to work? Will men who work in them always be looked down upon?

Some changes are being made to counteract the drudgery of the factory. John DeLorean, general manager of the Chevrolet division, insists—with much hyperbole—that at the new General Motors Vega plant in Lordstown, Ohio, the most automated plant in American automotive history, "Every tedious job has been eliminated from the assembly line." Chrysler Corporation experimented with S&H Green Stamps at its Mound Road plant, giving trading stamps each month to workers with perfect attendance records. Some foremen have been given sensitivity training.

The UAW has made specific proposals: voluntary overtime, so that only those workers who want additional hours will have to work them; inverse seniority, so that older employees can, if they wish, be home during layoffs and new employees can earn more. Nelson Jack Edwards would allow employees to declare how many days a week they wish to work. This would permit the younger employees, who add so much to absentee rates, to take off the time they wish, and allow the companies to plan for this. If, as John Kenneth Galbraith writes, overtime broke "the barbarous uniformity of the weekly wage" that assumed that "all families have the same tastes, needs," this "undertime" proposal would go far toward meeting particular needs of individuals and families. Yet such proposals go by the boards when the negotiations get down to money, and even if they were enacted, they do not get to the heart of the matter: the system. Auto and union men alike say that it is the system—the assembly line, the emphasis on productivity— that makes the auto industry, for better or worse, what it is.

The auto executives know there is discontent in the shops; the staff psychologists and psychiatrists say so. The company reports also say so by listing the number of seats ripped off toilets, the absenteeism rates, the vandalism, the parking lot crime, the turnover, the sabotage. The executives point out that millions of American workers, white- and blue-collar, are unhappy. Lee A. Iacocca, president of Ford: "What the hell. I have tough days. It's boring as hell up here sometimes. Some guys can't wait to get a white collar on and work in a computer center feeding cards. And *that's* monotonous. That's *really* monotonous."

Most auto executives believe that while, in the words of Ford's McKenna, "We're frank to admit that working on the line is different than working in a bank or supermarket," the drudgery, the physical exertion, the monotony of the shop are exaggerated. Or they believe, simply, that many jobs are tough—that it is time the workers, and the industrial psychologists, accept this. It is time that workers start showing up promptly, start giving their all—and stop complaining. "The truth of the matter," says Earl Bramblett, "is that GM jobs are good jobs."

To many people, however, the assembly line is a cruel, dehumanizing place, one that should not, need not, be tolerated in a nation as rich and technologically advanced and as professedly concerned with human dignity as America.

Through the years, critics have suggested many reforms:

job rotation, job enlargement, participatory management, Ken Bannon's "team" proposal. Walker and Guest, using suggestions of the workers themselves, proposed in *The Man on the Assembly Line* that rest periods be increased and, where possible, that the companies allow workers to create "banks" and to "work up the line"—that is, to work as fast as they wish so that they can get ahead of their job—say, build up a stack of fenders or tires, and then rest. They called for "real communication" of mutual interest to tell each other about the assembly of automobiles.

Bell, in *Work and Its Discontents*, recommended extensive use of multipurpose automatic machinery which, he said, would bring about "decentralization of the industry . . . [construction of] new plants away from major cities." He declared: "If one hopes to consider the worker as more than a part of 'human relations' . . . his job must not only feed his body; it must sustain his spirit."

Dr. Stanley Seashore, a psychologist with the Institute for Social Research at the University of Michigan, says that auto companies must learn to "minimize status differences and maximize learning." He says changes will come not by increasing salaries and fringe benefits—normal results of company–union negotiations—but when "some manufacturer takes a hell of a big risk and makes a dramatic change in the whole philosophy of the organization, the conception of the relations between the management and the employees, between the employer and the community."

Dr. Christopher Argyris, a Yale University psychologist, warns that people "must stop assuming that the humdrum, programmed life that a worker now leads is going to be changed" drastically, no matter what a company might do. But he says that while there are limits to change, much change can come. "You can make jobs attractive enough so that the worker has the chance to experience some meaningfulness, some growth in his life."

Dr. Edward Lawler, a Yale psychologist, says that a "sort of class racism—classism" exists in which managers say, " 'Those guys don't have anything to offer and therefore we don't ask. And when we do ask they don't really say very much.' Well, there are a lot of reasons why they don't say very much, including the fact that they're rarely asked." Ross Stegner, a psychologist at Wayne State University, says, "We may have to abandon some of the efficiencies of assembly line production and go back to small factories where people work as a congenial group."

Dr. David Whitsett, vice president of a Manhattan industrial consulting firm and a consultant to General Motors, says, "I always tell them [GM] that there are two things they ought to do. They ought to automate those jobs as fast as possible—and they're doing that, really—no human being should be required to do that kind of work . . . And the other thing is to stop kidding these people by giving them the big picture, this kind of nonsense where you go down and tell a guy he's building America, that kind of bullshit. The poor bastard ought to be left alone and not tortured with that kind of nonsense. He knows better. He puts bolts on wheels, that's what he does. Let's not kid him by calling it something else." In obvious response to this attitude, the Ford Motor Company has produced a film, called *Don't Paint It Like Disneyland*, which attempts to give the employee an accurate picture of the drudgery of factory life. It is perhaps the most candid look that a company has given its employees, and viewers are told, "It's a drag at first, but you realize you got to do it, so you do it."

Victor Reuther, the last surviving of the three Reuther brothers and long-time director of the UAW's international office, suggests that union and management join as partners to improve work conditions. "If the union is to be forced solely into a position of a negative attack on the corporate structure . . . then it will constantly remain in a combative position. If the trade union, however, is invited to play a constructive role in these areas—in the problem of absenteeism, the prob-

lem of drugs, the problem of joint participation in the training of workers—then I think the whole relationship between
the union and management can undergo a significant change."

Workers can, if they wish, be allowed to participate in what
are considered management decisions—how jobs and plants
are designed, how quality can be improved and costs reduced,
what products should be made and at what costs they will be
sold. Men and women can be promoted out of factories into
management positions, instead of giving virtually all these
jobs to college graduates who enter factories at wage scales
higher than those of men and women who have spent their
lives in the plants. Why should workers be condemned to
menial jobs in factories for the rest of their lives because of
mistakes or problems encountered in their youth—dropping
out of high school or marrying early? Difficult jobs could, like
medical internships, be considered steppingstones to a better
future. Factories can be designed to allow the workers to
establish human contact with other workers. Why can't plants
be air conditioned like offices? The executive who says that it
is too costly to air condition a plant is usually sitting in an
air-conditioned office.

Worker councils, inside or outside the union, can be created
to allow those workers who wish it a voice in running their
companies. Workers, inside or outside the union, can be placed
on boards of directors. The key to all this is to grant that men
and women in factories are not morons—not the oxen that
Frederick Winslow Taylor, father of the time study, called
them—but men and women of intelligence and aspiration and
importance. If this is done, industry and labor can make immense strides toward realization of that old picket line slogan
to which neither has given much importance: Humanize the
factories.

In mid-August 1970, as negotiations proceeded in low
gear, Irving Bluestone questioned just how sincere the company was when it talked about improving plant conditions: "To

say that a factory is an ugly, lousy place to work may be true, but that doesn't mean it can't be made accommodating to the worker's needs, accommodating to his comforts. Because it can be. They [the companies] take much greater pains to do this for their white-collar workers than they do for their blue-collar workers, because they still believe in the double standard." Bluestone went on: "It's just a matter of, are you willing to make the effort to make these comforts available to the workers? My own feeling is, it would make one hell of a difference in reducing absenteeism and in terms of the workers' attitudes toward the job." The problem, Bluestone said, is that the companies are in business not to serve people but to make money. They're not even, he said, in business to make autos. "If they could make more money making another product, they'd go into that line of business. They're in business to make money. This is the motivation of our system."

To automobile executives—top men like Henry Ford II, Lee Iacocca, James M. Roche, Edward N. Cole, Richard Gerstenberg, Lynn Townsend, and thousands of middle echelon executives, division managers, plant managers, sales managers, superintendents, accountants, engineers, the men from whose ranks the future generation of automobile leaders will come—to these men such criticism and proposals are, at minimum, impractical. At the extreme, they are utopian claptrap.

The intellectuals say the executives are difficult to work with. Dr. Louis Davis, a UCLA psychologist, says that one of the difficulties of working with management "is to try and convince them that what they are seeing is a consequence of what they have asked for." The executives, in reply, say they are doing what they can to improve plant life—new plants, noise abatement programs, elimination of unpleasant jobs—within the limits of practicality, their obligations as employers, and the finances they feel they can address to the problem.

Critics condemn the companies for negligence in improving factory conditions, but they also have harsh words for the union, despite the fact that the UAW is probably the most socially concerned of the major unions in the country.

Most unions, says Davis, see jobs only "in terms of the number of people who can be working and the amount of money per hour that can be gotten," and the UAW is in this sense culpable. Companies strive to reach accommodation with the unions, he says, and as the unions are mostly concerned with money, the result is that both sides help inflate wages and the cost of fringe benefits, and do little toward improving work environments.

Dr. Whitsett, the consultant to GM, says that the worker's reaction is: "OK, if you're going to make me do something this stupid, if you're going to torture me this badly all day long, then I'm going to make you pay through the nose . . . because all I can get from you is money." He says, "Then management looks at the workers and says, 'Look, what money grubbers— all they want is money.' That isn't all they want; it's all they can get."

Auto officials often imply—they never say it outright, only suggest it in private conversations—that the men and women who work in auto plants are unambitious, that if they had the characteristic American drive to get ahead, to better themselves, they would not be in the plants. To this, the UAW's Douglas Fraser replies, "When a guy tells you the workers are not like you and me, that's nonsense. It's precisely because they are like you and me that the companies are having the goddamn problem. The workers are thinking, 'What the hell am I doing here?' "

Chapter 8

Agreement

On the morning of November 5, 1970, Ernest Moran, Leonard Woodcock's assistant, wanted a coffee. He stepped into Shapero's Drugstore in the lobby of the General Motors Building, ordered one, black, to go, and walked out, carrying it in a paper sack. There, standing by the elevators, as if he were just another of the 3,500 blue- or gray-suited General Motors men who work in the building, was James M. Roche, corporation chairman. This was odd, Moran knew, for usually when Roche comes to work, he is driven into the basement garage, from which he takes an executive elevator to his office. But this morning, for no real reason, he had been let out on West Grand Boulevard, and had walked into the building.

The occasion presented an excellent opportunity for Moran. The union leadership had not yet decided how to make its request that Woodcock see Roche; certainly the leaders did not wish to anger the General Motors negotiators by asking to be allowed to go over their heads. Yet it was important that Woodcock see Roche—and here Roche was, motioning for Moran, whom he has known for years, to come over. Good morning, Ernie, Roche said. Good morning, Jim, Moran said. How long, Roche asked, is this strike going to continue? The two sides, he said, must work to end the strike by Christmas. Yes, Moran said, the strike must end. He asked: Would Roche mind if Woodcock came to see him? Of course not, Roche said. He said he had told Woodcock weeks ago that he could visit any time he wished. I hope he will come, Roche said. The elevator opened, Roche stepped in and rode to his office on the fourteenth floor.

Roche's remark that he had told Woodcock they could meet any time Woodcock wished was a reference to a conversation the two had early in August. Both men are members of the president's productivity commission, and after a meeting at the Executive Office Building in Washington and cocktails at the White House, Roche asked Woodcock whether he would like a ride back to Detroit in the General Motors plane, an invitation that piqued Bramblett when he learned of it. Woodcock and Nat Weinberg, the union's research director, who was with him, accepted the offer. Usually, the plane lands at Pontiac, a blighted industrial suburb north of Detroit, where the plane is berthed, but Roche directed the pilot to land at Detroit's Metropolitan Airport. A General Motors limousine met them and Woodcock and Weinberg were driven to Weinberg's car. While Woodcock was retrieving his luggage from the limousine, he told Roche that he would like to talk with him one of these days. Roche replied that they might talk any time.

During the negotiations, however, corporation negotiators made it clear to Bluestone and Moran that they did not believe it would be wise for Woodcock to bypass them and see Roche; progress could best be made, they said, through normal channels. Woodcock, recognizing that the negotiators were protecting their own positions, found this insistence on protocol amusing, and he mentioned Roche's invitation at the bargaining table to needle the corporation men. Of course, he was told, he could see Roche—he could do so whenever he wished. But Woodcock knew the negotiators did not mean this and he did not pursue the matter.

Now, on the fifth floor, shortly after Moran chanced upon Roche in the lobby, Bramblett approached Woodcock and said that Roche would be happy to see him, but if Woodcock wished to see Roche that day, the meeting would have to be

before 1 p.m., because Roche was scheduled to leave town
that afternoon—to attend another meeting of the president's
productivity commission.

The union leadership conferred to determine whether
Woodcock should see Roche alone or take a delegation with
him. It was decided that others would add nothing and Woodcock should go alone. At 12:55, Woodcock left the negotiation
rooms and walked down the corridor toward the elevators. In
front of him, in the hall, he saw a clutch of reporters, perhaps
thirty or forty; the media were carrying stories of an imminent
break in the talks, and many national reporters who had left
Detroit when the talks had settled into boring routine had
hastily reassembled. Woodcock dislikes reporters, but he also
dislikes subterfuge and did not wish to go out of his way
to avoid the reporters. But his aides intervened. He must not,
they said, be seen taking an elevator upstairs; there was only
one floor he could be heading toward, the executive floor, and
this would fuel speculation that a break in the talks was near.
Woodcock consented, turned, and walked to another bank of
elevators in the rear of the bargaining area where, unobserved,
he rode to the fourteenth floor.

The chairman's office is handsome and comfortable, car-
peted in light green and paneled in walnut, but it is an under-
stated office, understatement being a General Motors tradition. It is a home away from home: a few steps away is an
apartment where the chairman spends several nights each year
when the press of business becomes heavy. The practice dates
to the days of Alfred P. Sloan, Jr., who, when he came to
Detroit two weeks out of each month, often did not emerge
from the General Motors Building from the day he arrived
from New York until the day he returned.

Woodcock entered through a large outer office, walking
past Roche's secretary, Gertrude Wolter, a pleasant woman
who, like so many secretaries of top men in the automotive
industry, has worked for her boss many years—in this case,
ever since Roche was a personnel man at Cadillac. The automotive secretaries, unlike secretaries of politicians or kings,

take to their graves the many secrets and the private information which no doubt would bring them much money if they
wished to write of their years with the corporation.

Inside the chairman's office, Woodcock shook hands with
Roche, somewhat surprised to find Bramblett there, for he had
expected Roche to be alone. But Bramblett's presence did not
disturb him. The talk was between Woodcock and Roche:
Bramblett said little.

If anyone except Roche had been running General Motors,
the union would not have attempted to visit the chairman;
it would have been fruitless. This is not to say that visiting
with the corporation chairman or president is unique. The
president of the union and the presidents or chairmen of the
automobile corporations visit each other several times during
the year, in private meetings and at civic functions. Lower
echelon union and corporation men also visit with one another; some carry the telephone numbers of their counterparts
in their billfolds so they may call them when matters arise that
demand immediate attention. But the corporation chairman
and the union president had never met to discuss how to
settle a strike.

So they talked for twenty minutes, the president of the
United Automobile Workers, the nation's most ambitious,
robust union, and the chairman of the world's largest industrial
firm; the one-time Socialist and supporter of Norman Thomas,
and the quintessential American industrialist who, left father-
less as a child, unable to attend college, had through hard work
and dedication risen to the top of American business, risen to
become chairman of the nation's most important business enterprise.

Roche is the archetype of the General Motors man—
the model created by Sloan, Roche's predecessor—the man
who, as Peter F. Drucker has said of the modern corporation
executive, is both master and servant of the corporation.

Gentle, even shy, Roche was, from the corporation's point of view, the perfect man to deal with the problems that faced General Motors in the 1960s and 1970s, the problems of safety, pollution, and consumerism. He was the perfect man for the union to seek out to help bring a settlement in the 1970 strike: friendly, likable, respected, considered to have, within corporation definitions, a genuine interest in the lot of the workers.

While in many ways the complete General Motors man, Roche is personally unlike most of his predecessors. Sloan was aloof and impersonal; hard of hearing, he was embarrassed and often silent except in the presence of men he had known for years. Harlow Curtice was cold and tough, a man who liked to chop people up, who enjoyed making the unemotional decisions required in business. Frederic Donner, rough and demanding, delighted in obtaining information about his subordinates and tucking the information away for a time when it might be needed. If Roche resembles any of the past General Motors leaders, it is Charles E. Wilson, who, despite his tough exterior—when he went to Washington as secretary of defense in 1953, he antagonized senators by calling them "you men" —was a warm man, a man who welcomed Walter Reuther's visits, a man whose funeral Reuther attended because he sincerely wished to show his respect.

Roche was born in December 1906, in Elgin, Illinois, a quiet, tree-shaded town fifty miles west of Chicago, a town that harks of the writings of William Inge or Sherwood Anderson. His grandparents had come to America from Ireland during the mid-1880s, and his grandfather had become one of the community's leading citizens, an executive with the Elgin Watch Company, then the world's largest maker of watches, and a community booster, leading a campaign for good roads at the turn of the century when the automobile first appeared on Elgin streets. Roche's father was a successful undertaker and his mother a schoolteacher—the family was highly respected in the community.

In 1919, when Roche was twelve, his father died in the terrible influenza epidemic that swept America, his death coming a few days after he had gone to what is now Great Lakes Naval Training Center to help embalm the bodies of influenza victims. To this day people in Elgin recall the courage of the Roche family after the father's death. The family moved in with an uncle, and Roche's mother supported them by teaching. As a boy, Roche peddled the local paper, worked in a notions store after school and on Saturdays, and mowed lawns, all to make extra money. He considers this work a valuable experience; he says that today, when so many young people have so much given to them, "I feel very sorry for any kid who finishes high school and is sent off to college without having had some kind of job."

Young Roche was a good but not gifted student; perseverance, not brilliance, won him good grades. When he was graduated from Elgin High School in 1923, the yearbook, the *Maroon*, inexplicably called him "the sheik of '23." Because of the death of his father, he could not attend college, and when he finished high school he accepted a position as a clerk with the gas and electric company in Aurora, Illinois, twenty miles away; at night he studied accounting and economics from a correspondence school. The job was dull and Roche disliked it. He was attracted instead to the booming automobile business, and in 1927, he obtained a position as a statistician with the Cadillac Motor Car Division, which William Crapo Durant had brought into General Motors two decades before.

Soon Roche was recognized as an expert on business management. He was given positions in Boston and New York and, in 1932, he was brought to the Cadillac home office in Detroit.

In May 1943, as Cadillac was building up its work force for increased defense production, Roche was named to the new and important post of director of personnel, with responsibility for salary and wage administration, employment, and employee communications, for conducting negotiations with the still young, turbulent United Automobile Workers, and for handling problems that came with the influx of new workers —Southern whites, blacks, and women—who were coming to Detroit to earn big money in the car plants.

Roche performed admirably, a reserved, gentlemanly man, a welcome change to union men used to the tough, unbending corporation men like Sloan, Harry Anderson, and Harry Coen. In some ways Roche was ahead of the union, for he was appalled by segregation in the plants, by the separate black and white drinking fountains, the refusal of whites to eat with blacks, and the threats of whites to strike if blacks were promoted above them. When he appealed to the United Automobile Workers for help in combating these practices, the union leaders refused because they did not wish to confront the white membership. Roche went ahead on his own and succeeded in bringing some integration to the Cadillac plants.

Roche rose steadily, but not quickly. In 1949, he was made director of Cadillac public relations, in addition to his position as head of personnel. In 1950, he became general sales manager and directed the division to its first 100,000 car year. In 1955, when the automobile industry set a record of 7.9 million sales—this was the era of the tail light and tail fin—Cadillac sold 143,000 units, a record that was to stand until the 1960s. On January 1, 1957, Roche, then fifty, was named Cadillac general manager and a General Motors vice president. In 1960, after thirty-three years with Cadillac, he was promoted to vice president of what is now the corporation's marketing staff, with responsibilities for sales, marketing, service, advertising, parts, and dealer relationships.

By now Roche had caught the eye of Frederic Donner, the General Motors chairman, and in the 1960s he emerged as something of a Donner protégé. In 1962, he was jumped over a number of senior men and named executive vice president in charge of overseas operations; in June 1965, Roche was elevated to the presidency. And while Donner is remembered by most people as an acerbic, steely man, he is remembered by Roche, understandably, as one of the warmest, most friendly men Roche has ever met.

When he was named president, Roche was an anonymous man to most of the American public, just another name on the business pages, another face in the corporation's annual report. But this was to change.

Ralph Nader had just finished his book on the automobile industry, working feverishly, turning it out in ten weeks. General Motors runs an excellent intelligence network and knew as early as the summer of 1965 that Nader was preparing a book on automobile safety, that he was a foe of the auto makers, and had written anti-industry stories beginning in the late 1950s in *The New Republic* and *The Nation*. In November 1965, before Nader's *Unsafe at Any Speed* was published, an investigation was ordered into Nader's background; nothing was found. General Motors was not deterred. In February 1966, a New York detective, Vincent Gillen, a former FBI agent, was retained for another investigation, for which General Motors ultimately paid 6,700 dollars. Later, in congressional testimony, Aloysius F. Power, head of GM's legal department, said he ordered the inquiry because Nader was a "mystery man" and because, although Nader was a lawyer, he did not maintain a law office. He said the corporation wished to determine whether Nader was connected with lawyers pushing cases against General Motors involving GM's Corvair, which Nader vigorously attacked in his book. Such investigations were accepted, normal practice. "It was something you always do," says a General Motors executive of that time. "It wasn't a big deal."*

---

* David Lewis, the former General Motors public relations man, recalls a luncheon with a member of the General Motors legal staff, shortly after *Unsafe at Any Speed* was published. The staff member informed Lewis that the legal staff was investigating Nader and, Lewis recalls, that it would "make a case for him being a homosexual and an anti-Semite." Lewis says: "I

Nader began to report that he was receiving anonymous telephone calls and that he was being tailed. In early March 1966, stories broke in *The New York Times* and *The New Republic* that Nader was being investigated by private detectives. Industry men, including men at General Motors, denied that they had taken part in the investigation. "You can bet that if one of us was doing it, it would be a lot smoother," one man told *The New York Times*. "If we were checking up on Nader he'd never know about it."

The night of March 8, as lights burned late in the General Motors Building and yet another denial was being drafted, a corporation man contacted Roche, who was staying late to oversee this important matter. *There is something you must know*, he said. *We have had detectives investigating Nader*. The next night, shortly before eleven p.m., after the first editions of morning newspapers were on the streets, the corporation released a statement written at Roche's direction: General Motors, it said, had conducted a "routine investigation through a reputable law firm to determine whether Ralph Nader was acting on behalf of litigants or their attorneys in Corvair-design cases pending against General Motors." Such investigations, the statement said, were "a well-known and accepted practice in the legal profession."

This was one of the most embarrassing moments in the history of the corporation. Donner, the chairman, was away, visiting New Zealand and Australia, and he did not return during the affair. Some of the top men in the corporation wanted to camouflage what General Motors had done. Others, particularly men in the legal department whose necks were on the line, wanted to attack, to say, yes, the corporation had con-

---

replied that I found it difficult to believe that the corporation would conduct such an investigation—that GM could . . . stoop so low as to smear anyone in that manner. I was assured that the corporation was indeed going to smear Nader and that, after it had done so, Nader would stand discredited. Anything he might say or do afterward . . . would carry no weight with the great American public."

ducted the investigation, but this was what any corporation would do under similar circumstances.

Roche listened to the advice for a long time. Finally, he made a decision: there was, he said, but one course of action. *We must go to Washington and apologize.* Many were shocked; we must not apologize, they said. General Motors must never apologize. *Goddammit,* Roche replied, *what the hell do you want me to do? This is the only thing that can be done.*

Two weeks later, on March 22, Roche appeared before the Senate subcommittee, chaired by Senator Abraham Ribicoff, that was conducting hearings on automobile safety. "This investigation [of Nader] was initiated, conducted and completed without my knowledge or consent of any member of our governing committee," Roche said. The investigation, he said, was unworthy of General Motors. "To the extent that GM bears responsibility, I want to apologize here and now to the members of the subcommittee and Mr. Nader. I sincerely hope that these apologies will be accepted."

It was an excellent performance. Ribicoff and Senator Robert Kennedy, another committee member, praised Roche. Nader, who later settled, out of court, the 26 million dollar law suit stemming from the incident for 425,000 dollars—although he had said he would never settle out of court—concedes that Roche was the perfect man to make the apology—a "kindly, grandfatherly figure." Said a journalist who covered GM at the time of the apology: "Christ, he looked like he enjoyed it."

But Roche did not enjoy that moment. He had been a friend of Aloysius Power's; for years, Roche, Power, and two other General Motors executives had played golf together every weekend at the Orchard Lake Country Club. After the Nader episode, Roche and Power never golfed together again. Even today Roche cannot erase the incident from his mind. In the spring of 1971, when a reporter said to Roche, "I guess it is about five years this month since you were put in the position of going to Washington to testify before the Ribicoff subcommittee regarding Mr. Nader," Roche replied, "It's been five years ago March 22, ten a.m."

It is an axiom at General Motors that each chairman is named to his position—the choice is made by the outgoing chairman and a few top board members, the decision then perfunctorily ratified by the board of directors—because he possesses qualities uniquely suited to deal with the problems the corporation will face during his years in office. It is not clear whether this is luck or whether the corporation men, when it comes time to select a new chairman, look into the future and attempt to determine what the corporation's problems will be and who is best suited to lead the corporation during that time. Probably it is luck. Whatever, it is true that each top man has been admirably equipped to deal with the problems at hand: Sloan was a genius at organization and marketing at a time when the corporation needed an organization plan and needed to develop a full product line, and at a time when the market seemed saturated with automobiles; Knudsen was a production man in an era when the corporation needed to redesign the Chevrolet and establish new plans to overtake Henry Ford and his Model T; Charles E. Wilson was an engineer at a time—World War II and the postwar years—when engineering talents were needed, first to direct retooling for defense production and then to establish a postwar car line; Curtice was a master salesman, this in the 1950s, the time of American chrome, the big selling years when a salesman's talents were needed; Donner was a finance expert, well suited to lead the corporation first when money was tight and afterward when the corporation, making money easily, was expanding into markets overseas.

In the months following the Nader incident, a difficult period that brought intensified attacks on the corporation and the automobile industry, including passage of the Highway Safety Act in May 1966, Roche handled himself flawlessly. He made few enemies within the corporation and no key people

said harsh words about him. As Donner and other top men
looked around, sure that the pressures on the corporation
would mount, it was clear that Roche, with his long experience
in dealing with people and in public relations, could best meet
the problems of the 1960s and 1970s: safety, pollution, credi-
bility, consumerism. In November 1967, when Donner stepped
down, the board of directors, at his request, named Roche to
succeed him.

In his four years as chairman, Roche displeased many
people both inside and outside the corporation. He opened
new avenues for the corporation, yet was the target of more
vilification than any chairman since Alfred P. Sloan at the time
of the sitdown strikes.

In the opinion of many people within General Motors—
from the short-haired, middle class young men it recruits to
begin the forty-years' climb through its executive ranks, to the
men who have already made that climb, the top managers—
Roche has been too soft with the critics. What is more, as
chairman he must accept blame for the eroded profit picture
of the late 1960s. There are men in the corporation today who
still wonder why Roche did it, why he went to Washington to
apologize before the nation for the corporation's hiring of
detectives to trail Nader. That act, these men believe, made
Ralph Nader and, by so doing, made the safety issue, the
pollution issue, the consumer movement. That spectacle, that
tableau of Roche humbling himself and humbling the corporation, angers these men to this day. Similarly, many plant managers and foremen, the men charged with production, resented
Roche's decision that hard-core unemployed—blacks—be
brought into the work force, for this reduced efficiency and
gave them what they considered unneeded problems. Yet
Michael Hamlin, a leader of the revolutionary Congress of
Black Workers in Detroit, calls Roche "the Jay Gould of the
20th Century." Nader describes him as the "perfect organization man for the turmoil General Motors has gone through in
the last five years; he gives the demeanor of a venerable dea-
con. He doesn't alienate people . . . he's very dedicated; he's

got a personal life above reproach; he's religious, and so on."
But, Nader insists: "You've seen those people in charge of
concentration camps—by that I mean personal qualities have
nothing to do with a man's ability to assume an organizational
ethic which is very cruel and very fraudulent in its impact
upon people."

Nevertheless, it can be argued that Roche, directing the
corporation in a time of unprecedented attack, has done a
masterly job of blunting the corporation's critics and sending
some away demoralized, of holding the corporation together.
And while the corporation's efforts on the social front are
insignificant in light of the enormity of the problems that
confront the nation, and compared to the power and prestige
that General Motors could bring to bear to attack them, General Motors has made a number of advances during the Roche
regime, including the hiring of more blacks at both the white-
and blue-collar levels, the appointment of a black to the
corporation's board of directors, the donation of funds to
build low-cost housing, the deposit of GM money in black-
owned banks. He has done more to push the corporation than
his predecessors would have. "If Donner had been running
the corporation," says a scholar of General Motors, "I don't
know where the thing would be today."

Roche—an unlikely man for this captaincy, a soft-looking
man with soft arms and face, somewhat soft now, too, of neck
and stomach, with a bad leg because of varicose veins; a soft-
talking man whose voice sometimes breaks into stutters and
whose hands, when he is nervous, shake like summer leaves—
Roche believes there is no sacrifice that cannot be made, as
Alfred P. Sloan, Jr., said years ago, no demand that cannot be
met if one is to fully serve the corporation. In both Sloan's
terms and his own, Roche has fulfilled his responsibilities as
a General Motors man.

He was once asked what he wished to be remembered
for. What would he want to have inscribed on a plaque in the
lobby of the General Motors Building when he is dead?

"We do not erect plaques," he said.

But surely, he was asked, he would want his work recalled. Surely he would want to be remembered.

Yes, he said, he would. When he is retired, when he is gone, he would want the "satisfaction of having had the responsibility for guiding the corporation through this difficult period. And hopefully given some credit for having recognized some of these problems and doing something about them."

Now, in Roche's office, Woodcock told Roche that he was worried. Despite the news blackout and creation of the special probing committee, he said, the corporation and the union were not making sufficient progress to end the strike. If the talks continued to drag, he said, the attempt to end the strike in early November would fall apart; he said that if that happened the strike would not end until early December, if then, and this would mean that the bulk of General Motors employees would not be back at work before Christmas. Possibly, Woodcock said, the strike might drag on past Christmas, and this might mean the men would not be back at work until February, or perhaps later. If the strike dragged on that long, Woodcock said, the workers would be most bitter toward the corporation when they finally returned to their jobs, and it would take years to overcome this bitterness.

Moreover, he pointed out, by the end of November the union's strike fund would be exhausted; the union, for all practical purposes, would be broke. He said the union would continue the strike without strike benefits if it had to, but that a strike continuing into the first of the year would fasten a debt of more than 100 million dollars upon the union. The union did not wish to continue the strike, Woodcock said; the union wanted a settlement.

Woodcock explained that the union had decided to call a meeting of its General Motors Council for November 11, Armistice Day, the day after the deadline proposed by Bramblett and agreed to by the union. He hoped, he told Roche, the delegates would be able to vote to approve a contract, but, he said, if there was not a settlement by that time, he would instruct the delegates to return to their local unions and inform the rank-and-file members to prepare for a long strike.

Roche listened carefully to Woodcock; then he presented the corporation's position. General Motors, Roche said, was under intense pressure from the government and from business elements, including the steel industry (whose contracts would expire the following August) and other automobile companies and suppliers, to force as inexpensive a settlement as possible upon the UAW. The corporation was under particular pressure, Roche said, not to yield on the union's demand for unlimited cost-of-living. The industry, he said, believed costs had to be held down to combat foreign manufacturers.

Woodcock said he recognized the pressures on General Motors. But it was the obligation of the union and the corporation, he said, to reach an agreement that, while not injurious to the nation or to the other companies, would, as far as possible, be fair to the parties of direct concern, the workers and the corporation.

Woodcock explained that he had not come to see Roche to bargain, but rather to make clear the settlement the union needed to present to the rank-and-file with hope for ratification: a return to unlimited cost-of-living, movement toward the union's demand of full 30-and-out, more money for the supplemental unemployment fund. He said he saw no major problem on wages; a compromise could be arranged.

The two shook hands; the meeting ended. Roche thanked Woodcock for coming and said he would give every consideration to what Woodcock had said. He agreed that the strike must be ended before Christmas.

Woodcock walked to the elevators and returned downstairs. He was gravely concerned. Running through his mind were thoughts of the 1945–6 strike, of how the corporation had continued the strike for thirty days over one cent, and how the union had not won that cent. He was thinking, too, of how the corporation is fixed in a mold, how its policies are carried forward from one regime to the next. Roche, he thought, was different from many of the former corporation heads; still, philosophy and practice, he thought, do not change.

In the early days of the strike, it had been the union that had raised the specter of a titanic struggle against General Motors, a struggle like the one waged by the union twenty-five years before. Now, in recent days, the union had made it clear it was interested in a settlement: it had told first Bramblett and now Roche exactly what was needed in that settlement. Still, Woodcock did not know what the corporation's response would be. He is an intelligent, skilled man, but this was the first negotiation he had headed; he was unsure. He had great responsibilities: more than 500,000 men were out of work, perhaps as many as 1.5 million people were directly affected; the holidays were approaching. He believed that the situation was past the bargaining stage; the company must grant what the union had said it needed or the strike would have to continue.

Woodcock left the elevator and walked into the union bargaining room to report to the negotiating committee, not wishing the committee to learn of the Roche meeting through leaks to the press. As he was making his report, Bramblett called him into the corridor. Roche and Bramblett had conferred in Roche's office after Woodcock had left; now Bramblett asked Woodcock to refrain from publicly announcing the calling of the General Motors conference. Roche, Bramblett said, had been greatly impressed with Woodcock's presentation, and the corporation intended to give his demands serious consideration. Announcing the calling of the conference, Bramblett said, might throw up a roadblock to settlement. Woodcock agreed to Bramblett's request. He returned to the committee room and, laughingly, told the union negotiators what Bramblett had said. He was pleased by Bramblett's promise that Roche would give the union demands consideration, yet he was amused; hell, he told the union negotiators, he had not told Roche anything he had not been telling Bramblett for weeks.

Woodcock: "It is not that I believe there was a lack of communication between Bramblett and Roche. I'm sure the people we deal with directly believe it is their duty, their responsibility, to completely present our case." But, he says, "I think there is a difference in my being able to say directly what I feel about where our people are, and what their reactions will be going through a holiday period . . . that they'll be out of money, that they are not going to like it, but they will do it. I think there is a difference when a man hears it directly instead of it simply being repeated by somebody."

For months, General Motors had intended to make the 1970 negotiations watershed negotiations. Even if it took a long strike the corporation intended to teach a lesson to the UAW. It had decided it would, once and for all, win measures to ensure productivity: contract agreements to provide for penalties to combat absenteeism and tardiness, sanctions against workers who performed shoddily. Some of this talk was bluff, but still the corporation intended to hold the line on labor costs, for labor costs were cutting into profit margins and helping give price advantages to German and Japanese manufacturers.

General Motors saw itself, as it has for decades, as the defender of American business, of the American free enterprise system. It would confront the union, it had decided, because it had a responsibility to make the confrontation. Bramblett: "When we make a settlement, the UAW takes it around to the people they have contracts with and some of them don't have much choice but to take it. We understand that. We understand also the responsibility we have goes beyond our own. . . . We're not negotiating strictly in a vacuum."

But the strike was almost two months old and the situation had changed in those two months. Even for General Motors, this huge, profitable enterprise, the strike was beginning to hurt; 140,000 white-collar employees were drawing full wages, a drain of millions of dollars a week; the supply of automobiles in dealers' hands was almost exhausted. What would the corporation gain by continuing the strike? A strike through Christmas, Roche knew, would, as Woodcock had said, generate intense bitterness. If the workers were still on strike through the cold and snow of Christmas and New Year's, it would cause intense public relations problems for General Motors and indeed bring hardships to workers, a situation GM wished to avoid.

Most important was the fact that the union had indicated in precise terms that it was ready to settle and that Woodcock, whom Roche knows well and respects, had laid out exactly what he said he needed for ratification. It was more than General Motors had hoped the settlement would be, but not that much more. In fact, Woodcock was asking for nothing that the corporation, in the days before the strike, would not have given if the union executives had said they could sell the agreement to the rank and file. Woodcock's demands were reasonable, much more reasonable than the settlements won by the Teamsters, the building trades, the *New York Times* printers; it was a settlement the corporation could live with. The corporation understood Woodcock's situation in replacing the fabled Reuther in leading his first national negotiation. What effect would a continuing strike have upon his position in the union? What would the corporation win by inflicting a defeat upon Woodcock and upon the union? Would a continuing strike impair his position? Could he conceivably lose control? Roche, in consultation with corporation Vice Chairman Richard Gerstenberg, GM President Edward Cole, Bramblett, Donner, and a handful of other executives and board members, made the decision: give the union what Woodcock said was needed for ratification.

Despite Bramblett's assurances that the corporation would give serious consideration to Woodcock's proposals, no progress was made in negotiations the rest of Thursday or on Friday. Entrusted with winning the best possible contract, Bramblett was bargaining in the conventional fashion, making proposals but no specific offers, hoping the union would, in its enthusiasm for a settlement, accept less than the corporation was prepared to give. But for Woodcock, boxed in, it was too late for conventional bargaining. Woodcock: "We had no response except bits and pieces, which were most unsatisfactory . . . which were being put out in the traditional fashion . . . [to make] the UAW react to them. But since I had not laid out a bargaining position, there was nothing to react to. In other words, when I said we were not there to negotiate, just there to say what it takes, that when you've said—supposedly with honesty—what it takes, you can't move from there."

On Friday, November 6, hoping the move would force General Motors' hand, the union, despite Woodcock's agreement not to do so, announced it was calling a meeting of the General Motors Council for November 11, the next Wednesday. Telegrams went to the 359 delegates advising them to "come prepared to stay." The union declared that reports that an agreement was at hand were "currently without foundation" and appealed to the local union leaders to attempt to work out local settlements to "help achieve a national agreement." The telegram said: "If General Motors Corporation decides to force a continuance of the strike, plans must be made to meet the situation created when strike benefits are no longer available." A union vice president told *The New York Times* that the council would hear either "we've got a settlement or we've got to dig in for a long strike."

Woodcock, still disturbed, asked for a meeting with Bramblett. He told Bramblett he did not intend to "piecemeal this" —to bargain one item at a time. He had not gone to see Roche, he said, to lay out a bargaining position but to say exactly what items the union must have to end the strike. There was no point in playing games, he told Bramblett; if the corporation was not ready to grant the union's demands, it should say so—and the strike would continue. Bramblett was angered by Woodcock's abruptness. He said little—and gave no indications that the corporation was prepared to make the concessions demanded by the union. Woodcock was troubled. "We had the conference called," he said, "and I knew that the conference, having been called, that if they came in and there was no settlement, that going back home without it . . . we'd be in a jam." A negotiator: "Leonard sweat like I never saw him sweat."

On Monday, November 9, believing that the talks might fall through, Woodcock telephoned J. Curtis Counts, director of the Federal Mediation and Conciliation Service—the man who had not been welcome in Detroit two weeks before. Woodcock and Counts are long-time friends; before going to Washington to join the Nixon Administration, Counts was a labor negotiator with Douglas Aircraft, and Woodcock, at one time head of the union's aerospace department, had faced him in negotiations. Woodcock reached Counts in Miami, where he was attending a labor conference, and asked Counts to come to Detroit as soon as possible; he was, he said, most apprehensive; perhaps Counts could help the two sides reach a settlement. If the talks fell apart, Woodcock said, Counts should be in Detroit, for it probably would be necessary for the government to intervene.

Woodcock and Counts agreed that the union should keep its delegates to the General Motors conference standing by in Detroit; the government, they decided, would not openly intervene until it was certain a settlement could not be reached in the traditional fashion—without government assistance. Counts said he would come to Detroit, and the next morning he caught a plane to Atlanta, where, in a rare, driving snowstorm, he boarded a flight for Detroit. He arrived about 1:30 p.m., Tuesday, November 10, and caught a taxicab downtown, where he took a room in the grim Pick-Fort Shelby Hotel.

When Woodcock received word that Counts had arrived, he and Moran secretly left the General Motors Building, using the back elevators he had taken to see Roche, and drove to Counts' hotel. There, Woodcock conferred with Counts, David Tanzman, the federal mediator in Detroit, and James L. MacPherson, Tanzman's superior from Cleveland. The union still had not received a proposal, Woodcock said, or been informed that a proposal was forthcoming. Time was running out, he said; he feared there might not be a settlement.

Counts said he would talk to Bramblett, and as soon as Woodcock and Moran left the room, he telephoned Bramblett at the General Motors Building. Did General Motors intend to make an offer? he asked. Yes, Bramblett said: the company had put together an offer and planned to present it later in the day, sometime after dinner. He saw no problem, Bramblett said. Counts said he was pleased and hung up. By the time Woodcock returned to the General Motors Building, a message was waiting for him: Mr. Counts had called. Woodcock returned the call. The corporation had a proposal, Counts said, and it would be presented that night.

Still Bramblett, most skillfully, was waiting for the precise moment—the last possible moment—to make the proposal. "Earl was playing it real close to his vest," Moran says. Another negotiator: "Bramblett knew the game. Bramblett knew timing, so that when he gave it to them, they were so relieved, even the great Woodcock."

Finally, shortly after midnight, the special probing committee met once again. Bramblett, unsmiling, said there was no sense in wasting time. Woodcock had been abrupt the week before when complaining about Bramblett's attempts to piecemeal, he said; he intended to be equally abrupt. Matter-of-factly, without a trace of emotion, Bramblett laid the proposal point-by-point before the union, pausing only occasionally to ask an assistant for clarifying information or elaboration.

The company granted each demand Woodcock had made,

demands he could have had in September. The average wage
boost of 51 cents for the typical worker, the assembler, meant
that the union had reached what Woodcock called the "magic
fifty cent circle," the wage figure that would be most easy to
sell to the membership. Unlimited cost-of-living was restored,
although the union agreed to a corporation demand that payments not begin until December 6, 1971. Woodcock also won
the compromise he had been seeking on 30-and-out. Beginning
October 1, 1971, workers with 30 years' service would be
allowed to retire at any age; they would receive a pension of
500 dollars a month if they were age 58 or over, and the 500
dollars would be reduced by 8 per cent for each year the
worker was under age 58. At age 62 and again at 65, the pension would be reduced as the worker started receiving social
security benefits. The important concession was that beginning
October 1, 1972, workers with 30 years' service would be
eligible to retire on the full 500 dollar pension at age 56. The
corporation also agreed to Woodcock's demand for an increase
in supplemental unemployment funding, raising the corporation's contribution from a maximum 7 cents an hour per person to a maximum 10 cents an hour.

In what was described as an attempt to combat absenteeism and tardiness, the two sides agreed to establish a joint
orientation committee to instruct workers on the conditions
they could expect when they went to work in the automobile
plants, on their responsibilities to their employer, and on their
rights as union members. To provide an incentive for new
employees to stay on the job—and to provide a large savings
for the corporation—the union agreed to a company demand
that the starting wage of new employees be 20 cents below
the standard wage instead of 10 cents below as it had been
for years; not until the employee had been on the job 90 days
would he receive the standard wage.

The union's demand for an unbroken holiday between
Christmas and New Year's was compromised. General Motors
said this year that it needed the working days for production

to make up for the strike. The union won the unbroken holiday in the second and third years of the contract, and an extra day's pay—a holiday bonus—each year.

Much work remained to be done. Union technicians spent hours analyzing the offer to see precisely what it contained. Demands were matched against what was in the contract; items that were included were checked off as achieved, other items were forgotten. A number of noneconomic items were settled in subcommittee sessions.

Shortly after 5 a.m., so tired he had difficulty making himself understood, Moran telephoned Counts to say that a settlement had been reached. Woodcock and Bramblett and assistants on both sides—the special probing committee— met again early the next morning. The union, Woodcock said, understood the corporation's offer; the union would caucus, he said, and take the proposal to the General Motors Council. Does this mean you will recommend ratification? Bramblett asked. Yes, Woodcock said.

Chapter 9

Getting it by the boys

The twelve members of the United Automobile Workers' General Motors negotiating team had much time on their hands while the union and corporation executives put together the settlement. Once Woodcock and Bramblett agreed on October 25 to establish the special probing committee, there was nothing at the General Motors Building for the negotiators to do. Many returned to their home locals to assist in pushing toward local settlements or to check sentiment of the rank-and-file.

Then, on the weekend of November 7–8, when it appeared that an agreement was near, the negotiators were contacted by Bluestone and other members of the union's international staff and directed to report to Detroit. In the final hours before settlement they were at the General Motors Building, milling in the corridors, sitting with their feet on desks in the union negotiation rooms, or at their hotels, the Belcrest Hotel near Wayne State University in the shabby central part of the city or the Leland Hotel downtown. Three negotiators had moved from the Belcrest, its attraction being a pleasant cocktail lounge, to the recently renovated Leland because it had a swimming pool and because it seemed more exciting. Young girls, including stewardesses, lived there, as did a number of Detroit Lions football players, and the negotiators enjoyed watching them and chatting with them.

The negotiators played no part in reaching the agreement.

"Frankly," says Roy Goforth, of Local 1005 in Parma, Ohio, a Cleveland suburb, "it was in the Detroit papers prior to us having one official inkling from anyone that there was a settlement." Woodcock had attempted to keep the negotiators posted but he was too busy to provide more than a brief outline of the confidential talks, and sometimes he did not do that. Sal Astorga, of Local 216 in Southgate, California: "We had to read the papers to find out what we were doing. We'd be back at the room at the hotel, and we would get in, say three or four, whatever. And the papers would come in, either early in the morning or late at night. And we'd read the papers down there and we would see we were in intensified negotiations. . . . Here we are sitting, you know, at the bar or something, and we were reading of what we were doing. Hell, we had no knowledge of what we had been doing."

Woodcock says that when he and Bluestone asked the negotiation team for permission to establish the probing committee, they asked only for permission to deal with economic matters. The negotiators, he says, instructed him and Bluestone to attempt to work out the complete agreement. He says: "I said to them, well, look, if we're going to do this, we can't come back to you every night and say 'this happened' and 'that happened.' The advantage of exploratory talks is you can try things out and if they don't work, you can recede from that position, whereas if you do things like that in public— put something out—you can't pull it back." He says, "They understood that." Robert Johnson says: "We had no objection. I knew they would go up there and do the best job they could . . . Had I been there or not wouldn't have made a whole lot of difference." Goforth: "We were at an impasse. Nothing was being accomplished." The probing committee, he says, had his full "faith and confidence."

Kermit Stiles, another member of the UAW's negotiating team: "In order to probe General Motors you've got to have trust in somebody. This is one of the things the union has always done, have the top negotiators do the negotiating.

. . . As Walter Reuther said one time, 'If you're going to take that shot at the moon, you've got to go by yourselves.' " But Stiles states a truism: "I'm sure the international sometimes wishes there wasn't any negotiating committee."

After Woodcock had been informed by Counts that Bramblett intended to make the corporation's proposal, Bluestone alerted the committee that a settlement seemed near. But there was nothing for the negotiators to do; late during the night of November 10 and the morning of November 11, they stood or sat in the corridors and rooms of the General Motors Building, ignorant of what was happening. "We sat around and drank coffee and bullshitted," Astorga says. The negotiators noted the union and corporation secretaries scurrying by, working industriously, walking briskly through the rooms with copies of the agreements. At 6:30 a.m., a committee meeting was called, and the negotiators shuffled into the main conference room where they had met so many times during the past four months. Bewildered and tired, the negotiators had no idea what Woodcock and Bluestone had accepted from the corporation.

It occurs in almost every negotiation: an agreement had been reached between the union leadership and the corporation negotiators; now began the difficult task of gaining an endorsement from the committee—a committee almost completely ignorant of what had taken place. "It was dumped on them," a union assistant says. "The economics at least—the money, the cost-of-living, the 30-and-out. These pieces fell in abruptly, as they always do in any negotiations . . . there are certain things that flow out of the intimate meetings that you don't dare divulge until all of it is out there. Then it comes all at once, one big dump operation."

Woodcock, who had bargained and won a settlement from the corporation, now was forced to bargain and win approval from the union. A mediator: "Woodcock had to buy and sell. He had to buy from the company and sell to the committee. Woodcock was the enemy at this point."

A number of the negotiators, talking among themselves as they waited, took the position that if they were to recommend that the union ratify the agreement, the union must fully achieve its two main goals: immediate restoration of unlimited cost-of-living and complete 30-and-out. Astorga: "Some of the guys had said, 'Well, look here, if we don't get *this* and *this*, fuck it. We ain't going to sign it." The union negotiators had not settled upon a specific wage figure. They had, in fact, no idea the figure would be as high as fifty-one cents; they would have accepted a much lower increase.

The most militant negotiators were Goforth and Astorga. Stiles supported them, as did Eunice Williams, from the Chevrolet Grey Iron Foundry in Saginaw, Michigan, the lone black negotiator. These men believed that four other negotiators—James Hensley, Gomer Goins, Robert Murphy and Bud Grant—also intended to reject any agreement that did not give the union its complete demands. Williams: "If you would have heard the discussion before some of the brass came into the room, you would have said it didn't have a snowball's chance in hell of passing."

Shortly after six-thirty, Woodcock and Bluestone, with Moran and three assistants, Frank James, William Colbath, and James Ogden, walked into the room. Everyone was weary; they had been up all night; Woodcock seemed especially tired. The probing committee, he said, had a proposal to submit to the negotiators.

Bluestone spoke first, outlining the agreement. He went to the blackboard, diagraming that while the cost-of-living agreement did not become effective until October 1, 1971, if the proposal were rejected and the strike continued, it would take eight weeks or more for General Motors to improve its offer. During that time, he said, strikers would lose more wages than they could gain by forcing General Motors to make cost-of-living effective immediately. Bluestone said that to hold out for more, after eight weeks of strike, was absurd.

Goforth was the first member of the negotiating committee

to speak. He was adamantly opposed to the contract. He
proposed that the committee recommend that the General
Motors Council reject the settlement, and that this recommendation be taken to the meeting scheduled for 10 a.m. in
the Veterans Memorial Building. The council, Goforth argued,
would then reject the package, and Woodcock, with the votes
of the two advisory bodies as a mandate, could return to the
negotiations and inform the corporation that the price of
peace would be immediate restoration of cost-of-living and
a complete 30-and-out retirement program. Eunice Williams
agreed with Goforth. The men in the foundry, he said, wanted
and deserved immediate 30-and-out; they worked hard, he
said; they deserved retirement. The proposal, Williams said,
should be rejected.

Woodcock was disturbed as he listened to the discussion.
While he had repeatedly and emotionally talked of carrying
on an "old-fashioned strike" without strike benefits if the
strike fund were exhausted, he knew this would be a dangerous and even foolish venture. After a week or so without benefits, the workers would be bitter and angry; much of this bitterness and anger would be directed against the union, not the
corporation. The dissident leaders, small as their number is,
would attack the international; some of the workers might listen to them. Most importantly, however, Woodcock simply
believed it wrong to continue the strike. He had won from
the corporation the demands he had sought, demands he believed he could sell to the workers. He wanted the workers
back at their jobs for the holidays. He knew they were ready
to return to work: he had received many letters from workers
and their wives asking him to end the strike.

As Woodcock listened to the negotiators, it seemed that
they did not understand what an excellent contract the
leadership had extracted from the corporation. The talk of
rejecting the proposal, of going back for more, upset him. He
was tired from many hours of negotiations—and now the
settlement seemed in danger of being rejected.

Woodcock took the floor, his voice quavering. The proposal must be accepted, he said. He could not conceive how any of the negotiators could vote to reject the proposal in light of the hardships that more than 400,000 General Motors workers and the hundreds of thousands of wives and children had endured for nearly two months. He reminded the negotiators that the strike fund was nearly exhausted, and that the union would be in great debt if the strike continued. He said that if the union did not accept this proposal it was likely that the corporation would not make another proposal until early in the new year, perhaps not until February. In the 1945–6 strike, he recalled once again, the union and the corporation had fought thirty days over a single cent—and the union had not won that cent. He said he was convinced that the majority of the union's rank-and-file would accept the agreement.

Astorga: "I got the impression that he was not satisfied, not completely satisfied. I could tell by his expression . . . I got the impression that he and Bluestone were pleading with the council to buy it. In other words, if we rejected this one, why, hell, we would have to wait until February to get another one from the corporation. . . . They were telling us in other words that if we rejected this one, we wouldn't have no offer until February. And the strike fund was depleted and so forth."

Astorga says he wished to continue the strike. What, he was asked later, happened to the idea of staging an old-fashioned strike without strike benefits? "Beats the shit out of me," Astorga says.

Woodcock delivered a forceful and effective address but he was not aware of its effectiveness. He asked Johnson, the committee chairman, to excuse him and his staff, telling the negotiators as he left the room that they should discuss the proposal and decide whether to accept or reject it. Woodcock met with Bluestone and the international assistants; he told them he wanted to postpone for a day the General Motors conference scheduled to begin at 10 a.m. If the committee members were confused, he said, the delegates to the conference would also be confused—even more so.

This was a dark moment for Woodcock. It seemed as if all the work, all these weeks, was for nothing. It seemed as if the proposal, won after so much effort, after so much thought, would be rejected.

Frank James, an assistant, looked at him and said: My God, the conference will tear it apart.

Yes, Woodcock said. This was possible.

The committee members began discussing the proposal immediately after Woodcock and his aides left the conference room. Most speakers urged that the proposal be rejected. Then Johnson, the chairman, made a strong speech supporting Woodcock's arguments for accepting the contract. This was a crucial moment, because Johnson influenced a number of negotiators who had seemed opposed to the contract. The tone of the talk changed; slowly, increasingly as moments went by, the thinking changed. We must, the negotiators said, support Woodcock; we must accept the contract. Astorga: "You could see that the guys who were with you were all of a sudden not with you."

It was time to vote—even though most negotiators had no real idea of many of the details of the contract. Neal Madsen: "Nobody had time to analyze it. I mean, what was catch-up pennies and what was make-up money. . . . There was too much to digest in too short a time. You've got to understand that everybody was tired." Astorga: "At the time they gave us the proposal, after going around the clock, they just laid it down there in loose papers. And no member of the committee knew exactly what we had, to be truthful . . . not even the people who told what we got—they were not certain either."

Johnson began the roll call. Astorga: No. Williams: No. Goforth: No. Goins: Yes—he would go along with the chairman. Stiles: No. Now three of the negotiators who had seemed likely to vote against the contract, Hensley, Murphy, Grant:

All voted yes. Then the four who had been firmly in support of the contract, Madsen, John Niemeyer, Carl Bartlett, and Johnson: All voted yes. The vote: eight to four for acceptance. Woodcock had won.

Woodcock suggests that the men who opposed the contract were confused. That was not the case. The men who voted against the contract simply did not like it. "I've been in negotiations a long time," says Kermit Stiles. "I've practiced some law and things . . . it's pretty hard to confuse me in a contract situation. We could have gone very easily into February or maybe March. I was willing to take that chance, but I have no complaints that I was outvoted."

Goforth, while opposed to the settlement because he did not believe it was large enough, also hoped to win prestige in his home local and region by appearing as the tough negotiator who stood up to General Motors and the UAW, and helped win a larger settlement for the workers. A reporter: "May I say you are politically ambitious?" Goforth: "You may say I am politically ambitious." Astorga opposed the contract because he believed it fell short of union demands, yet he also displayed a fondness for Detroit and for the negotiation limelight, and seemingly, at times, no real wish to hurry back to California.

James Hensley, the committee vice chairman, says there was a "real good possibility" that the committee would recommend against ratification. "The closeness of the whole thing was really closer than the actual vote. I mean, you're saying two more votes, and the whole thing might go the other way. And I think there were several guys who were real close to voting the other way." It was not, he says, that the agreement was a poor one; it was a matter of politics. The negotiators had been elected in their subcouncils with instructions to obtain specific items—immediate restoration of unlimited cost-of-living, say, or complete 30-and-out. Hensley says: "The things that the sub-councils wanted them to get, they didn't. This is what really disturbed them, what they were really worried about—going back to the sub-councils."

Ernest Moran, Woodcock's aide: "Hell, yes," there was a possibility the committee would vote against ratification, even though this has never occurred in UAW negotiations. "You are dealing with a lot of people," he says, and each individual was concerned with his own political future and with the specific problems that confronted the men he represented. Many of these problems were not met, and the negotiators were disappointed.

Goforth, the most forceful of the delegates opposed to the contract, says "there was real hope" on his part that the contract would be rejected. "You must understand the struggle that was going on with our membership. They were suffering, there was no question . . . and the pressure was insurmountable from the local unions. Mr. Woodcock—Brother Woodcock —was under extreme pressure to the extent of receiving many letters and phone calls from people who were vitally concerned and in financial despair. But," he says, "I felt as though, if we would recommend unanimously to the conference that it be rejected, and then from the remaining issues select two, perhaps three . . . that we could have taken these back to the corporation and said, 'look here's the price of peace.' And I think this strategy would have worked."

It was Woodcock who sold the contract, Goforth says, wryly—exercising "his good office, his good voice, his good ability," doing what "any forceful leader would have done," taking the floor and demanding acceptance. Woodcock, he says, believed he "could explain it more forcefully" than his subordinates, "pound the table, do whatever was needed to explain the contract, to sway the vote. I believe that there was a time just before all of us getting together to hear the corporation's offer that the committee had said, we will settle for not less than *this*, and that the committee ended up somewhere below that, after having the thing outlined to them and kicked around." The committee, he says, "settled for what was there."

· · · ·

Johnson, the committee chairman, was elated with the vote. The contract, he believed, contained "all that we could really obtain from a seven-week strike." He walked across the hall to inform Woodcock that the proposal had been accepted. But Woodcock was not completely pleased. What, he asked, would happen if the four men who voted to reject the proposal issued a minority report at the conference? This had occurred in 1967, when a General Motors negotiator, Joseph Malotke, of Local 160, the technical center local, issued a one-man minority report calling the General Motors contract skimpy and recommending its rejection. The report, it turned out, had no effect, but its issuance was disturbing. Now there seemed a possibility that four members might issue a minority report. Woodcock did not want to go to the General Motors conference with a divided committee. He wanted no bars to acceptance. He wanted solidarity.

Johnson had not thought of the possibility of a minority report—neither, for that matter, had the dissidents. But Johnson and Woodcock did not know this. Worried, wishing to please Woodcock, Johnson returned to the conference room. What, he asked, were the main objections to the proposals? The negotiators said they were largely concerned over the union's failure to win immediate cost-of-living and full 30-and-out. Johnson asked whether they were satisfied with the rest of the package. The negotiators said they were. In that case, Johnson said, would they agree not to make a minority report to the conference? This, he explained, might impair ratification. The dissident negotiators agreed to make no report. Johnson walked back across the hall to tell Woodcock there would be no minority report.

It was nearly 11 a.m. Woodcock was late for a meeting of the union's international executive board. He left the negotiation suite and started walking toward the corridor jammed with perhaps a hundred newsmen and two hundred to three hundred General Motors white-collar employees who had left their offices hoping to obtain word whether a settlement had been reached.

Woodcock did not wish to talk to the press, but he was intercepted by a General Motors publicist who pointed out that the reporters had been waiting for him for several hours. Woodcock gave in and went to the press room where, tired, unsmiling, thinking of the opposition to the proposal, he faced the reporters and the cameras.

Woodcock did not appear to be a man who had won a victory: he was curt and rude, the opposite of Walter Reuther, who would emerge triumphant and fresh from each negotiation and proclaim that the union had won the largest settlement in its history, that the working man had won another victory in his fight for dignity and improved living standards.

He made the announcement: "A tentative agreement has been reached covering the U.S. plants of the corporation. At the union's request the details are being withheld."

A reporter: "Are you happy?"

"I am giving no details beyond that statement," he said. The agreement, he said, was "tentative as far as the union is concerned" until ratification was completed.

A reporter: Would local unions be allowed to continue their strikes?

All locals, Woodcock said, would be allowed "to prosecute their strikes."

A reporter began another question. Woodcock was angered by what he considered this waste of his time. "I'm sorry to be rude, gentlemen, but this is getting us nowhere," he said. He walked from the room, went to his car, and was driven to Solidarity House.

Bramblett, smiling slightly, walked in to face the reporters.

Selecting what he later conceded were "carefully chosen words," Bramblett, asked whether he considered the agreement inflationary, declared, "I would say the cost of the settlement is substantially more than the anticipated increase in productivity of the country."

But was the agreement inflationary?

Bramblett: "That's the definition—the general definition —of inflation."

and the next morning stated or implied what Bramblett had
said: the agreement was inflationary. The agreement, to be
sure, did meet the standard definitions of inflation. What Bramblett had failed to point out was that the settlement was a
most reasonable settlement. Bramblett knew it was a reasonable, responsible settlement—just as he knew it was necessary
not to call it reasonable or responsible but to call it inflationary,
for this would help sell the agreement to the rank-and-file. For
four months the corporation had fought to achieve as inexpensive a settlement as possible; for nearly two months it had been
struck. Now that was past, and Bramblett was doing his best
to help achieve the common goal of the union leadership and
the corporation: ratification.

Two months after the settlement, in an interview, Bramblett was asked whether he believed the settlement was truly
inflationary. "If you're just talking about the money," he
said, "it exceeded the projected productivity increases of the
country." However, he said, "Take the cost-of-living out of the
settlement and it's three per cent a year."

But was the agreement inflationary?

"Just putting the blinders on, obviously it's more than
three per cent," he said. "Then you back off and take a second
look, and you say, well, thirty-three cents of this, take that
out, and you've got three per cent a year plus six cents. And
three per cent a year plus six cents is really not a big earth-
shattering settlement."

These were words, obviously, that Bramblett would not
use the morning of the settlement. What worker, after two
months on strike, would have voted for a settlement that
General Motors called *not a big earth-shattering settlement*?

The agreement increased General Motors' labor costs just
an estimated 1.10 to 1.40 dollars an hour over the three years
of the contract. Moreover, GM continued to raise its prices
during 1971 and 1972 to allow for inflation, thus offsetting this
inflation. And it must be noted that the unlimited cost-of-living provisions only returned General Motors to a condition

... lion dollars in 1948 until

...ars in 1967.

... later the Nixon Administration declared its displeasure ... the settlement. In the administration's second inflation alert, the White House charged that the contract was not only inflationary, but that the increased costs it forced upon General Motors Corporation and the other automobile manufacturers would impair the industry's campaign to combat the foreign car invasion. The forty-one page report, issued by the Council of Economic Advisers, said: "It is clear that this settlement, if generalized through the economy, would crowd further upward costs per unit of output and therefore the price level."

The report declared that "inflation would go on endlessly" if "everyone in his turn gets as big a wage or price increase as the biggest obtained by others during the height of the inflation." Cost-of-living increases were criticized by the council as "particularly harmful to the economy." The report: "To embody in wage agreements covering two or three future years provisions for wage increases which assume that prices will continue to rise at recent peak rates is not a reasonable response to our present situation. If it were done generally, it would be a recipe for permanent, rapid inflation and also for persistent unemployment, because the government would be bound to try to check the inflation by generally restrictive policies."

Woodcock resented this government criticism, as did George Meany and James Roche. Woodcock said that the White House's claim that the GM–UAW pact was inflationary was "not well-founded."

"We deliberately restrained and restricted increases in years two and three to a three per cent figure," he said, "which is below national productivity and therefore considerably below the General Motors productivity. And wage increases that come through cost-of-living will come after the prices have increased and not before, and therefore cannot possibly force price increases. And any price increases that are caused by cost-of-living increases at General Motors will be because the Nixon Administration is not following proper fiscal and monetary policies and is allowing the inflation in the United States to go unchecked. We resent and reject the attempt of the Administration, through its inflation alert, to shift the blame for the failure of its misguided economic policies to the shoulders of the General Motors workers."

Meany said that the automobile settlement provided a needed "catch-up and modest gains in buying power," nothing more, and was "a most responsible agreement." He said: "Workers and wages did not cause this inflation and they have not profited by it. They are among its chief victims and they are not happy about it."

Roche, in an address at the Manufacturers Hanover Trust Business Conference in New York on December 6, took the union leaders' side, saying the agreement was noninflationary —a responsible statesmanlike settlement. It was, again, a description the corporation had not chosen to use the morning of the settlement. He said: "We are asked if our economic settlement is inflationary. If we measure wage increases against the productivity gains in the economy, the quick answer is yes. But the full answer is not so simple." He noted that of the 51 cents average wage increase 33 cents "can be attributed, not to the inflation that is to come, but to the inflation of the past three years." Roche said that 26 of the cents represented "makeup for the increase in cost-of-living to April 30," the catch-up money that had received so much attention early in the talks. The 26 cents, he said, "was provided for in the 1967 agreement." Seven cents, he said, "reflects the cost-of-living increases from April 30 to the time of the strike. Another twelve cents . . . is equivalent to the annual improvement factor which has been part of the General Motors–UAW agreements since 1948. This leaves an increase of only six cents in the first year that is not tied in some way to past inflation or to productivity."

The next spring, this same analysis of the settlement—so unlike the analysis made by the corporation or the union when the agreement was reached—appeared in the General Motors Corporation annual report to assure stockholders that the corporation leadership had protected their rights and negotiated a settlement fair to all concerned parties.

After his terse exchange with the press on the morning the union's GM negotiators had approved the settlement, Woodcock arrived at Solidarity House for the meeting of the international executive board shortly before noon. By now an atmosphere of confusion and misunderstanding was creeping into America's most important strike in a decade, perhaps the most important strike in twenty-five years. When Johnson, chairman of the General Motors negotiating committee, informed Woodcock that the four negotiators who voted against ratification had decided not to make a minority report, Woodcock took this to mean that the delegates had made the ratification vote unanimous. He said: "I thought he meant they had taken a vote, that it was 8–4 in favor, but that the four had then agreed, okay, we'll make it unanimous." Accordingly, Woodcock reported to the twenty-four member executive board that the committee had voted unanimously for ratification. The board members, who favored an end to the strike, were heartened by this information. The board unanimously recommended ratification.

Meantime, Woodcock had dispatched Bluestone to inform the General Motors Council delegates, who had been milling around the downtown hotels since the day before, and were now jammed into a basement room at the Veterans Memorial Building, that the council was postponed until 10 a.m. the next day. Bluestone said that the union wished to put the proposal in writing so that it could be more intelligently dis-

cussed by the delegates. Mostly, however, the union leadership wished to discuss the proposal so that it could logically
and forcefully present its arguments to the delegates. The
delegates were disturbed but there was nothing to be done.
"It's up in the wind," a delegate said, "and it could blow
either way." Jack Wagner, president of Buick Local 599 in
Flint, one of the leaders in the 30-and-out movement, said he
would not recommend ratification. "This is an old game,"
Wagner said. "They keep you out eight weeks and they think
you're going to buy anything." Outside the building, some
one hundred pickets from Local 160, the technical center local,
and from the United Caucus—the small, antiadministration
caucus that had supported Art Fox, the dissenter from the
Ford plants, for UAW president against Walter Reuther at the
April convention—marched in demand of a dollar an hour
wage increases, immediate restoration of cost-of-living, and
complete early retirement.

That night, word spread in the hotels downtown that
Woodcock had informed the executive board that the vote
was unanimous, not eight to four. What was going on? Had
Woodcock lied? The newspapers were on the streets with
accounts of the settlements, obtaining their information from
union vice presidents, board members, and publicity men
despite Woodcock's insistence that details be withheld until
the agreement had been ratified by the General Motors Council. Most of the details were correct, but where they were incorrect they were usually low; this heightened the feelings
of some delegates that the proposals were inadequate. Yet
this worked to Woodcock's advantage, for next day, when he
explained the contract in full, it was clear the agreement
called for more than the newspapers had said—and this erased
some of the delegates' resentment.

Woodcock did not realize the error in the report of the
committee vote until the next morning when he arrived at
the Veterans Memorial Building to take the settlement to the
conference delegates. Johnson approached Woodcock to ask

when he would speak. After the staff officers reported, Woodcock said. Woodcock said Johnson should make a motion that
the conference, based upon the unanimous endorsement by
the twelve member negotiating team, recommended that the
rank-and-file accept the contract. Johnson was surprised: the
vote, he said, was not unanimous. Woodcock was startled but
he quickly recovered. He told Johnson merely to say that he
recommended "on behalf of the committee" that the conference accept the proposal. If anyone wished to bring the
matter of the divided vote to the convention, Woodcock said,
it would be up to them. The leadership would not mention it.

The meeting was a wearisome affair, the delegates crowded
into the damp basement room for more than five hours. In
the past, the union had discussed contracts, section by section,
the leaders explaining each provision and calling for debate.
Now, perhaps to ensure that delegates would be tired by the
time for debate, the union leadership presented the explanation of the entire contract—a process that took more than
three hours—before allowing the delegates to ask questions.

Shortly after 1 p.m., Woodcock arose to an ovation to
make his report to the delegates. "I am not satisfied with this
agreement," he said, a statement that brought applause and
cheers from the handful of union dissidents. "But at all times
during a strike there must be continuing decisions made . . .
[in which] one must weigh the additional gains that might
be possible against the sacrifices that are required of the
soldiers of the battle who are carrying on the strike.

"We have constantly asked ourselves," he continued, "can
sufficient progress be made in vital areas and [can] the battle
of principles be won? We called a convention on the 24th
of October and at that convention, reporting to all of you
through the delegates who represent the membership of this
union, I outlined the area in which there had to be substantial
progress for there to be an end to the General Motors strike.
I emphasized wages, cost-of-living, the resistance that we
had to have to the corporation's demands that we go back on

the cost-sharing of hospital, surgical, medical and drug insurance. There had to be arithmetical progress on the question of 30-and-out. And that this union was never going to abandon its retired members. And that we had to strengthen our SUB [supplemental unemployment benefits] financing.

"How," he asked, "have we done?" How, he asked, do the gains the union had won weigh against "what more might be won and against the sacrifice to the families and to this union that might be entailed?"

He said: "First of all, there is nothing in this agreement which will haunt us in the future . . . and there is much on which we can build.

"Let us take cost-of-living. That principle has been fully won. . . . It is true there is a lag in the quarterly implementation for one year. To that degree it was a compromise. But on and after the 6th of December, 1971, it's just like it used to be. On the 6th of December, 1971, whatever the accumulation of the cost-of-living—and at the rate we're going now it will be twenty cents—will be added to the wage rate. . . . And in March of 1972, and every three months thereafter, whatever the cost-of-living may have gone up, or come down, will be added to the wage rate.

"And," he said, "the victory in cost-of-living will be with us for years and years to come. It is not just a victory for this contract." The union, he said, had been forced to give up unlimited cost-of-living. Now, he said, to much applause, the union had gone to General Motors and won it back and it would never be taken away.

The December 1971 starting date for cost-of-living, he said, was a compromise—"not in principle but in practicality." But, "assuming the cost-of-living went up by five cents in each quarter, the wage loss by December 6, 1971, would be 156 dollars for the average worker. That's less than the cost to the worker of one week of strike."

Woodcock continued, "Now the first-year wage increase of fifty-one cents is ten cents less than can be rationalized. . . .

There is no question about that." But, he declared, "with the cost-of-living [settled] so we don't have to go through that fight again, then the bargaining of 1973 can focus on the real gains in the areas of wages and other things because the phony battle of cost-of-living—which was so difficult to win—will be behind us."

Thirty-and-out, he said, "doesn't go all the way . . . but it doesn't sacrifice the principle." He explained that in October 1972, the age at which workers could utilize 30-and-out retirement would drop to fifty-six—"and that points the direction. That gives meaning to the whole program. And I would say to the supporters and leaders of the 30-and-out movement they should recognize their own victory when it is before them."

The settlement, he said, was an "honorable settlement . . . a solid settlement. It represents solid gains for the families we all represent . . . This settlement represents a solid achievement for this union. More than that, it benefits the whole labor movement. . . . I hope that what we are doing here in cost-of-living will enable the steel workers, when they have their turn next year, to win back from the industry the cost-of-living clause that was taken away from them in 1959.

"Getting back the cost-of-living and making the General Motors Corporation put better arithmetic with 30-and-out, making the General Motors Corporation move that program so what will be done next is so obvious you can write it down now—getting it from GM is worth everything. It's much better than getting it from somebody else."

To continue the strike, Woodcock said, "would bring questionable possibilities" and "take us into a most dangerous area. We have benefits we have reached that are there to be collected for a great time in the future."

His voice softening, the union men silent, Woodcock declared, "It is a victory. We took on the world's mightiest, most powerful manufacturing corporation. They said we wouldn't dare. And when we did they said we couldn't win.

Well, they were wrong on both counts. We did win. We spent all our money. But we've got a better union. That is what it's all about." The workers rose in tremendous applause that lasted nearly five minutes. When the workers quieted, Woodcock, who had remained at the microphone, said, "We have come a long way together. I love you guys. And you're the greatest." The applause rose again, and Woodcock sat down. Bluestone came to the microphone. "I want to speak for the membership, Leonard," he said, "that we love you too."

It was over. Months of planning, months of negotiation. Two months of strike, millions of dollars in strike benefits, millions of dollars in lost profits. It was over. It had been close, and Woodcock and Bluestone and the other union executives had been gravely worried, worried that the settlement, achieved at the last possible moment, might be junked. But Woodcock had gotten it through; he had sold the contract. Bluestone called for a vote. Emil Mazey said it was nine to one; Bluestone said it was four to one. No one knew, for no one counted. The General Motors conference, for all practical purposes, had unanimously recommended that the agreement be ratified. Next week, the 385,000 General Motors workers across the country voted on the contract; the vote took a week, but the margin was clear—"a landslide margin," the United Automobile Workers said—367,533 to 11,546. On November 20, shortly before 5 p.m., Woodcock and Bluestone drove to the General Motors Building and formally notified Earl Bramblett that the General Motors strike, the most costly strike in history, was ended—sixty-seven days after it had begun.

Was the strike worth it? Woodcock was asked.

"Yes," he said. "It was a strike that may prevent strikes in future years."

The corporation and union had agreed that work would resume on Monday, November 23; if it did not—if it went another week, into December, another month's payments on

Blue Cross–Blue Shield insurance would come due, a 23 million dollar debt for the UAW. There were, however, a number of local agreements that remained unsettled, including two important local disputes that stood in the way of production—one at Local 549 at the Fisher Body plant in Mansfield, Ohio, which manufactures door and roof panels, fenders and truck decks, and one at Local 909, a key Chevrolet parts plant in Warren, Michigan. Woodcock had pledged that the locals would be allowed to continue their strikes, but the UAW, desirous that the corporation resume full production as quickly as possible, stepped in to ensure settlements.°

Emil Mazey had already announced that because the strike fund was so low—it had fallen to about 28 million dollars—

° International union pressure also helped produce a settlement in November at General Motors' new expensive plant at Lordstown, Ohio, where the sub-compact Vega is produced. A year later, in late 1971, a highly publicized dispute broke out at Lordstown, after the tough-minded General Motors Assembly Division took over the Vega complex and laid off some 300 workers while maintaining the line speed of about 100 cars an hour. The local union charged that this constituted a speed-up, and the 7,800 Lordstown workers went on strike, this in the newest, most advanced plant in the automobile industry. The 21-day strike, which ended when GM agreed to return many of the laid-off workers to their jobs, was caused by old-fashioned issues: authoritarian rule and management drive for high production on top of the ever-present issues of monotony, repetitiveness, and meaninglessness. (GM, in search of high production, has, with automation and advanced engineering, made the jobs at Lordstown as simple, as effortless—as routine and mindless—as modern technology will allow.) Ironically, General Motors sought out the Lordstown location for the Vega plant because it seemed to offer the perfect work force. The steel and manufacturing industries in eastern Ohio and western Pennsylvania have been badly depressed by foreign competition; many men had lost their jobs. GM believed that it would thus acquire a work force that would be happy with the relatively high wages and that would do all tasks that were asked. Moreover, GM knew, many workers would be young and inexperienced in auto manufacturing, and thus, unlike the older workers, would not contest the new automated methods or the high speed of production. And here, in mid-America, GM believed, the nation's traditional work ethic would still be alive. But the Lordstown workers, mostly white, with an average age in the late twenties, nevertheless revolted against the speed, the monotony, and the meaninglessness of their work, and against the lack of participation in decisions—a revolt with many lessons for American industry and labor as they consider the work force of the 1970s and 1980s.

strike benefits would be halted November 30, an action taken
as much to prod local unions as to protect the strike fund.
Woodcock summoned the leaders of Local 549 to appear at
Solidarity House at 1 p.m., November 21, to "review the situation" at Mansfield. The Mansfield local is historically recal-
citrant. In 1966, two wildcat strikes at the plant almost halted
General Motors production: 94 plants were closed, forcing
the layoff of some 220,000 General Motors workers across the
country. The strikes ended only when Walter Reuther appointed an international trusteeship over the local; the day
that the international representative arrived in Mansfield to
take the union over, the local's members flew the American
flag at half staff. Now, Woodcock said, the international was
again considering placing the union in trusteeship. But on the
21st, after 60 hours of continuous bargaining, the local buckled
under international pressure, and a local agreement was
reached.

The same day Local 909 was placed under command of
the international; continued bargaining brought a settlement
hours before the General Motors Corporation was to resume
production.

Monday, November 23, across the country, General Motors
workers began returning to their jobs (some locals took more
time to settle, and a dispute at the Lakewood plant in Georgia
kept GM's Pontiac division from resuming full production
until February). The next day General Motors flew a plane-
load of journalists to its Vega assembly plant at Lordstown,
Ohio, to observe the first scheduled poststrike automobile come
off the assembly line. The car, a lime Vega ordered by a woman
library employee in Bloomington, Illinois, had been sitting on
the line, ten minutes from completion, for more than two
months. It was driven from the line at 7:40 a.m. The cameras
recorded the event and newspapers published the story across
the country. General Motors, however, neglected to inform
executives at its Framingham, Massachusetts, assembly plant
of the plans at Lordstown. At 7:12 a.m., twenty minutes be-

fore the Vega was finished, and with no photographers present, a Pontiac LeMans came off the Framingham line.

Later the same day, General Motors Corporation announced a price increase of 24 dollars on its automobiles, this in addition to an average 208 dollar increase that, in anticipation of the union settlement, had been made three months before the strike—the highest increase in more than a decade.

Chapter 10

"A continuing relationship requires no loser"

The strike ended, UAW negotiators, using the General Motors settlement as a pattern, resumed talks with the Ford Motor Company and Chrysler Corporation—these talks had been canceled in September when the contracts expired—and continued negotiations at General Motors of Canada, where 23,000 workers remained on strike.

The main issue in the Ford talks was a dispute over when 25 cents of the wage increase should be paid—that portion of the 51 cents average wage increase beyond the 26 cents cost-of-living money owed to the workers under the old contract. The UAW said that the 25 cents, like the 26 cents, should be made retroactive to September 15, the expiration date of the old contract; Ford said that the 25 cents should not be paid until the UAW's 101 Ford locals ratified local and national agreements.

Executives on both sides insisted that it would be incorrect to assume that a settlement at Ford without a strike was assured, but it remained for Henry Ford II to state the obvious; the Ford agreement, he said in Chicago, "probably would follow General Motors one hundred per cent" and he "would be surprised if we were struck."

At 3 p.m., December 7, after more than twenty-four hours

of negotiation, the company and the union reached agreement granting the Ford workers the same wage increases and increased pension benefits that had been negotiated at General Motors. A compromise was reached on the payment date of the disputed 25 cents: November 2, virtually midway between the date the union had insisted upon, September 15, and the date of the agreement. Ford agreed to pay the money immediately, meaning the workers would, on the average, receive an extra 25 dollars apiece—a total of 20 million dollars—before Christmas.

To force quick local settlements, the company and the union stipulated that the money be paid to workers only when their locals had ratified local and national agreements.

In accordance with negotiation custom—the custom is intended to heighten the status of the union negotiators and help ensure ratification—the Ford contract went a step farther than the General Motors agreement. Kenneth Bannon, director of the union's Ford Department, won what Walter Reuther would have called frosting on the cake: agreement by Ford to deduct funds from workers' paychecks on a voluntary basis to establish a dental care plan—the plan the UAW had surrendered at General Motors. The voluntary deductions, Bannon said, represented a major breakthrough. The union's health insurance plans had developed from such a voluntary, worker-paid program set up at General Motors in 1941; Bannon said the 1970 Ford plan would constitute the basis for an industry-wide dental plan funded by automatic deductions, perhaps as early as the 1973 negotiations.

Malcolm Denise, the Ford negotiator, agreed to set up the voluntary plan to please Bannon and to adhere to custom. But when the dental plan was trumpeted as a major breakthrough, the industry was disturbed, and Denise issued a statement discounting the plan's importance—even though he knew it would be the forerunner of a mandatory program.

The Ford union conference overwhelmingly approved the contract December 8, and the next week Bannon announced that the 161,000 Ford workers had ratified the agreement. By Christmas, agreements had been reached at all Ford plants except the stamping plant at Woodhaven, Michigan, where three deaths had occurred in recent months and the dispute continued over safety conditions. All Ford workers except those at the Woodhaven plant received their bonuses by Christmas.

The night the Ford agreement was ratified by the Ford Council, Woodcock took a late plane to Toronto, hoping to guide a settlement of the General Motors Canadian strike, which constituted a 900,000-dollar-a-week drain on the union's nearly depleted strike fund. The Canadian strike was blocking a settlement at Chrysler Corporation, since Chrysler, alone in the automobile industry, has a single agreement with the UAW covering its American and Canadian plants. It was necessary that a settlement be reached at the General Motors Canadian plants to set a pattern for a settlement at Chrysler's Canadian facilities.

The major issue in the General Motors Canadian talks was cost-of-living, but the strike was also prolonged by a leadership rivalry between Dennis McDermott, the union's vice president and director of Canadian operations, and Gordon Lambert, chairman of the union's General Motors negotiating team in Canada. The dispute broke into the open November 23, the day General Motors workers began returning to plants in the United States, when Lambert demanded that General Motors make an offer to end the talks before midnight or the union would break off negotiations. The corporation refused, and Lambert canceled the talks and departed on a round of meetings at the company's seven Canadian plants. McDermott complained, "You don't get a settlement by hopping across the country." But settlements are also not reached unless top leaders involve themselves in negotiations, and McDermott, hoping that Lambert would get out on a limb and destroy himself, had attended just two meetings since negotiations began in July.

Many Canadians charge that the Canadian negotiations are worked out by Americans, and this is true—even though it is denied by the corporation and the union. American corporation and union executives have directed the settlements in Canada since 1947, and both sides knew a settlement would not be reached until top American officials came to Toronto, where General Motors of Canada has its headquarters.

The cost-of-living dispute in Canada was brought about by the fact that, while the cost-of-living in the United States had increased 33 cents during the three year life of the contract, the cost of living in Canada had risen only 12 cents. The union insisted that the Canadian workers be granted the full 33 cents. The corporation refused, saying this would import inflation into Canada.

Once the top leadership—Woodcock for the union, George Morris for General Motors—arrived in Toronto, the two sides began moving toward settlement. The corporation had made a third offer, proposing wage increases of 42 to 51 cents an hour —the figures including the 12 cents of cost-of-living. Woodcock said the proposal was unacceptable, but did not formally reject it. On December 10, he suddenly left Toronto and returned to Detroit, requesting a meeting with James Roche, the General Motors chairman, as he had done in the main General Motors talks a month before. The meeting, on Friday, December 11, lasted thirty minutes, Roche and Woodcock engaging in a general discussion of the Canadian situation. Woodcock returned to Toronto and Monday, December 14, General Motors made its fourth proposal, offering an average wage increase of 38 cents, 13 cents less than the American workers received, but giving Canadian workers wage parity with American workers in the second year of the contract. A news blackout was declared, and the two sides entered intense negotiations. The union accepted the company's offer on December 16.

One nettlesome issue had been the demand by the predominantly French workers at General Motors Ste. Therese plant that French be made the official plant language. Mc-Dermott complained: "We cannot get GM to comprehend what the problem is in Quebec. The French language question is no longer a private squabble between the UAW and GM. There is great social unrest in Quebec." But the union settled without winning the French workers' demands, agreeing in a private session that the issue would be withdrawn. Sometime later, in a mellow mood, Morris described how the language dispute was settled. "I just told them," he said, "there was no fucking way that plant was going to speak French."

By dragging on into mid-December, the Canadian dispute made it impossible for the UAW and Chrysler Corporation to negotiate a settlement before the holidays, so the Chrysler talks were postponed until after the first of the year. January 3, Douglas Fraser threatened that the Chrysler workers would strike if necessary to ensure that they received the same contract as negotiated at Ford. Fraser emphasized that Chrysler would not receive any special treatment because of its precarious financial position. The corporation had lost some 15 million dollars during the first nine months of 1970; however, under a cost-cutting program directed by Chrysler President John J. Riccardo, the corporation seemed to be strengthening its position, earning a 7.6 million dollar fourth quarter profit, which held its full-year losses to 7.4 million dollars.

An agreement was reached January 19, the union gaining the same contract it had won at General Motors and Ford, with the 25 cents in new money again retroactive to November 2. Chrysler estimated that the settlement would cost 1 billion dollars in wages and fringe benefits and that Chrysler workers would receive some 30 million dollars—an average of 311 dollars apiece—in back pay.

Fraser, like Bannon, won a concession not in the General Motors contract: an agreement to explore the possibility of instituting a four day, forty hour week in an attempt to combat the problems of absenteeism and tardiness, and to make the automobile work more appealing. This was a novel item, possessing what Woodcock called "very exciting possibilities."

Talk of the four day week began early in the negotiations as Fraser chatted one day with William Bavinger, one of the Chrysler negotiators, about the many problems associated with the automobile work place. Fraser had just finished reading an article about a new book that had been receiving attention, *4 days, 40 hours,* by Riva Poor. The idea of the four day week flashed through his mind: he described the idea to Bavinger and told him that perhaps this was an answer to the automobile workers' complaints. Bavinger said perhaps it was, but, although the idea was raised a few times in negotiations in the weeks that followed, no special importance was attached to it. Then, the final morning of the talks, after the two sides had worked out major items, Fraser again brought up the four day week to Bavinger, and also said the union wanted to set up a voluntary dental plan like Bannon had won at Ford. Bavinger said that the UAW could have one or the other, but not both. Fraser thought about the matter. Ford had already won the dental plan; perhaps, therefore, it would be wise to take a different item. He said that the UAW wanted to explore the four day week.

The Chrysler package did not cover the ten thousand Chrysler white-collar workers who belong to the UAW, because the two sides had been unable to agree on wage increases. The white-collar agreement took another two weeks, and came on February 2, after a three hour strike, the shortest in automobile negotiations. After 30 hours of negotiations, Woodcock announced with Fraser that the workers would receive a 13 per cent increase and that, as in the other pacts, the 25 cents would be made retroactive to November 2.

One more automobile company contract remained: American Motors. On April 12, the union concluded a contract with AMC for a wage increase of 49 to 61 cents an hour. The union also won unlimited cost-of-living and the 30-and-out retirement program it had negotiated at the Big Three. In an attempt to give the corporation—always financially troubled, existing in large measure only because General Motors and Ford make no real effort to seize its sales and likely make it known to bankers that they wish to have loans extended to American Motors—more time to work out its financial problems, the union agreed to extend the contract to four years.

In the months that followed, the United Automobile Workers took the contracts as patterns to the many supply firms whose members belong to the union. Because of the recession, and because many of these firms are not as profitable as the automobile companies, the union found the suppliers resistant to matching the agreements. Many disputes arose, and at one point more than 50,000 supply workers were on strike, costing the union about 1.7 million dollars a week in strike benefits. Negotiations were particularly difficult in the tool and die industry, which was in a severe recession because the automobile companies had reduced styling changes, and hence tool and die orders. The tool and die firms were especially opposed to the union's cost-of-living demand, because tool and die contracts with the automobile companies contain no provisions for fees to rise with increases in the cost-of-living.

By late winter and early spring, unions and firms in a number of other industries had begun negotiating agreements that paralleled the General Motors agreement.

The can workers won a 50-cents-an-hour first year wage increase and an unlimited cost-of-living formula from the can manufacturers. The copper and aluminum workers received large wage increases and unlimited cost-of-living. In the summer the Communications Workers of America won a large wage increase and unlimited cost-of-living for the more than 500,000 workers at American Telephone and Telegraph. The new U.S. Postal Service signed an agreement calling for a substantial wage increase and unlimited cost-of-living for the nation's 640,000 postal workers. In August—in the most expensive settlement of 1971, even though finally agreed upon after the administration's wage-price freeze—the United Steel

Workers won a 50-cents-an-hour first year wage increase and unlimited cost-of-living. The aerospace industry won contracts almost identical to the auto industry.

By the end of 1971, the number of workers covered by cost-of-living clauses jumped from 30 million to 57 million, the largest annual increase in history. Previously, the increase ranged from 1.8 million to 3 million a year.

The General Motors strike of 1970 was one of the largest and most expensive strikes in American history. General Motors lost 1 billion or more dollars in profits. The corporation says it lost production of some 1.5 million cars and trucks. Dividends in 1970 were down from an expected 5 to 2.09 dollars a share, a gap of 600 million dollars.

The strike had a crippling financial effect upon the UAW. It paid out more than 160 million dollars in strike benefits. It was forced to mortgage its recreation and education center at Black Lake. In repaying its bills it paid more than 2.5 million dollars in interest, chiefly 496,000 dollars to the General Motors Corporation for its insurance payment loan, and 2 million to the Teamsters Union. A check for 15 million dollars, part of the money the UAW owed General Motors for payment of its medical and life insurance premiums, was the largest check Emil Mazey had ever written. To ease its financial situation, the international union, at a special convention in November 1971, in an action that was strongly contested, pushed through a restructuring of its dues, directing that local unions be allowed to keep 37 cents out of each dues dollar instead of 40 cents, the union's practice for many years. The 3 cents went to the international to help in the financial crisis.

Other automobile manufacturers did not, as might have been expected, gain sales during the strike. The industry had predicted a big year for its 1971 models, which went on sale late summer and early fall of 1970, but production rates were only slightly higher than in 1969. The American automobile buyer is a comparison buyer. He likes to compare a Chevrolet against a Ford, a Ford against a Plymouth. With General Motors out of production, the buyer—frightened too by the recession—could not make this comparison and stayed home, his money in the bank. Additionally, General Motors buyers are loyal; many waited for the strike to end rather than switch to a Ford or Chrysler automobile. Finally, General Motors canceled much of its advertising, and this depressed automobile demand. Lee A. Iacocca, Ford executive, told the *Wall Street Journal:* "I would like to say that things never looked better, but I can't. The longer the strike goes on, the less confidence anyone has to buy any kind of a car."

The strike hurt the American manufacturers' campaign to recapture their markets from the foreign car makers. The American manufacturers had hoped to skim the foreign producers back from 15 per cent to perhaps 11 or 12 per cent of the market—or at least hold the line at 15 per cent. But because General Motors was not in production, the automobile buyer —the comparison buyer—was unable to compare the Vega with Ford's Pinto, Chrysler's Colt or Cricket, American Motors' Gremlin. Purchases were postponed. Without General Motors leading the way, the American small car campaign never got moving. The continuing success of the foreign auto makers was a major reason the Nixon Administration moved to force a revaluation of foreign currencies when it imposed the wage-price freeze.

The steel industry, already depressed because of increasing sales of cheaper foreign steel, was forced to reduce production. Many workers in steel, glass, and rubber were placed on four day weeks. More than 300,000 people, in addition to the strikers and those laid off by the strike, were on reduced hours or forced to accept reduced wages.

The federal government, according to General Motors, lost more than 1 billion dollars in taxes due to the strike. The nation lost hundreds of millions of dollars in retail sales. In Michigan, where 170,000 strikers lived, the largest concentra-

tion of men and women on strike, the state government lost
more than 90 million dollars in corporate and personal income
taxes and suffered a retail sales loss estimated at 375 million
dollars. More than 80 million dollars was paid out in welfare
payments in Michigan because of the strike. Other states with
large concentrations of automobile workers—New York, Ohio,
Indiana, Missouri, Georgia, California—also suffered severe
losses. A 1972 study at the Wharton School of Finance estimated that the GM strike cost American citizens at least 30
million dollars in tax monies in the form of welfare payments.
The two researchers who did the study raised the possibility
that unions will increasingly rely upon welfare payments instead of union strike funds. They said such a tactic would
cost American taxpayers more than 330 million dollars a year.

The strike helped thwart hopes for a recovery from the
recession. In September, the month the strike began, the nation's unemployment figure jumped from 5.1 per cent to 5.5
per cent, the largest monthly increase in a decade. By November, more than 500,000 people were on strike or laid off because
of the strike, one of the largest numbers idled by any single
strike. During the fourth quarter of 1970, government economists said, the nation's real output of goods and services rose
1.4 per cent instead of the predicted 2.5 per cent, the strike
being the major cause of the low growth.

Yet, the automobile industry in 1971 and 1972, shored up
by federal economic policies, soon largely shook off the de-
pressing effects of the strike. Sales soared, some of the high
volume consisting of units lost because of the strike. The sales
—and increased prices—brought profits to almost embarrassing levels.

The strike was a political strike, a strike not to win
agreement but to win ratification. General Motors would have
signed the same agreement in September if the UAW had
made known that it was prepared to settle. But Woodcock

is unsure whether the final settlement could have been ratified without a strike. He says: "You could have had the response, 'Well, if it's so easy, there's got to be something else . . .' I think we could have sold it, but there would have been difficulty, particularly in the 30-and-out area." Eunice Williams, of the union's GM national negotiating team, says, "If we had brought that settlement to the rank-and-file on September 15 they would have told us to go to hell."

Bramblett: "I think inflation was the root of the problem. The big settlements by the Teamsters, the building trades, *The New York Times*. They raised expectations of people and made the price so high—kept the bar up there so high—that there wasn't any chance to reach it until things were down for ten weeks. Only then were we able to reach a settlement that they thought they could get ratified and we thought we could live with. It's about that simple."

Woodcock, in July 1971, speaking to some three thousand delegates to the Teamster convention in Miami Beach, said:

> When the UAW struck the General Motors Corporation in the middle of September 1970, we had one hundred and twenty million dollars in our strike fund, and most of our members thought that was all the gold at Fort Knox. But it is not much against General Motors . . .
>
> Now people sometimes say to me, "Why General Motors? Why take on the toughest? Why take on the biggest? Why take on the one that could run you out of money so fast and so quick?"
>
> Well, we had two excellent reasons: one was that ever since the Big Three were all on the same date [since 1955, when GM, Ford, and Chrysler contracts first expired simultaneously], we had always turned to some other company. . . . There was . . . beginning [a] feeling in our union— more than a beginning feeling, a strong feeling among the General Motors workers and among the Ford workers and among most of our members—that we were afraid of the General Motors Corporation.

When we have that kind of feeling in the membership that a union is afraid of the biggest employer with which it deals, you have a situation where the union becomes demoralized. . . .

The other thing was that one of our chief things was to get back the cost-of-living in its old form, and we lost it in 1967 under understandable circumstances, and the place to go to get it back was the place where we first had got it in 1948, because they proposed it and all their publications were full of propaganda which we could use—their program—against them, and we figured that that would be valuable. . . . So there were two excellent reasons why we went to General Motors and I might say that our union today stands twenty feet tall because we did.

The corporation demand that the UAW help increase productivity by combating absenteeism, tardiness, and sloppy workmanship—the demand that General Motors enunciated so forcefully—was largely ignored by both parties, just as were the union's urgently stated demands for improvement in working conditions. The union's pollution demands—Reuther made pollution an issue only because he wanted to appear up to date—were likewise forgotten.

The corporation's demand for increased productivity is in large part a means for winning antiunion publicity—a tactic to give the corporation the appearance of toughness at the bargaining table. For productivity is not substantially increased by instituting work rules to make men work more diligently, although that is part of the productivity formula. Productivity is increased, by and large, through increased investment in plants and machinery. Talk of sanctions against tardy or absent workers or against workers who do not perform their jobs according to work standards is mostly that—talk. The corporation cannot insist upon penalties against the workers, for it knows that the union cannot agree to them; if the union did, the workers would accuse the union of being allied with the corporation. The two sides know this; they are victims of the relationship they have fashioned.

The union is aware of the problems of absenteeism and tardiness and shoddy workmanship, but whatever it does in this area must be done with great tact, if anything is done at all. The corporation and the union agreed to establish a special worker orientation program at a large urban plant. The Cadillac plant in Detroit was selected as the pilot plant, and Ford and Chrysler instituted similar pilot programs. Bramblett, Woodcock, and Bluestone praised the program as the possible forerunner of a corporation-wide plan to improve worker attitudes, by explaining to workers what factory work is like and to point out their responsibilities. But this effort was all that was done in this area, and can be expected to have no real impact. After the strike, absenteeism, one indicator of worker discontent, returned to prestrike levels of about 5 per cent.

The idea at Chrysler, which received so much notice, of exploring the four day week was abandoned. Some discussions were conducted between union and corporation executives, but the corporation was not interested in the plan; it agreed to the discussions largely because Fraser asked company executives to do so, and the corporation did not wish to offend Fraser. It knew he needed something extra and gave it to him. Fraser called off the talks in December 1971, after a handful of meetings, saying that it was obvious the corporation was not enthusiastic about the concept, and that to continue the talks would delude union members and the public.

No large number of workers utilized the 30-and-out retirement program in the months after it went into effect in October 1971. The continuing recession made the workers wary of accepting retirement. Overtime was down, and workers had little opportunity to put money away. Some men and women wished to build up savings accounts that had been reduced during the strike, and they also wished to stay with their companies during the Christmas and New Year's holidays to enjoy the ten day paid vacation.

But many workers also decided against taking early retirement when it became known that if they retired at age 58, their Social Security benefits would be greatly reduced when they turned 65. In computing Social Security benefits, the five lowest years of a worker's earnings are disregarded; if a man retires at 60, for example, he can disregard the years between 60 and 65, the years he will not work, and still receive maximum Social Security benefits. If he retires at 58, as he can under the 30-and-out agreement, the additional two no-earning years cannot be dropped in computing Social Security benefits. Union economists estimated that the extra years of retirement would reduce an average worker's Social Security benefits from about 213 to 188 dollars a month. Although union negotiators were aware of this—they know the laws and corporation bargainers had called them to their attention—they did not make it known to the twelve member General Motors Council or to the rank-and-file when the General Motors agreement was presented for ratification. The union leadership decided to keep quiet; after ratification had been achieved, the union had a measure introduced in Congress to amend the Social Security law so workers could retire early without losses in Social Security benefits.

A central question: What of the working conditions that the union leaders condemn so vigorously and dramatically as negotiations open but which have been forgotten by the time contracts are reached months later? If what the union leaders say of the plants is true, that in so many cases they are miserable oppressive places; if what so many workers say is true, that factory work is boring and meaningless, that they wish they had never gone into the plants, that they believe they have wasted their lives; if what the corporations say is true, that they are aware of the difficulties of plant life, that they read the writings of the sociologists and psychologists, that they wish to make plants as livable as possible—if all this is true, why is so little done in negotiations to change plant life?

The answer is that fundamental changes in the factory system can occur only when fundamental changes are made in the philosophy and practices of the corporation and the union—and the corporation and the union believe their philosophies and practices are correct.

The corporation is not a humanistic institution, nor seemingly a particularly wise one. It exists to maximize profits, yet it does not feel compelled to truly work to reduce the extensive costs of employee dissatisfaction, the costs of tardiness, absenteeism, turnover, of extensive quality control programs, of the high wages demanded by workers to compensate for jobs they dislike so intensely. The corporation knows that factory life is difficult, but it believes that this is the nature of factory work and that this truth should be recognized by the men and women who work in the plants.

Edward J. Lawler and J. Richard Hackman, sociologists at Yale University, write that corporate profits and employee satisfaction need not be conflicting goals. "A desire to maximize profits should cause organizations to become more orientated towards designing jobs to fit the needs of employees. The assembly line worker has no real skill he can market . . . Rather than seeing his work as a part of him or as an expression of himself, he sees it as a place to remain as short a time as possible and to earn as much money as possible so that life off the job can be made enjoyable. Unions are supporting this view by demanding shorter and shorter work weeks and early retirement, as if to say to management, 'You can make work unpleasant, but we will do everything we can to see that our members spend a minimum time working.' "

Factory work likely will never be completely interesting or meaningful, even with increased reliance on automation. "It is almost morally wrong to think of making jobs totally attractive," says Dr. Chris Argyris, the Yale psychologist. "What can be done, though, is to make jobs attractive enough so that the worker has the chance to experience some meaning and fullness, some growth in his life, a chance to grow." What is needed are sensitive, humanistic men in positions of power at General Motors and other corporations, for this is the key: sensitivity and humanism. But the men at General Motors, like those at most other large corporations, are, most of them, narrow, unintellectual, unconcerned, unknowledgeable, profit-seeking men. Thus, except for increased wages, fringe benefits, additional time off the job—those concessions granted at union request—factory life remains unchanged.

It is a fact, too, it can be argued, that the company need not work to bring change, for this is, according to the relationship between the corporation and the union, the province of the UAW. But the UAW does not work for change, not meaningful, fundamental change; it works for the perpetuation of its position, for the status quo.

The UAW, like nearly all large American labor unions, works for little more than a larger share of American abundance, a larger piece of the American pie. It makes no effort to win progressive achievements: the placing of workers on boards of directors or the establishment of worker councils to allow workers to have important voices in production and management. The idea of worker participation in management or worker management—industrial democracy—is as foreign to the UAW as it is to General Motors.

Little bargaining skill is required to win large wage increases in the automobile industry, the richest industry in America, one of the richest enterprises in history. The UAW does what it believes the rank-and-file wants it to do—ask for more money, more time off the job. The leadership seemingly has little trust in the rank-and-file; it will not go to the workers and say that a large wage increase is unjustified, or that there are goals of greater importance than winning increased wages —let us change the factory system rather than increase wages or take more time off the job. A Pontiac foreman says, "Most guys actually don't believe that pay raises are the answer to

their problems." A utility worker at Cadillac: "To get a raise
ain't worth it. You get more money today and prices go up
tomorrow."

Humanism would make of the plants what they can be.
It would promote men out of the ranks; it would encourage
corporations to make products to serve the national good, not
merely the corporations; it would create structures in which
workers could make decisions in the manufacturing and assembly process, in cost and quality control, in the layout of factories and jobs.

It is the ethic that is wrong: workers, young, old, men,
women, all of them coming into factories each day, five days
a week, 50 weeks a year, to build cars, nine million cars a year
—down the line, out the door, to be used for a year, two years,
four years, and junked. Is this the American genius? If it is,
it is a wicked genius. The double standard is also wrong—
that working men and women are second-class people of no
talent, aspirations, or importance. This, too, must change.

Surely, without humanism, the problems of the work place
will become intensified in the years ahead. To be sure, the
work force is changing as the proportion of industrial jobs,
typified by auto industry work, decreases; however, workers in
some of the new service jobs, the technical and professional
ranks, will face many of the problems industrial workers have
so long faced in the auto industry: boredom, repetition, power-
lessness, meaninglessness, second-class status.

Bramblett says that no one wins, everyone loses in a
strike such as the General Motors strike—a huge, costly shut-
down. But a man who has watched these talks for years, a
neutral man, says, "Nobody lost; both sides won." He explains:
"A continuing relationship requires no loser."
The relationship between the General Motors Corporation

and the United Automobile Workers has altered—they are not enemies, nor, in a large sense, adversaries. It is true, as Bramblett says, and Woodcock agrees, that the two, General Motors and the UAW, have a *greater community of interest than of conflict.*

Archie Walker, a UAW member, a black: "The union and the company, they are more or less business partners."

Epilogue

No job is perfect, James M. Roche of General Motors Corporation said in an interview in Louisville, Kentucky, on the matter of worker discontent. Look at my job, said Roche, who as GM chairman earned about three-quarters of a million dollars a year, asking, "What's more boring than lugging home a big briefcase of papers to be read before going to bed?"

UAW leaders had little enthusiasm for provisions of the new Occupational Safety and Health Act that permits workers to complain directly to the Department of Labor about unsafe working conditions. This was the finding of the Ralph Nader study team in its book *Bitter Wages*. The UAW sent a letter to locals suggesting that, instead of complaining to the government, workers forward their complaints to the UAW regional director, who would decide whether complaints should be passed on to the Labor Department. "Without this chain of command," a UAW officer said, "we would run the risk of having self-appointed experts in hundreds of plants operating singly, on the one hand, or [of] being inundated with requests here at headquarters, on the other."

Negotiators should lie to reporters, John Dunlop, head of the federal Cost-of-Living Council and a long-time labor expert, told a group of Nieman Fellows at Harvard University.

Some reporters were outraged at this suggestion, and Dunlop was asked how such a philosophy could be defended. He replied that negotiators always use reporters and that reporters are usually too stupid to realize this. Anyway, he said, lies serve the negotiators, the truth often does not.

A skilled tradesman told a Detroit reporter of the feelings of fellow workers: "They say Solidarity House is just like the White House."

How does this book stand up, two years after it was completed and after another round of negotiations between the automobile companies and the United Automobile Workers?

The auto companies and the auto union are locked in a partnership. Their relationship, their understanding, was demonstrated, as it was in the negotiations of 1970, by the negotiations in 1973.

The workplace and the manner in which corporations are run are not challenged. Not challenging the corporations is among the rules of the game—the scenario, the ballet. But while the UAW likes to say that it is a partner with the auto companies, it has no power. The companies have the power. Product policy, marketing, design and location of factories, organization of jobs, employee policy, line speed, discipline, manpower, automation, factory closings—all the important decisions are made by management and management alone.

General Motors, Ford, and Chrysler are conservative institutions led by insulated, profit-minded men who lack vision or social responsibility? Safer cars? Auto pollution? The need for a balanced transportation system? The companies resist change or act minimally in these areas. If they act they do so when forced by government decree or by events, such as the hullabaloo over the fuel situation, which has brought a decrease in large car sales, in turn prompting the manufactur-

ers at least for the time-being to reduce production of larger
cars and increase production of smaller cars. Soon, however,
the industry was again huckstering big cars. Normalcy was
returning.

Democratization of the workplace and of the industry
itself? This is absurd idealism or socialist claptrap to the auto
executives.

The UAW is a right-of-center union with a left-of-center
reputation? The 1973 negotiations demonstrated, if further
demonstration is needed, that the UAW is an undemocratic
institution led by self-righteous men out of touch with the
rank-and-file.

Despite its reputation as a socially concerned institution,
the UAW is in reality irrelevant in the fight against the major
problems that confront America, such as racism, poverty, unemployment, economic concentration, lack of economic planning.

The union leaders talk of the dignity and intelligence of
working people, but they are unwilling to lead or challenge
them. In reality, the UAW does not believe in confrontation,
in bargaining or social reform. Its leaders prefer moderation,
progress by degree. In a large way, the UAW leadership has
come to accept the ideology of the industrialists who are the
union's avowed enemies. They do not fight for social change.
They are, in large part, content with improving the lot of
the worker through expansion of the economy, that is,
through gaining a larger piece of an expanding pie.

The UAW leaders do not believe in democracy, in the
union or the running of the corporations. As I said in this
book, worker democracy is as alien to the UAW as it is to
the corporations. The UAW executive board is controlled by
conservative, aging, often racist white men. The legal, education, health and safety, recreation, conservation, and organizing departments are unimaginative, unaggressive, and
short-staffed. The much-praised Public Review Board is a
fraud, without authorization to act in many areas.

A final point: What I have said about the auto industry—
that because of its lack of concern for safety and its refusal to
combat pollution and to lead the way toward a balanced
transportation system it is a damaging force upon American
life; what I have said of the UAW—that it refuses to challenge the workplace or the way corporations are run, that
it is undemocratic, and that it is not a militant fighter for
social reform; these same statements are also true for much
of the rest of American business and labor.

In recent years, auto sales and profits have hit record
levels. Still, the companies complain that profit margins are
low—profits plummeted during the Arab oil embargo—and a
number of critics contend that the industry's great days are
over, that it is in a period of decline and possible extinction.

These criticisms are not well-founded. Perhaps the industry may never again know the gigantic growth of the
1920s or the burst it received after World War II, when
pent-up demand was great, or that of the 1950s, when national and state governments spent massively on roads and
expressways. Yet, while the industry faces problems in years
ahead with possible limits on energy and what may be a
growing feeling that the nation must reduce its dependence
on the auto and build a rational transportation system, the
auto industry remains—and will remain for decades ahead—
a dominant force in American life. Americans are accustomed
to mobility. Many citizens in large cities, towns and rural
areas depend upon the automobile for transportation.

Even a balanced transportation system will depend in
large measure upon individual vehicles of some sort, and it
is logical to assume that GM, Ford, Chrysler, and American
Motors will build them. Even if one disagrees with the philosophy of men like Richard Gerstenberg of General Motors
Corporation, Henry Ford II and Lee Iacocca of Ford Motor
Company, and Lynn Townsend of Chrysler Corporation, one
should not doubt the business abilities of these men or their
subordinates. They do not intend to see their corporations

become extinct; it is vacuous to think that the corporations will become extinct.

Years ago, Alfred P. Sloan, Jr., the architect of the modern General Motors Corporation, wrote that the "primary object of the corporation . . . [is] to make money, not just to make motor cars." GM, like the other auto companies, probably will continue largely to make transportation vehicles, no matter what kind of motors—gas, steam, turbine, nuclear or solar energy—will propel them. And they will continue to make money. Henry Ford II has written: "For all its flexibility, the car is not the best possible way to get to or move around in very busy places. For all its efficiency in carrying large numbers of people along busy corridors, mass transit is not flexible enough. What we need and are now beginning to see, in addition to cars and mass transit, are new kinds of vehicles and systems designed to carry people quickly, conveniently and efficiently where neither cars nor conventional transit can do the job as well." It is only wise to assume that the auto companies, in addition to making cars, will build those vehicles and transportation systems—and reap the profits from them. Many businesses depend upon the automobile industry—gas stations, franchise food parlors, motels, road construction companies, insurance companies, the trucking industry. In a nation of corporate socialism, can it be expected that the government will let the auto companies and these scores of other industries go out of business?

For the worker, life is unchanged despite the 1970 and 1973 contracts. Absenteeism remains at 5 per cent or more on most days, and well above that on Fridays and Mondays. Drinking and drug usage continue to be major problems. Boredom, drudgery, lack of democracy, the repetitiveness and meaninglessness of auto assembly work—none of this has been altered.

Despite the pay and cost-of-living advances, workers' wages continue to be eroded by inflation. The auto companies and the auto union boasted in late 1972, when they said the average hourly wage in the industry reached 5 dollars—a far cry from Henry Ford's fabled 5 dollar day. (The 5 dollar an hour figure was misleading: the typical worker, the assembler, was making about 4.50 dollars.) But what auto or union executives raise families on 170 dollars or less in weekly take-home pay?

Although the companies suggested in 1970 that the contracts they negotiated were inflationary and would impair the companies' profitability, the increased labor costs did not harm the corporations. General Motors, for example, continued to earn about 20 per cent on investment throughout the years of the contract—far greater than the rest of American industry. In 1973, GM earned nearly 3 billion dollars, a corporate record.

Experiments in enriching the workplace, which have received attention in the last three years, are minimal at best. Those corporation executives who back them are not likely to end up in positions of power. And the job orientation program negotiated in 1970 and touted by both the companies and the union as a way to combat worker dissatisfaction is a failure—a quick briefing, a propaganda session for each side, nothing more.

Meanwhile, the federal government charged General Motors and Ford with price-fixing on fleet sales and attempting to pressure Chrysler into eliminating its fleet sales discounts. The companies were found innocent of the charges. But through subpoenaing the appointment calendars of chief corporation executives, the government was able to disclose that top executives of GM, Ford, and Chrysler met several times during 1970 in what were called "summit" and "foothill" meetings—summit meetings were attended by chairmen and presidents, foothill meetings by lesser executives—discussed the 1970 negotiations and assumedly settled upon some sort of strategy to combat the UAW. The UAW has long contended that such meetings occur. This was the first formal proof.

The federal government brought action against two automobile companies, among other firms, and the UAW, among other unions, for what the government called discrimination against minority workers. The UAW joined the automobile companies in asking the federal government to delay stringent federal emission standards. A Washington, D.C.–based organization, Health Research Study Group, affiliated with Ralph Nader, said that death and injury due to work-induced heart and lung diseases are high among auto workers, and that neither the companies nor the union adequately protect the workers. "Many auto factories and other workplaces where UAW members work are unhealthy and unsafe," the report said, and its main researcher, Dr. Janette Sherman, noted that the UAW does not employ a single physician on its health staff.

The 1973 negotiations brought gains for the UAW—restrictions on mandatory overtime, wage increases, an improved cost-of-living formula, a dental plan, greater pension benefits, and what the UAW described as strengthened health, safety and grievance procedures.

But the gains were not the great victories described by the UAW. The negotiations also saw three major wildcat strikes by workers in Chrysler plants in Detroit—strikes that were as much, or more, against the union as against Chrysler. They did not involve money or more time off the job—but the health and safety issues.

During the strikes, union executives resorted to a tactic that corporation executives had used against the founders of the union years before: tarring the strikers as radicals. One wildcat strike also saw the UAW muster 1,000 union loyalists at the gates of the struck Detroit Mack Avenue Stamping plant, to ensure, union executives said, that radicals would not block workers from going to their jobs. Newspapers praised this flexing of union muscle as reminiscent of the flying squadrons of the old days of the union. But, it seems fair to ask, what is the difference between a company goon squad and a UAW loyalty squad?

At Ford, in a bitter ratification struggle, the UAW suffered the first rank-and-file contract rejection in the union's history. This was by skilled tradesmen angered by a provision —the existence of which was not made known by the UAW but had to be discovered by the tradesmen—that Ford could place production workers in skilled trade jobs if tradesmen made use of voluntary overtime provisions.

The UAW withheld the vote count until, climaxing a boisterous day of argument at Ford Local 600 where a second vote was going on, a unit president, David Mundy, shot a skilled tradesman—luckily in the buttocks. The tradesmen believed that the UAW constitution gave them veto power over the agreement. But the international, interpreting the constitution to its benefit, ruled that the contract had been ratified because production workers, who constitute the majority of Ford workers, had approved the agreement. The international went ahead to renegotiate the overtime provisions that had angered the tradesmen. It refused to allow the tradesmen to vote on the renegotiated provisions.

It is the position of many people that production methods cannot be changed, even if the companies favored change, because it would be impossible under any other methods to build cars to sell at reasonable prices. But the auto companies, to hear them tell it, have never been able to afford anything, beginning with the gains won by the workers during the Flint, Michigan, sitdown strike in 1936–7; and they are not counting the costs of present production methods—the costs of drugs, alcohol, absenteeism, bad workmanship. David Jenkins, in his book *Job Power*, asks if quality production can ever be obtained from a disenfranchised workforce.

According to the UAW, progress by degree—the nature of collective bargaining, its leaders claim—is how progress is made in America. Why, the UAW asks, aren't workers revolting against the leadership if it is so out-of-tune with workers? Why aren't contracts rejected if they are inferior? But the union's philosophy of progress by degree, progress every third year, is a philosophy of moderation that may be

similar to the philosophy that blacks should practice moderation because blacks have made great gains in America over
the last one hundred years. The UAW was not founded on
moderation. Its leaders do not talk of moderation when they
make their speeches to union conventions or tell the press
the gains they plan to make in the upcoming negotiations.
They only practice moderation in the bargaining suites and
in their efforts in behalf of social reform. It is not, says a
long-time union member from Ohio, that the international
has lost fights, but that it has not made fights.

Moreover, the workers do rebel. Unable to reach international officers, whose jobs are guaranteed by union elective
practices, they continually oust local leaders. They rebel
against the workplace by not showing up, by doing their jobs
poorly. Through the use of drugs and alcohol, they rebel
against the workplace and against the society that the UAW
allegedly wishes to change.

The structure of the union and the process of ratification
practically guarantee that contracts will be ratified. The international controls the locals, which do the ratifying. Contracts are not fully explained to rank-and-filers. Still, the Ford
skilled tradesmen rejected their contract. Overturning a contract or challenging the UAW leadership in elections is a difficult task. Dissidents are co-opted into the international structure or purged from the union. It is not enough to say that
the UAW is the most liberal, the most robust, the most democratic of labor unions. The UAW cannot be judged by the
Teamsters or the steel workers. It must be judged by its own
standards, by the words and promises of its leaders—like
Walter Reuther who, in 1947, at the Atlantic City convention
where he consolidated his power, declared to the UAW members: "We are the vanguard in America in that great crusade
to build a better world."

The UAW leaders are, in many ways, decent men. They
wish the workplace were better. They believe that the nation
should end poverty, that there should be better schools and

social and economic equality. But these men are old, and
they have mellowed. They are compromisers, and they have
settled far short. If they were radicals in their youth, they are
not now.° Leonard Woodcock—more progressive than many
members of his executive board—does not make 75,000 dollars
or more a year like George Meany. He does not have a big
stomach and smoke cigars and play golf in Miami Beach. But
he earns about 36,000 dollars a year and lives in a handsome
high-rise apartment. His is a life of good food, good drinks.
Not a lavish life but a comfortable life. And he has settled
into it. Reform does not burn in him, for he is not a zealous
man, if he was one in the Socialist days of his youth. Privately, I suspect, he believes that America, while in need of
progress in a number of areas such as housing, guaranteed
annual income, health care, is not a bad place.

He has lost his combativeness. Consider the remarks of
Woodcock in 1971, before the Detroit Economic Club—an
organization of business leaders and one of the prestigious
speaking forums in the country. President Nixon had come
to Detroit shortly before, and Woodcock was asked why the
UAW had not picketed Nixon shortly after new economic
policies had been announced. Woodcock explained he did not
believe that picket lines "add very much to the democratic
process." The UAW, he said, had been able to present its
points of view to the Administration and Congress. He said:
"I just don't think this growing tendency to have demonstration picket lines adds a thing to the democratic process. . . .
I think if you've got something to say, go hire your own
hall and see what kind of a crowd you can get." The remarks
were followed by generous applause.

What is true of Woodcock—he wants to take the UAW
back into the conservative AFL-CIO—is true of other UAW

° Indeed, they want to forget their pasts—and their colleagues of those
days. In spring 1974, not a single UAW leader attended a tribute in Detroit
to Maurice Sugar, the one-time UAW counsel and legendary labor figure
who had died some weeks before.

leaders. They are brokers, accommodationists—in the end, leaders not of a militant union, an instrument for social reform, but of an insurance company that provides a work force for the corporations; leaders of a moderately progressive institution for reform in American life.

In the 1973 negotiations, the UAW was pledged to mount an attack upon the problems of the workplace. The course was largely chosen because of federal wage guidelines which, limiting wage and fringe benefit increases to 6.2 per cent a year, forced the union to turn from solely economic gains.

The bargaining year began in February, 1973, when the UAW conducted a production workers' convention, the first convention of its kind in union history, in Atlanta.

The UAW did not want the convention. At a meeting of its twenty-five-member executive board in New Orleans, Woodcock said there was no reason for the convention. But he said the union was committed to it by resolution of the 1972 convention. So the UAW did the next best thing to not having the convention: the union rigged the convention. The seven hundred–odd delegates were handpicked local union officers, men and women, who said Douglas Fraser would break their backs for the leadership. Convention hours were set as ten to five, with an hour and a half off for lunch. It was to be a boondoggle, a few days drinking and dining on the union expense account. As Stephen Schlossberg, a UAW counsel, remarked: "You don't need a convention when you have a majority."

Yet, one by one, these union loyalists rose to condemn factory conditions, to attack, as one delegate said of the assembly line, "that black devil chain." They said overtime must be made voluntary, that health and safety problems must be solved with dispatch—on the factory floor—and that there must be no disciplining of workers until workers could

tell their side of any incident. The 1973 negotiations, they
made clear, must concentrate on factory conditions, not just
wages and hours. "The only kind of protection we are going
to get," said one delegate, "is the protection we give ourselves."

The delegates knew the union did not want the convention and were worried that the leaders would adjourn it and
forget the workers' demands. Woodcock went out of his way
to promise that the union would give attention to what he
called the production workers' fair grievances. He had learned
a "great deal" from the delegates' remarks, he said, and factory
conditions would be an important issue in the 1973 negotiations.

Then Woodcock made a stunning declaration. The problems of the workplace had been much discussed in academic
circles and in newspapers, magazines, books, and on television.
The 1972 local strike at Lordstown, Ohio, had received an
amazing amount of coverage in the United States and abroad,
with many observers seeing it as an illustration of how
America's growing young work force would act in the future.° A study, *Work in America,* by a Department of
Health, Education, and Welfare task force, concluded that
worker discontent not only existed among blue-collar workers
but also was widespread among white-collar employees. Auto
workers, the task force said, rank sixteenth in satisfaction,
last among listed categories. And at this convention, UAW
members were complaining about the workplace. For Wood-

° It cannot be denied that the Lordstown strikers were predominantly
young—the average age was about twenty-nine, the company and union say
—and that the walkout occurred in a depressed Midwestern area, a place
picked by General Motors because the company believed it would offer labor
peace. Yet, while the strike may suggest how many young workers look at
their jobs, and will look at them in future years, a main point of the strike
is that the Lordstown workers were revolting against the speed-up, an evil
that helped bring about the union years before. The lesson: despite thirty-
seven years of existence, the UAW has been unable to control the speed of
the line, the most basic aspect of automobile production, and perhaps the
most fundamental point of contention between workers and the companies.

cock it was as though he had been challenged. He lashed out, not at the delegates, whom he could not attack, but at the "academics"—those professors and journalists who were examining the workplace.

Woodcock told the delegates that these "academics" were writing "elitist nonsense" about the workplace, or what the press, with the news magazines' zest for the snappy phrase, had come to call "blue-collar blues." These people, he said, seemingly were attempting to create a "new intellectual and academic discipline to deal exclusively with the problems of worker alienation." Woodcock declared, "They would like to create a professionalism which would give more jobs to some people who have never done any real work in their whole lives. If some company said to us tomorrow, 'Okay, you do it, humanize the plant,' we wouldn't know where to start. We don't have the answers. Nobody does."

A similar attack came in March of 1973, before some three thousand union members gathered to give approval to the UAW's bargaining platform. This time Woodcock condemned the "enemies of our union," who "say we have never addressed ourselves to the workplace." Woodcock said that anyone who said that was either a "liar or a fool." He added, "We have had to fight every inch of the way" to improve work conditions and he called the effort a "never-ending fight." He then cited these gains the union had negotiated: in 1958, written guarantee from the corporations of local negotiations, and in 1961, 21 minutes of relief time a day, expanded to 36 minutes a day in 1964 and to 46 minutes a day in 1967. It was not an expansive list.

Then Woodcock outlined the union's 1973 bargaining goals:

> An end to mandatory overtime: "If we are on a collision course on this question, so be it," he said.
>> Increased pay for overtime
>> Higher wages
>> An improved cost-of-living formula

Profit-sharing

A company-paid dental program

Stronger health and safety measures, including guarantees for the immediate shutdown of unsafe machines
or assembly lines

"Watchful attention" to the problems of work pace

Methods to combat the "inverted system of plant justice," in which the "worker is presumed guilty . . . until
proven innocent"

Protection against subcontracting, in which the automobile companies contract work to outside firms, often
taking work from UAW members. Skilled tradesmen are
particularly hit by this practice; moreover, many outside
factories are more unsafe than Big Three plants

Better financing of the supplemental unemployment
fund, which provides up to 95 per cent take-home pay,
less 7.50 dollars for lunch and other work-incurred expenses, to laid-off workers

Increased vacation time

An improved 30-and-out pension system, including re-
insurance for workers in supplier firms

Woodcock declared: "We will go from this convention,
I am sure, together, united, because we face the most powerful economic adversaries on this earth and we need all our
unity, determination and strength to gain the victory—the
realistic, sensible victory—that will be ours in 1973."

Woodcock, in his Atlanta and Detroit speeches, was engaged in a curious exercise. He was, at once, condemning the
"academics," who had helped raise the workplace issue as
people who knew nothing of the workplace, and saying that
the workplace, the issue the "academics" had raised, would
be the key issue in the 1973 negotiations.

He was, to be sure, rejecting such academics' proposals
as job-rotation, in which workers are shifted from one job
to the other to reduce boredom; and job enlargement, where,
instead of breaking jobs down into their smallest components,
as in the time study of Frederick Winslow Taylor, jobs are

expanded, so that a worker's assignment and responsibility
are broadened. Yet, Woodcock, a smart man, surely knew
that the academics were not limiting their calls for "humanization of the workplace" to such proposals. Woodcock was
engaging in the self-righteousness of Walter Reuther, assert-
ing that the UAW, not elitists in the universities or the New
York magazine offices, understand the workplace issue and
what could—and could not—be done about it.

He was simultaneously seizing the workplace issue and
running with it—a tactic at which the UAW is extremely
skilled. Ironically, the UAW had helped fuel the workplace
issue. The leaders told reporters of the problems of auto
production and the drudgery, hard work, noise, filth, monotony, the authoritarian foremen and supervisors. But then the
stories, from the UAW's view, got out of hand, or, as then
U.S. Labor Secretary James Hodgson remarked, were blown
out of proportion by "pop sociologists and their media sisters
under the skin." Indeed, this same view was taken by George
Morris, General Motors vice president for industrial relations,
who told *Newsweek* that the clamor over the issue of job
dissatisfaction reminded him of the great attention given
automation a decade before when, he said, "the academics
started talking about it and pretty soon they were quoting
each other." Morris said: "They said people were on their
way out, which simply wasn't true." Now, the same kind of
reporting was occurring, he said: "There is a lot of writing
being done on this subject of 'alienation' by people who don't
know what they are talking about."

The UAW had to counter the issue. It would be foolish
and dangerous to let it lie unchecked. As Douglas Fraser
remarked to a reporter in 1970, during a discussion about
militant black workers, "You've got to be prepared to take
issues away from them, not allow issues to arise upon which
they can exploit the situation. Unless you do that they're
going to grow and grow." The reporter asked Fraser whether
this was a democratic tactic, how it might differ from when

GM is under attack and appoints a safe black or a safe woman to its board of directors. Democratic or not, Fraser said it was leadership.

Finally, the federal wage-benefit guidelines of 6.2 per cent lay in the background. And while Woodcock said the UAW would not be bound by the guidelines, that he was not in favor of federal guidelines or controls, he knew that while they could be stretched—as the Teamsters had done, with a 7 per cent settlement—they could not be ignored.

Yet, despite the importance that Woodcock and other union executives placed on the negotiations, the UAW president, like the auto executives, said he saw no reason for a strike in 1973.

Union and company officials had made similar remarks in 1970, but that year they were largely sham, the responsible remarks of responsible labor and business leaders, at best made in hope. There were too many factors in 1970: a new union president, the need to put the workers on the street, Woodcock's lack of knowledge as to what he could sell the rank-and-file, the fact that the UAW had not struck GM in twenty-five years, the pressure for a large wage increase and for restoration of the cost-of-living formula. Now these pressures were gone. The issues that remained were not strikeable. They could be hashed out, hopefully, by reasonable men from both sides.

Woodcock said, "There is not the same feeling of inevitability now as there was in 1970 and 1967 [when the UAW struck Ford for 67 days]."

Richard Gerstenberg, the GM chairman, took the same position. He said: ". . . this year, unlike 1970, carries no built-in factors that make a strike almost inevitable. We in General Motors agree fully with Mr. Woodcock that there is no need for a strike in 1973." Restating a theme that Woodcock and Earl Bramblett, then GM vice president for labor relations, had voiced in 1970, Gerstenberg said: "I now suggest that we have come to a time when we can acknowledge

that we have so far more in common than in conflict, when
we can jointly pay our respects to the buried animosities of
the past even while we pay tribute to what we have jointly
achieved despite them." He continued, "These differences
have no place in our country today: they have gone the way
of the sweatshop."

Such a statement was in marked contrast to the warlike
address that James Roche had made before the 1970 negotiations, when Roche said GM workers were shortchanging the
company with absenteeism and poor workmanship. Indeed,
what purpose would a strike serve this time? The workers
did not appear restive. The UAW had no points to prove,
having struck the nation's largest industrial firm for ten weeks
just three years before. As *The New York Times* observed, the
atmosphere was one of conciliation and optimism.

But the 1973 negotiations were not to be peaceful. In
the summer, three large Chrysler facilities were shut by
wildcat strikes, demonstrating that the sweatshop had not
been eliminated, that the UAW leadership was out of touch
with many of the rank-and-file, and that the union had not
been aggressive in combatting health and safety problems.

The first strike broke out July 24, a few days after formal
opening of the talks, at Chrysler's Jefferson Avenue Assembly
plant on Detroit's east side; two young black workers, Isaac
Shorter and Larry Carter, barricaded themselves in a wire
cage housing a power system and shut off the power, stopping
the assembly line, idling some five thousand workers. It
lasted just thirteen hours and had a most unexpected ending:
the firing of Shorter and Carter's foreman, whom the two had
accused of using racist language and of authoritarian practices. Perhaps even more surprising: the company refused to
discipline Shorter or Carter.

Douglas Fraser, the UAW Chrysler Department head, and
GM and Ford executives were stunned by the strike, but more
by the firing of the foreman. Fraser even conceded admira-
tion for the audacity of the two workers, calling the wild-

cat the first hijacking of a plant in his memory, although apparently forgetting the 1936–7 sitdowns at Flint that won the union recognition from GM.

To the Jefferson workers—two hundred of whom surrounded Shorter and Carter in the cage to ensure they would not be removed by police—the two were genuine folk heroes. When the strike ended, they were carried from the plant on the shoulders of fellow workers, the air full of clenched black fists.

The companies and the union had feared that the Chrysler capitulation would bring more sitdowns. On August 7, workers left their jobs at Chrysler's Detroit Forge plant after an accident in which one worker's arm was crushed on a conveyer belt and another's finger was smashed by a crane. A shutdown at the plant—whose workers produce torsion bars, engine and suspension system parts—could close the corporation, Chrysler officials said, and the firm went to court to force a return to work. Fraser left the bargaining suites to tour the plant, emerging with oil on his clean coat. He looked, he said, like he had just spent two years in a coal mine and that the workers had "legitimate and pressing grievances," that the plant was dirty and there was grease on the floor.

The wildcat forced Fraser into other action. Calling off the Chrysler–UAW bargaining, he sent international staff members into Chrysler's twenty-one Detroit area plants to inspect for dangerous health and safety conditions. The staff members found fifty-nine "distressingly bad" conditions. On Sunday, August 12, Fraser urged a meeting of Forge workers to return to work and promised that the union would authorize a strike if conditions were not corrected. "We'll stay on the company's back," Fraser said. "Give us a chance to clean this thing up." He said, "We'll put an international representative on all three shifts and we'll stay with them until we're satisfied that the plant is clean." A show of hands indicated that the workers were about equally divided. But on Monday, under federal court order to refrain from participating in an organized work stoppage—the judge ruled that individuals could refuse to work dangerous jobs, but that collective action was illegal—the strikers returned to work.

Peace was short-lived. Next day, August 14, the nearby Chrysler Mack Avenue Stamping plant was shut down, idling about 4,800 workers. Some 70 wildcatters, led by a twenty-five-year-old fired white worker—William Gilbreth—staged a sit-in.

According to Chrysler, Gilbreth—he is a relative of the famous efficiency expert, Frank Gilbreth, the scientific management pioneer and hero of the book and movie *Cheaper by the Dozen*—had been fired August 10 for giving false employment information and, later, for trying to lead an unauthorized work stoppage. The company said he returned to the plant and with a friend climbed onto a conveyer belt, shutting down the department, a framing unit. When two guards attempted to eject Gilbreth and his friend, according to Chrysler, the guards were belted with pipes. One required sixteen stitches for a head wound, the other received bruises on the head, neck, and shoulders.

Both Chrysler and the UAW were enraged by the third strike. Chrysler said it would use "every legal means" to end the disruption, and the union claimed it would support all "reasonable action" by the company. On August 14, the day after Gilbreth—he was described as a leader of the Workers Action Movement, a small group of young radicals—sat down on the line, police entered the plant and ejected Gilbreth and some forty sitdowners who remained in the plant. Workers returned to their jobs on the first shift on August 16 as, in an action laden with irony, the UAW marshalled one thousand loyalists at plant gates.

With them were union officials Fraser, Secretary-Treasurer Emil Mazey, and Vice Presidents Kenneth Bannon, Irving Bluestone, and Olga Madar, plus numerous assistants. A Detroit police inspector said of the loyalists, massed at each of the six plant gates: "I'm glad we're on the same side." The loyalists had been cautioned against violence, but Gilbreth was beaten, although not severely.

That was the end of the wildcats. Later, when Shorter reportedly attempted to stage a wildcat, he was rebuffed by workers and fired by Chrysler. Fraser said the incident demonstrated that Shorter had "no support" in the plants.

When William M. Farrell, a *New York Times* correspondent, interviewed workers outside the Mack Stamping plant during the sitdown, he found that the union was repeatedly singled out for criticism. One worker complained, "The reason this all started is we don't have a union in the plants that is meeting our needs." The union executives, he said, were "too old to fight." As Fraser conceded to a reporter: "There is something fundamentally wrong with the system when you don't know you have a problem until it explodes."

All along there had been speculation that Chrysler would be the 1973 negotiation target. GM had been singled out in 1970, Ford in 1967. Unlike 1970, Chrysler's financial picture was good, with profits of 198.4 million dollars in the first six months of 1973, up 52.5 per cent from the first six months of 1972. Its 1973 sales were expected to hit 9.8 billion dollars. The union executives believed Chrysler did not want a strike, because a shutdown would affect its comeback from the lean years of the late 1960s and early 1970s. Moreover— and this was an important factor—Chrysler had old plants, knew it had a problem with them, and, as Fraser remarked: "Chrysler has had the least knee-jerk reactions to proposals this union has made on working conditions."

The wildcats constituted another reason for selecting Chrysler. To go to GM or Ford, after turmoil had broken out at Chrysler, would have meant that the UAW had avoided the company where militancy was high and workplace problems were perhaps the gravest. There was some speculation that the wildcats had demonstrated that Chrysler workers lacked the discipline to be the negotiation's leaders, and perhaps there was that fear. But to have avoided Chrysler would have opened the UAW to charges that it was frightened of the Chrysler workers.

At a UAW executive board meeting in Milwaukee on August 21, despite the usual exclamations from Bluestone and Bannon that GM and Ford workers were willing to make whatever sacrifices the UAW would demand of them, Chrysler was named the target. Bargaining began August 25. Chrysler made an offer of a wage increase of 3 per cent a year which Woodcock rejected as a "mockery of collective bargaining," just as three years before, Bluestone had described an initial GM offer as a "hiccough."

On September 14, in what seemed a surprise, Woodcock and his assistants—a farcical touch was added by a tape recorder playing "Solidarity Forever" in the background— emerged from Chrysler's bargaining headquarters and Woodcock announced that there would be a strike. Time had just run out, he said. Chrysler's vice president for personnel, William O'Brien, agreed. But it was not a real strike, although workers were to lose a week's pay—more if they were scheduled for overtime—and there were to be no strike benefits.*
Perhaps the UAW did not want to direct Chrysler workers to stay on their jobs without a contract, which would have saved their pay but opened the UAW to charges that it was not militant. However, it is likely that the negotiators bungled. The strike was surely not a tool for an agreement. Woodcock announced that bargaining would resume at 10 A.M. Saturday, the next morning. Early Monday, less than sixty

---

* The loss of wages did not occur during the strike—but after the strike. This is because each week's paycheck is for work performed the previous week. Each worker thus received the week's regular paycheck during the time spent home. It was the week back at work that the worker was docked the week's pay. However, that loss was cushioned by payment of an average 200 dollars to each worker in cost-of-living payments, which Chrysler workers receive quarterly. Thus, the workers were not really hurt by losing a week's work. This made calling the strike easier.

hours after the strike began, an agreement was reached. As detailed by UAW executives, it brought these breakthroughs:

> Overtime: No worker would be required to work more than nine hours a day. Sunday overtime would be voluntary, provided the worker had been present for all assigned work the preceding week, and a worker could refuse to work every third Saturday provided he had worked the two previous Saturdays and been on the job the five previous days. This stipulation, Woodcock said, was an attempt to assist Chrysler in reducing its absenteeism. The union assured the company it would not allow collective action, that is, workers collectively refusing overtime to force changes in work rules or to settle grievances.
>
> Wages: An increase of 3 per cent the first year, plus an additional 12 cents—in all, a 25-cent first-year wage increase for the typical worker, the assembler. Three per cent increases in each of the second and third years of the contract.
>
> Cost-of-Living: Improvement in the cost-of-living formula—a one cent wage increase for a rise of each .35 points in the Consumer Price Index, compared to a penny for a rise of each .4 points in the old contract.
>
> A Dental Plan: To finance the plan, a penny an hour would be subtracted each quarter from every worker's cost-of-living allowance beginning in March, 1974, and for the next ten quarters of the contract. The plan would begin in October, 1974.
>
> Health and Safety: According to Fraser, each Thursday union stewards and committeemen along with representatives of the company would examine work areas for "cleanliness and orderliness." On Friday, the union's plant safety chairman would be allowed to tour the plant and consult with district committeemen. Problems could be placed on agendas for discussion with Chrysler. If a problem was urgent, a representative of the UAW's international safety committee could be summoned to the plant.
>
> Grievances: A strengthened grievance procedure, with a pilot program for instant arbitration of discipline matters if a worker selected the arbitration.

Epilogue

Subcontracting: Th̶...
over subcontracting.

Supplemental Unemploym̶...
an hour, depending on the size of ...
5 to 10 cents an hour under the 1970 c̶...
also agreed to pay extra money for over̶...
nalize itself, the UAW said, for overtime.

Holidays: A guarantee of twelve days off at ...
and New Year's plus a new holiday, the day after 'T̶... ...s-giving.

Pensions: An expanded pension program, which, through a combination of company pension benefits, a company supplement after age sixty-five and social security payments, would, beginning October 1, 1978, guarantee each thirty-year worker 700 dollars a month in pension benefits regardless of age.

In other matters, the company and the union agreed that the union would be a party to any job enrichment programs. Chrysler agreed to pay all medical insurance premiums for laid-off workers from the company treasury, not from supplemental unemployment funds, to strengthen the unemployment fund.

Chrysler also added 35 cents of the present 40-cent cost-of-living payment to a worker's base wage. Therefore, if the cost-of-living index fell, the worker could have no more than 5 cents deducted from his pay. The 3 per cent wage increases in the second and third year of the contract would be figured on an expanded base wage, thus giving the worker a higher second- and third-year increase.

To combat the absenteeism problem and to save the company money, the UAW went along with a company proposal to reduce a beginning worker's pay to 45 cents below the normal classification for the employee's first three months on the job. The company agreed to a UAW–Chrysler study of foundry workers, beginning in the third year of the contract. If the study demonstrated that foundry workers suffer disability because of their work, they could receive

......ents after twenty-five years of service. The
..y offered to pay both the company and worker share
of a national health insurance, if such a program were enacted by Congress.

Woodcock expressed satisfaction. "It is most certainly a
breakthrough," he said. He refused to place a figure on its
cost, although it appeared that the contract was larger than
the 6.2 per cent a year federal guideline, and it was soon estimated at 7 per cent a year or more. "I'm not going to get into
the percentage game," he said. "I have no idea what the percentage is." O'Brien, the Chrysler vice-president, released
this statement: "Chrysler is very pleased with the terms of
the new contract. . . . We are hopeful that ratification will
be completed this week and the company will be able to
resume normal operations as soon as possible." Newspaper
stories and editorials hailed the agreement, as exemplified by
this *New York Times* editorial: "The Chrysler accord is a
pacesetter in what will undoubtedly be the major motif of
industrial relations in the nineteen-seventies, a movement
away from the sterility of the traditional 'battle for the buck'
to union involvement in joint efforts with management to
'humanize' factory life." Only *Newsweek*, among major publications, took a less euphoric view. "As fat as the contract
was," *Newsweek* said, "a close look showed that Chrysler
got as well as it gave." On Wednesday, September 19, the
UAW's two-hundred-ten-member Chrysler Council endorsed
the agreement and, as Woodcock and O'Brien had hoped,
ratification came quickly with, according to the UAW on
Sunday, September 23, only seven of the sixty-nine locals
voting against the contract. Work resumed Monday, September 24.

But the contract was sold by an international union that
controls every step of the voting procedure and which has
great assistance from the press. It was not the breakthrough
described by the international, for it does not alter the job
nor fundamentally challenge management's right to run the

company as its executives see fit. Ratification procedure—
as it is called, not, as it should be, a vote on a proposed
contract—began immediately after Woodcock, Fraser, Ernest
Moran (a long-time Woodcock assistant), and Chrysler's two
top labor officials privately worked out the agreement. As
in 1970, elected negotiators were absent. First the contract
was submitted to the thirteen-member negotiation committee.
They accepted unanimously. Then the contract went to the
union's twenty-five member executive board, all international loyalists. They approved unanimously. Next the contract was considered by a special group composed of presidents of the union's sixty-nine Chrysler bargaining units.
Bringing them to Detroit was a skillful move. The union paid
for their travel, food, drinking, and lodging. For them it
was a visit to the big city, a chance to belong, a place in the
sun. They had no documents before them; all they knew was
what Woodcock and Fraser told them. They gave the document overwhelming approval.

Monday evening, Woodcock and Fraser conducted a press
conference at Solidarity House. They applied such phrases
as "historic" and "precedent-setting" to the contract and went
on to describe it in general terms. Most reporters face deadlines; they wanted terms of the settlement and preferred not
to bother with analysis. And so, the next day's stories—the
most important, for they were the first accounts of the contract and set the pattern for how it would be received—described the contract according to the words of the union
executives, in fact often going beyond what the executives
said. Terms like "historic" and "precedent-setting" were used
without attribution. Most reporters, in effect, let the union
executives write their stories for them.

For the rest of the week, stories and editorials were based
on information provided at the Monday night press conference. During this week of ratification, only one article, in
The New York Times, compared the union's demands along
with its gains; but the *Times* is not available to most of the

workers. *The Detroit Free Press*, whose coverage was decided from the perspective of the international, published stories saying that the contract was not a total union victory, that there were some trade-offs, that both sides would benefit, and included some details that union executives had neglected to mention at the press conference. But these articles did not appear until after most contract votes had been conducted. The Detroit *News* provided no analysis of the contract, nor did the wire services or any other major newspapers, although the Chrysler press room was packed with reporters.

Most of the press looks at labor negotiations and contracts from the point of view of businessmen: that settlements by strike deadlines are positive, quick ratification and a quick return to work are positive, strikes and rejection of contracts are negative. Reporters feel pressure to report terms of the settlement in the next day's paper. Such adjectives as "historic" and "precedent-setting" assure page-one play, so reporters like to use those kinds of words. Negative stories cut off sources, making reporting more difficult. Labor reporters, like other reporters, become friendly with their sources—both union and company men.

With this as the background—media coverage that heralded the contract as a breakthrough, plus approval by the negotiation committee and the executive board—the UAW took the contract to the union's two-hundred-ten-member Chrysler council and then, Thursday through Sunday, September 20 to September 23, to the local unions. Talk was of ratification, nothing else. Make-ready workers were already being called back to the plants.

At their meeting at Detroit's Veterans Memorial Building, the council members, mostly union loyalists, were provided with copies of parts of the new contract plus an eight-page pamphlet—*Chrysler Newsgram*, published by the UAW's publicity department. The newsgram gave some details that union officers had not revealed at the Monday press conference. But it was not a fact sheet as much as a propaganda sheet that described the contract as a significant victory in every area. Woodcock and Fraser and other top staff members ran the meeting, extolling the contract. Delegates with questions or criticism rose from the audience when recognized by the international officers. The speakers on the platform said critics were misinformed or unaware of the larger picture. At no time was there a full discussion of the contract —a presentation of good points and bad points, gains and trade-offs. Expectedly, the contract was approved, 203–7. Local ratification followed, at meetings that largely were copies of the Detroit meetings.

But even with these procedures, the contract was not ratified as overwhelmingly as the international suggested. The UAW does not merely count votes. It follows a unit voting rule in which all possible votes from a local are awarded according to how the votes are cast. Thus in a local with, say, 10,000 members, the 10,000 votes go to the side that carries, no matter how many votes are cast. This procedure simplifies the international's ability to control an election, for it will concentrate on large locals; if it can get majorities in those locals, the vote of the smaller ones does not matter. Moreover, the unit rule makes it appear as if the turnout is not only extensive, but complete, for under this rule the turnout is always 100 per cent of each department's membership. The UAW does not release the numbers of workers who voted—neither the local counts nor the actual national count. Instead, it gives the percentage of yes and no votes, the percentage according to the unit rule.

Actually, in the Chrysler vote, it appears that 20 per cent to one-third of Chrysler workers went to the polls. For example, of some 9,000 members at UAW Local 3, the Hamtramck Assembly plant, or Dodge Main, only about 1,200 workers—or 13 per cent—voted. The contract carried 613 to 528 for production workers, 25 to 23 for skilled tradesmen. But all 9,000 votes were counted for ratification. Of 1,400 members at UAW Local 47, 499 workers voted—35 per cent of

the membership. Among production workers, 180 voted for
the contract, 117 against; skilled trades voted 117 for ratification, 85 against. All 1,400 votes were counted as affirmative
votes.

Obviously the vast majority of workers were not moved
to go to their union halls to vote. For many the contract
was probably satisfactory. For some, it was good enough. For
many others it was not particularly good. After the Ford
skilled-trades rejection, Emil Mazey, UAW secretary-treasurer, argued that dissatisfied workers vote, that satisfied
workers stay home. This was not an argument he would have
used after the Chrysler contract was ratified. Most workers
probably stayed home because it appeared that their votes
would make no difference. Most auto workers do not participate in the affairs of their union anymore. Even Mazey
says he is concerned about low turnouts not only at contract
votes but also at membership meetings, where, he says, local
unions often have difficulty in marshalling a quorum. Most
workers are as alienated from unions as they are from their
jobs or from society.

Surely the contract was large, somewhat over the 6.2 per
cent federal guidelines. In fact, Mazey told a group of union
financial secretaries that the UAW "deliberately steered away"
from fully describing gains of the agreement because the
union wanted to guard against an "unnecessary struggle" with
the Cost of Living Council over whether the contract should
be approved. But as David Jenkins writes in *Job Power,* auto
workers have always had comparatively high wages, not un-
related to the fact that they are asked to perform wearisome,
difficult, monotonous work.

Let us examine the contract:

Overtime. The union sought voluntary overtime, that is,
an end to mandatory overtime. It did not win this, but instead won some overtime restrictions. As with 30-and-out,
or early retirement, which was a key issue in 1970, many
workers probably will not utilize this gain. They will not want

to give up the overtime pay, which has become part of family
budgets. But for those who wish to trade money for time
off, the overtime restrictions are an overdue reform, even
for those workers who will only occasionally take days off
to lessen work strain.

But overtime rules, which went into effect January 1,
1974, contain provisions designed to assist the corporations
in two major areas—absenteeism and the corporations' need
for overtime at critical times and at critical plants. In regard
to absenteeism, William Luneburg, president of American
Motors Corporation, which has had no mandatory overtime
since 1969, told newsmen in little-noticed remarks in 1973
that voluntary overtime was not a "basic problem" for the
industry. The "real problem," Luneburg said, was absenteeism. He said: "You can't really count on the stability of the
work force. It seems to have disappeared because of a change
in the way of life or how people look at work." The UAW,
as even Woodcock conceded, attempted to assist Chrysler
with this "real problem," by the provisions that a worker must
not only work all assigned hours Monday through Saturday to
refuse Sunday overtime, but also must work two consecutive
Saturdays and Monday through Friday of the third week to
refuse overtime on the third Saturday. Excused absences are
counted as time off the job—the same as unexcused absences
—and will prevent workers from refusing overtime.

To guard against concerted action, or group refusal of
overtime, the contract allows the company to lift the overtime restrictions for up to two weeks at plants where workers
have resorted to concerted action. Dissidents said this action
introduced the doctrine of "collective guilt" into union contracts, meaning that all workers would be punished for the
actions of others.

The contract also stipulates that overtime restrictions do
not apply for up to four weeks during model changeover
time, when companies begin producing the next year's model,
and at model build-out time, when the last of the old model

line is manufactured. Additionally, plants designated "critical plants"—facilities where overtime is judged a necessity—are exempt from the restrictions for up to ninety days at a time. The "critical" status of these plants will be examined by the company and the union at the end of each ninety-day period. Finally, the restrictions may be suspended if Chrysler gives notices of supply problems or other emergencies that might impair production if the company is prohibited from scheduling necessary overtime.

The companies guard their overtime figures as company secrets. But it is likely that it is at these "critical plants" that the greatest amount of overtime is worked, for they are key plants. Typical workers on overtime probably were working fifty- to fifty-four-hour weeks, meaning that in many cases the restrictions will only limit workers to those hours they already were working. As the contract was explained by Emil Mazey to the local financial secretaries, Woodcock and Fraser made clear to Chrysler bargainers that the union must have voluntary overtime on Saturdays and Sundays. The company executives said that the company could not operate under those conditions. Five-day weeks in critical manufacturing plants, the executives said, would mean three and one-half or four-day weeks in assembly plants. So the union executives, Mazey said, accepted overtime regulations Chrysler claimed it needed to maintain production.

According to the *Wall Street Journal*, citing government figures, the average work week in the automobile industry in 1973 was forty-seven hours. And, *Newsweek* suggested, the overtime restrictions might not be worth a great deal if the companies, as they planned to do, reduced overtime due to decreased demand for large autos brought about by the scare over the shortage of gasoline. This was exactly what happened in the months following the negotiations.

The *Journal* pointed out before the contract was reached that the auto industry was one of the few major industries in America in which mandatory overtime was not curbed years ago. The *Journal* said that the UAW, with some seven hundred thousand workers, probably represented the largest single unionized work force in the country subject to mandatory overtime. Woodcock could say in March that the UAW would eliminate mandatory overtime and that if the company and the union were on a collision course, "so be it." But on September 23, the day ratification was completed, a union official was quoted in the Detroit *Free Press:* "What the hell, it's a start. We got the guys some manhood."

Wages. While the new wages, 25 cents in the first year plus 3 per cent increases in the second and third year of the contract, seemed large, particularly given the 5.5 per cent federal wage guidelines, they actually represented an increase of 4 cents in "new money." This is because 13 cents of the 25 cents represents the 3 per cent annual productivity increase that workers have been receiving every year since 1948. This raise is equal to the typical productivity increase in heavy industry, although it is probably somewhat less than the productivity increase in the high-efficient auto industry. The industry has never said what the rate is, but has suggested it is about 3 per cent. The UAW believes it to be about 5 per cent. The 3 per cent increases in the second and third years of the contract also are productivity increases, and have been going to auto workers for years.

Of the remaining 12 cents of the 25-cent first-year increase, 8 cents was due workers as cost-of-living for the months May, June, and July. Neither the 1970 or the 1973 contracts provided for cost-of-living increases for those three months, but both sides knew that the 8 cents would be part of the new wage increase.

Cost-of-Living. The union had sought a penny wage increase for each .25 point increase in the cost-of-living index. What it got was a penny increase for each .35 point increase, instead of each .4 point increase as under the 1970 contract. Yet, as Woodcock admitted, one cent of the cost-of-living will be deducted from each worker's wages to pay for the dental

plan, 30-and-out, additional holidays and other benefits—
meaning that the workers are paying for those benefits themselves.

Dental Plan. This represents a true benefit for workers and
their families, who now will be able to receive much of the
dental care they have missed because often they cannot afford
it. But workers are helping finance the plan, and it does not
go into effect until October 1, 1974.

Health and Safety. Local unions had wanted to be able
to "red flag," or shut down, unsafe machines, equipment or
assembly lines. Instead, the UAW negotiated the "right" to
have a special health and safety representative in each plant
who had the "right" to conduct weekly plant inspections and
meetings with management after the inspections. In addition,
members of the UAW's international health and safety staff
"will be given access" to Chrysler plants for inspections. It
won all this, the international said, "for the first time in the
history of the auto industry."

But the UAW already had the right to "inspect plants."
Any conscientious committeeman had done that for years.
And it could conduct meetings with management on health
and safety problems. To combat health and safety problems,
dissidents say, local unions ought to have the right to strike
with minimum bureaucratic procedure. They do not have
that right, nor will they get it if the international can avoid
it, the dissidents say, because the international believes in
discipline and control over its members as much as General
Motors does over its employees. The UAW is a political institution, and international officers fear that if local leaders
had the right to strike, they would lead their locals out all
the time in quest for political power. But a wise official does
not lead workers out for transient reasons, because workers
can lose money; strikes can last a long time. If the strike
leader fails, he is likely to be voted out of office.

Under the 1973 contract, the power of local unions may
be reduced, for health and safety problems will be tied up

in new machinery. While those problems are in that machinery, locals cannot strike even with Solidarity House authorization.

Grievances. The UAW and Chrysler agreed to establish a joint committee to study standards for a pilot program for acceleration of grievances by discharged employees. The contract does not address other matters—workplace conditions, manpower practices, what workers consider arbitrary actions by foremen—that lead to grievances, and because they are not resolved, to worker discontent.

Subcontracting. The union negotiated the "right to strike" for all workers when the company violates outside contracting provisions of the contract.

Supplemental Unemployment Fund. The increased funding, from 7 to 12 cents an hour compared to 5 to 10 cents an hour under the 1970 contract, will protect employees in time of layoff. This will be of particular importance if auto layoffs caused by the shut-down of large-car production lines last for any extended period of time.

Days Off. The union received the Friday after Thanksgiving as a holiday, beginning in the second year of the contract, plus guarantees of twelve days off at Christmas and New Year's. The union did not win the other holidays it had sought, the birthdays of Dr. Martin Luther King, Jr., and Walter Reuther. Auto-worker holidays outnumber those that most workers, blue- or white-collar, receive in America.

Pensions. In 1970, the day the General Motors contract was ratified by the GM Council, a journalist remarked to Woodcock that the UAW had not won 30-and-out. The UAW certainly had, Woodcock replied. It had, but with restrictions. Although, beginning October 1, 1971, a worker with thirty years' service could retire at any age, the worker would be docked 8 per cent from his pension for each year the worker was under age fifty-eight. Beginning October 1, 1972, the last year of the contract, a retiree's pension would be reduced by 8 per cent for each year he was under age fifty-six.

Moreover, workers choosing 30-and-out retirement were also faced—at age sixty-five—with what became known as the "cliff effect," a reduction in company pension benefits when social security payments set in.

In 1973, the UAW negotiated an end to penalties for early retirement as well as to the "cliff effect" (the UAW had known about the "cliff effect" when the 1970 contract was being ratified, but it did not inform the workers). The 1973 pension agreement provides four pension rates: workers retiring after March 1, 1974, will receive a monthly pension of 550 dollars a month; workers retiring after October 1, 1975, will get 625 dollars a month; workers retiring after October 1, 1976, will receive a pension of 650 dollars a month; and workers retiring after October 1, 1978, will receive 700 dollars a month.

Moreover, while it is clear that the 700 dollars represents a pension gain, no one knows how much money the 700 dollars will be worth in 1978, when it goes into effect, or in 1979, when it can be renegotiated. Further, the 700 dollar pension guarantee includes not just a worker's company pension, but, beginning at age sixty-two, the worker's social security benefits and, beginning at age sixty-five, the worker and his wife's social security benefits. Nevertheless the system is one of the best in American industry.

In regard to pensions, the UAW negotiated a six-year contract—September 1973 to September 1979. This is a great advantage to Chrysler, because for the next six years the company will be protected against further union pension demands. Secondly, provisions that the longer a worker stays on the job, the greater that worker's pension benefits will be, are designed as an incentive for workers not to take 30-and-out but to remain at work. This would reduce Chrysler's employee turnover and keep experienced workers on the job.

In October, the UAW reached a similar agreement with Ford. In accordance with the "frosting on the cake" doctrine of adding improvements at each subsequent company to make the union executives look good and to prevent ratification problems, the Ford agreement contained 25-and-out retirement for foundry workers. At Chrysler, the UAW contract had provided for a study of foundry workers and enactment of 25-and-out for them if the study showed their health was affected by their work.

It appears that about one-third of the 185,000 Ford production workers and skilled tradesmen voted on the contract, probably a higher turnout than at Chrysler. The UAW said the vote among production workers was 112,154 for the contract, 38,684 against it. Skilled workers rejected the contract 20,089 to 5,943. But these figures were according to the UAW's unit rule. Again the impression was that the turnout was 100 per cent.

When the Ford skilled tradesmen rejected the contract, second votes were ordered at some key units, including some at UAW Local 600, the gigantic Ford Rouge plant local in Dearborn. Woodcock and Bannon, the UAW Ford department director, denied that the international had ordered the second votes. Bannon said he had called off the second votes when he realized they were in violation of the union's constitution. But The New York Times reported that some Local 600 officers disagreed with Bannon's interpretation. These leaders pointed out that the second votes were called off when key units, such as the Ford maintenance unit, were voting against the contract by margins of about 20–1.

One local leader said Walter Dorash, Local 600 president and an international stalwart, told unit chairmen that if the second votes were not held and the contract was not passed, the local leaders would have to wear steel vests in the plants. It would be made clear to workers that if a strike occurred and the men lost money, the local leaders were to blame for not adequately explaining and pushing the contract. When anti-international sentiment appeared in the newspapers, Woodcock and other leaders blamed the press for stirring up the tradesmen's opposition, saying that the press had not

pointed out how union leaders had been shouted down when
they tried to explain the contract. Woodcock complained that
the skilled tradesmen were confused, that they did not understand the contract. The tradesmen said they understood
perfectly. With the rejection standing, Woodcock and other
UAW leaders said that while the constitution provided for
separate skilled trades voting on proposed contracts, it did
not give the tradesmen power to veto contracts. He ordered
that the provision authorizing Ford to fill tradesmen's jobs
with production workers be renegotiated.

(In late 1973, dissidents appealed the international interpretation of the constitution to the UAW's Public Review
Board. In April, 1974, in a decision that the UAW's publicity
department neglected to make public, the press obtaining the
decision when dissidents gave it to them, the board upheld
the international. A 5-member majority of the 7-member
panel held that the UAW, in giving skilled tradesmen separate voting power in 1966, only meant to give "more attention" to the tradesmen's "special problems," not allow them
to veto a proposed contract.

However, the two dissenters, the two law school deans on
the panel, asked what was the purpose of the separate vote
if tradesmen did not have rejection power. The two panelists
noted that Woodcock said in May 1966 that if a rejection occurred when workers were not on strike—as was the case in
1973—"the nature of the reason for rejection will determine
. . . the tactics to be followed." But the two board members
held that the statement "did not contemplate" implementation of a rejected agreement. The dissenting board members
noted that while the UAW had blamed the "popular press"
for the idea that tradesmen had veto power, the union house
organ, *Solidarity,* reported in May, 1966 that production and
skilled workers would have "separate ratification balloting,"
and that if either group rejected a proposed contract, there
would be no agreement.

The dissenters asked, "Was separate ratification merely a

temporary expedient to assuage a restless minority—a grant
of illusory power now to be withdrawn with the passing of
the exigencies responsible for its proposal?" A study of the
matter suggests this was exactly the case.)

In late November, the UAW concluded an agreement with
General Motors Corporation. It was similar to the Chrysler
and Ford agreements, although GM and the UAW, to ensure
that there would be no opposition from skilled tradesmen,
eliminated the overtime provisions that had angered the
Ford tradesmen. Woodcock stated that the agreement was
good for the industry, which, he said, faced an uncertain
future. Morris, the chief GM negotiator, said he had never
seen such businesslike negotiations. As with the Ford agreement, the contract was retroactive to September 15. And GM,
to provide an inducement for ratification, announced that if
the agreement were quickly ratified, the company would pay
the retroactive pay—amounting to about 125 dollars for as-
semblers—before Christmas. GM suggested this was a Christmas bonus, although the money was no bonus, but money
the workers had earned. In December, Woodcock announced
that GM workers—he meant those who had voted—had
approved the agreement by a margin of more than 9–1. The
number of workers who voted was not announced.

In all three contracts, the UAW won agreement from the
corporations to pay both the company's and the worker's
share of national health insurance if a health insurance plan
is enacted by Congress. The union has been pushing for some
years for national health insurance. *The New York Times*
described this as a major breakthrough and the envy of other
unions. But the newspaper also noted that the steelworkers
have had a similar clause in their contracts for years. Moreover, the auto companies already pay the complete costs of
workers' health insurance through private insurers.

The UAW had been worried that if national health insurance were passed, the union would lose money—the difference between the private insurance and government in-

surance, the premiums on which probably would be lower than those under private plans. That matter was not resolved, although it is likely that the companies will agree to pass the money along to workers in the form of other benefits.

The company and the union also agreed to a starting wage for new employees of 45 cents below the standard wage. This reduction was designed to save the corporation money, to reduce the costs of the contract, and to provide an incentive for new employees to stay on this job. This company benefit—it will save millions for the corporations—went largely unnoticed, and was not mentioned in the UAW brochures sent to local unions.

Other demands were forgotten altogether: profit-sharing, an end to air and water pollution from auto factories, protection against speedup, preferential hiring rights for workers who lose their jobs because of plant closings, the end of racial and sexual discrimination, substitution of a salary for the hourly wage, investment of pension funds for socially useful purposes, medical insurance for treatment of alcoholism and drug addiction, company-paid training for workers who lose their jobs because of new technology.

A number of proposals have been advanced for reforming General Motors and similar giant enterprises. Some observers say that GM and similarly powerful institutions should be broken up. I suspect that there are many GM executives who, knowing first-hand how stifling and unprogressive the bureaucracy can be, are private trust busters, believing that the public would be better served if GM and similar enterprises were broken up. Ralph Nader, the consumer advocate, has called for federal chartering of GM and other large corporations. The chartering would force companies to disclose to the public virtually all information on products, research and development, and corporate tax returns. He says corporate officials should be made accountable for actions of their companies; he would jail corporate executives responsible for corporate crimes and force corporations convicted of fraudulent advertising to suspend advertising. Nader told *The New York Times:* "We should have a concept of social bankruptcy, [in which] the company is thrown into receivership. If a company can be thrown into bankruptcy because it's not paying its bills, why shouldn't it be thrown into bankruptcy for making thousands of people sick and destroying and depreciating other people's property without compensation, which is what contamination and pollution do."

Nader said, "One thing the Federal charter would do would be to begin to distinguish much more clearly between individual rights and corporate rights. A corporation doesn't have the right of privacy, like an individual." General Motors, he said, cannot be treated with the "same constitutional sensitivity as a person."

A key to reform is democracy: all segments of a society must be involved in the running of a corporation, blue- and white-collar workers (if blue-collar workers are exploited, so too are white-collar workers, whose desks stretch on for acres in places like the GM Technical Center; and if the talent of these men and women were unleashed, they could make valuable contributions), consumers, racial groups, the poor—all people who are affected by a corporation's acts but who presently are essentially powerless in determining a corporation's policies. Boards of directors could be broadened to include such representatives, or other instruments could be created; in either case the key is representation and real power.

It seems clear that the UAW, like other unions, has reforms of its own to make. Woodcock and other UAW officers —Bannon, Bluestone, Greathouse—do not seem to trust the rank-and-file, whom they privately believe are never satisfied. So these UAW leaders resort to undemocratic tactics to sell their contracts.

They regard themselves as true reformers, for they be-

lieve that they accomplish things, win gains for their members. But they really believe in nothing more than that
workers should gain as the economy enlarges. They will not
support true reform or industrial democracy. A perfect meta-
phor for the UAW—indeed, for American labor—is Mazey,
the secretary-treasurer, whose idea of a good day is to be
on the job from nine to five, lunch at Little Harry's (a restaurant not far from Solidarity House), and perhaps a dinner
at Carl's Chop House (a restaurant favored by Detroit union
leaders). Mazey was a giant in his day, a lion among men,
a rank-and-file leader who led wildcatters from the old Briggs
plant at the drop of a hat—a man so radical he was arrested
not *at* the famous Battle of the Overpass at the Ford Rouge
plant, where Reuther and Richard Frankensteen were beaten,
but *on the way* to the Overpass. The Detroit police department knew him on sight; they simply pulled him over and
arrested him. But now Mazey, like the union, is a tired,
toothless lion, taking the sun.

The UAW executives long ago humanized their Solidarity
House offices with carpets, air-conditioning, music, the pleasant view of the Detroit River and green Belle Isle. The
bargaining suites are humanized too, with soft chairs, carpet-
ing, air-conditioning, pictures on the wall. But the factories
are not humanized. While Woodcock can say that "we
wouldn't know where to start" if the company gave the union
the opportunity to humanize the workplace, the fact is that
plants can be humanized, workers can have decision-making
power in their jobs, their companies, and their union.

Here are reforms that could be instituted:

International officers should be elected by direct vote,
not by convention.

The international should pay election costs of all serious candidates for international office, and local unions
should do the same for serious local candidates. A can-

didate for office should be judged "serious" by any number of formulas—for example, if the candidate for international office had the backing of five locals, or if local candidates had the backing of 10 per cent of local memberships.

Workers now do not have the time or money to challenge Woodcock or other international officers. Even at the local level, campaigns for presidencies can run into the thousands of dollars. Moreover, local officers have use of secretaries, copying machines, mailing lists, plus the assistance of the international and regional officers. Insurgents have none of this available.

Federal laws should require certification and public disclosure of all ratification votes. Presently, federal law does not require that unions conduct ratification votes on contracts, much less that votes be certified.

Referendums should be conducted to determine which political candidates will receive UAW support. Now the international makes these decisions. While the officers supported first Edmund Muskie and then George McGovern for the presidency in 1972, many union members backed George Wallace. In Detroit in 1973, the union was behind Mel Ravitz, a white liberal councilman, for mayor; most Detroit auto workers, largely black, as well as a number of local leaders, supported State Senator Coleman Young, a black. When Ravitz lost to Young in the primary the UAW switched to Young.

Salaries of international officers should be reduced to no more than the straight-time salaries of the highest paid union members or, better yet, to the straight-time salaries of the typical auto worker, the assembler.

All international officers and international representatives should be required to return to the auto plants for six months every three years.

Local unions should be given the right to strike upon approval of the local executive board, not the international union.

The UAW should sell Black Lake, its multimillion-dollar retreat in northern Michigan.

The UAW's health and safety department should be greatly expanded, and experts should be retained to lead the fight against the corporations.

The UAW's social action departments—such as law, education, recreation, and civil rights—should be expanded into aggressive, imaginative arms of the union.

The rules of collective bargaining must be changed, with the union contesting management rights in such areas as hiring, firing, production of safe cars, promotion, location and closing of plants, subcontracting, automation, pollution, job design, plant design, profit margins, prices, products, marketing. The union must vigorously attack the problems of line speed, manpower and discipline.

Negotiation sites should be alternated, one year in corporation headquarters, the next year in Solidarity House. It would be a valuable experience for company officers to come to union headquarters.

Workers should be placed on boards of directors, and worker councils should be created. The representatives ought to be representatives of workers, not of the international union.

Solidarity, the UAW's news organ, and *Washington Report,* its Washington newsletter, should be transformed from house organs into publications that reflect the views of all union members.

The unit vote rule should be eliminated; issues and contracts should be decided only by the votes cast. Whenever possible, voting should take place in the plant, to make it as convenient as possible for workers to vote.

Workers should have profit-sharing, as corporation executives do.

While Woodcock says that "we wouldn't know what to do" if the corporations suddenly offered the unions the opportunity to humanize factories, the fact remains that the workplace can be changed, that jobs themselves can be altered. Dozens of work psychologists have important contributions to make, if unions and corporations would listen to them, instead of denigrating them as Woodcock did in

his Atlanta speech. Workers themselves probably have the
best ideas. Humanization begins with fans and water coolers
and goes on to include amenities like postal and banking
facilities; union vigilance in combatting the speed of the line
and company manpower and discipline regulations; the training of shop stewards so they are the equal of their company
counterparts; power to local unions; and industrial democracy—the real redistribution of power.

Perhaps, too, money should be removed from the realm
of labor negotiations and made the subject of arbitration by
labor courts or based wholly on cost-of-living increases. When
wages are omitted from talks, labor unions are forced to give
attention to other matters. As George Morris, GM's industrial
relations director, told the Conference Board in New York:
"The more control there is from the outside on wages and
economic matters, the more pressure there is from the union
on all the other issues"—meaning work conditions. He said,
"If management is to retain any control over the resolution
of all issues, then it must retain its hold on the purse strings."
The point is: when wages are not a negotiation issue, the
company can less easily defend against encroachment in
workplace issues.

Corporation and union executives are removed from the
consequences of their decisions. The corporation leaders use
their positions and their company's great economic means
to protect the auto as the dominant mode of transportation in
this country. They defend the highway trust fund against
diversion. But they do not sit in un-air-conditioned cars in
huge traffic jams on expressways. Nor do they travel great
distances hour after hour on expressways, eating in Howard
Johnson's and Fred Harvey's. These men have chauffeured,
air-conditioned limousines and private jets—wonderful private transportation systems. No wonder auto executives have
helped block rapid transit; they *have* rapid transit. And while
executives like Richard Gerstenberg can say that the sweatshop has been abolished, and that GM jobs are good jobs,

these executives spend no time in hot or noisy factories; they
do not live in bungalows under the smokestacks of their
factories. They lead wonderful—isolated—lives in green-
swards like the Grosse Pointes and Bloomfield Hills, making
occasional incursions through the black inner city to appear
at charity bazaars.

Union executives do not work long hours on a machine,
stamping out fenders, or on an assembly line. The authoritarian foremen, the dirt and noise of auto production, line
speed of sixty to eighty cars an hour, the boredom, drudgery and meaninglessness of installing seats in cars on an assembly line, take-home pay of 160 dollars a week, the long
hours—none of this is part of the lives of the union executives.

That blacks, who compose perhaps 40 per cent of UAW
membership, cannot get ahead; that white workers who plunk
down their life savings for a new home do not get a dream
house but some tract bungalow on a hot, treeless lot surrounded by strips of gas stations, shopping centers, and drive-
in theaters; that workers must drive many hours to find
open spaces; that schools are bad; that children must go to
segregated schools—these are not the experiences of Woodcock, Fraser, Greathouse, Bannon, or Mazey. These men have
mellowed, if indeed—as with Mazey—they once had revolutionary zeal. Their fires were banked long ago. With their
reverence for solidarity they reject criticism; they do not
question their actions.

But it does not seem likely that change will occur. The
UAW, under the present brand of leadership, is unlikely to
attack the fundamental problems of the workplace or how
the corporations are run, nor will it push for industrial democracy. The leaders are convinced that their philosophies
of progress by degree ("Management prerogatives are only
those things we haven't gotten around to taking away,"
Douglas Fraser likes to say) are correct. The main issues in
the coming years will probably be the conventional issues of

wages and benefits. In the area of social reform, the UAW is likely to continue to function as part of the liberal establishment, supporting liberal Democrats, sending Woodcock to Washington to testify before Congressional committees, getting behind such reforms as national health insurance or welfare changes. But the UAW is unlikely to make bold, imaginative moves; to stop compromising; to challenge its own membership.

According to the UAW constitution, Woodcock must step down when he reaches age sixty-five, in 1976. His successor, in all probability, will emerge from the top leadership, what remains of the old Reuther caucus—Fraser, Greathouse, Bannon, or Bluestone. The only hope for a more progressive union under any of these men, it seems to me, is Fraser. Some observers of the union believe that Fraser, while he has not fought Woodcock, is privately unhappy with his leadership. The question is, Would Fraser act courageously and lead the union to new ground? or would he be the Fraser who refused to run for the Senate from Michigan, bowing to counsel of people like Stephen Schlossberg, who held that if Fraser refused to take a stand against busing—as his conscience would have dictated—such a position would have turned white rank-and-filers against him and thus against the union leadership?

There is a paucity of aggressive, imaginative middle-echelon UAW leaders who might someday rise to the top. Most UAW leaders are men who, masquerading as reformers, are, when their disguises are remolded, capitalists.

It is not far-fetched to look at them, GM and the UAW, at the auto companies and the workers, and think of what Kurt Vonnegut wrote in *Harper's* of the American political system: that there are two sides, not the Democrats and the Republicans, but the winners and the losers, and the fix is on.

A Bibliography

ALINSKY, SAUL: *John L. Lewis.* New York: Putnam, 1949.

BARBER, RICHARD J.: *The American Corporation.* New York: Dutton, 1970.

BEASLEY, NORMAN: *Knudsen.* New York: Whittlesey House, 1947.

BELL, DANIEL: *Work and Its Discontents.* Boston: Beacon, 1956.

BENNETT, HARRY: *We Never Called Him Henry.* New York: Fawcett, 1951.

BERNSTEIN, IRVING: *Turbulent Years: A History of the American Worker, 1933–1941.* Boston: Houghton Mifflin, 1970.

CHANDLER, ALFRED D., JR.: *Strategy and Structure: Chapters in the History of the Industrial Enterprise.* Cambridge: Massachusetts Institute of Technology Press, 1962.

CHINOY, ELY: *Automobile Workers and the American Dream.* Garden City, N.Y.: Doubleday, 1955.

CHRISTMAN, HENRY M., ed.: *Walter P. Reuther: Selected Papers.* New York: Macmillan, 1961.

CORMIER, FRANK, and EATON, WILLIAM J.: *Reuther.* Englewood Cliffs, N.J.: Prentice-Hall, 1970.

DRUCKER, PETER: *The Concept of the Corporation.* New York: John Day, 1946.

FINE, SIDNEY: *Sit-Down: The General Motors Strike of 1936–1937.* Ann Arbor: University of Michigan Press, 1969.

FORD, HENRY: *My Life and Work.* In collaboration with Samuel Crowther. New York: Doubleday, 1922.

FOUNTAIN, CLAYTON: *Union Guy.* New York: Viking, 1949.

KEMPTON, MURRAY: *Part of Our Time.* New York: Simon & Schuster, 1955.

KRAUS, HENRY: *The Many and the Few: A Chronicle of the Dynamic Auto Workers.* Los Angeles: Plantin, 1947.

MacManus, Theodore F., and Beasley, Norman: *Men, Money, and Motors.* New York: Harper & Brothers, 1929.

Mortimer, Wyndham: *Organize!* Boston: Beacon, 1971.

Michigan: A Guide to the Wolverine State. New York, 1941.

Nevins, Allan: *Ford: The Times, the Man, the Company.* New York: Scribner's, 1957.

Nevins, Allan, and Hill, Frank Ernest: *Ford: Expansion and Challenge.* New York: Scribner's, 1957.

————: *Ford: Decline and Rebirth.* New York: Scribner's, 1963.

Pflug, Warner W.: *The UAW in Pictures.* Detroit: Wayne State University Press, 1971.

Pound, Arthur: *The Turning Wheel: The Story of General Motors Through Twenty-Five Years, 1908–1933.* Garden City, N.Y.: Doubleday, 1934.

Rae, John B.: *The American Automobile.* Chicago: University of Chicago Press, 1965.

Sloan, Alfred P., Jr.: *Adventures of a White-Collar Man.* New York: Doubleday, 1941.

————: *My Years with General Motors.* New York: Doubleday, 1963.

Sorensen, Charles: *My Forty Years with Ford.* With Samuel T. Williamson. New York: Macmillan, 1956.

Swados, Harvey: *On the Line.* Boston: Little, Brown, 1957.

Sward, Keith: *The Legend of Henry Ford.* New York: Holt, Rinehart, 1948.

Walker, Charles R., and Guest, Robert H.: *The Man on the Assembly Line.* Cambridge: Harvard University Press, 1952.

Widick, B. J.: *Labor Today.* Boston: Houghton Mifflin, 1964.

Widick, B. J., and Howe, Irving: *The UAW and Walter Reuther.* New York: Random House, 1949.

Index

A NOTE ABOUT THE AUTHOR

William Serrin is a reporter for *The Detroit Free Press* and a member of that newspaper's team of reporters which received a Pulitzer Prize for its coverage of the Detroit riots of 1967. He also shared in a 1970 George Polk Award for coverage of the killings at Kent State, and recently was cited by the Sidney Hillman Foundation for outstanding labor reportage. His articles have been published in *The Atlantic Monthly, The New York Times Magazine, Newsweek,* and other magazines. This is his first book.

50 44